New Jersey Day Trips

A Guide to Outings in New Jersey
and Nearby Areas of New York,
Pennsylvania, and Delaware

10TH EDITION, REVISED AND UPDATED

Barbara Hudgins and Patrick Sarver

RUTGERS UNIVERSITY PRESS
New Brunswick, New Jersey, and London

LIBRARY OF CONGRESS CATALOGING-IN-PUBLICATION DATA

Hudgins, Barbara
    New Jersey day trips : a guide to outings in New Jersey and nearby areas of New
    York, Pennsylvania, and Delaware, 10th edition, revised and updated.
      p.   cm.
    ISBN 0-8135-3351-1 (pbk. : alk. paper)
    1. Family recreation—Middle Atlantic States—Guidebooks.   2. Middle Atlantic
    States—Guidebooks.   3. New Jersey—Guidebooks.   4. New York—Guidebooks.
    5. Pennsylvania—Guidebooks.   6. Delaware—Guidebooks.   I. Hudgins, Barbara.
    II. Sarver, Patrick.
    F106.T835 2003

                           2002208823

British Cataloging-in-Publication data record for this book is available
from the British Library

Manufactured in the United States of America

Contents

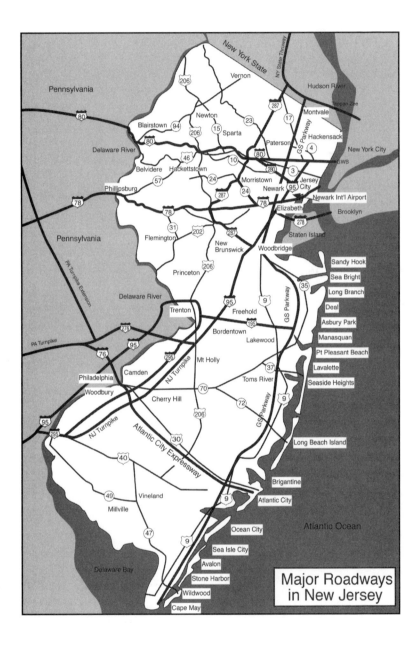

Major Roadways
in New Jersey

Preface

The first nine editions of *New Jersey Day Trips* were published by the Woodmont Press and were written solely by Barbara Hudgins. With this edition there is, for the first time, a new publisher, Rutgers University Press, and a new coauthor, Patrick Sarver. Because this is a new beginning of sorts, we have made some changes in format. But the book is still basically divided into subject categories, such as museums, zoos, gardens, flea markets, and so forth. In the chapter on unique towns we have changed the structure somewhat and now include diverse attractions within a specific town.

Another change has to do with the way that admission fees are listed. In the last few years, admission fees for many New Jersey attractions have gone up with the same regularity as the state's property taxes. In fact, Tuckerton Seaport was the only destination that has actually lowered its price. With a publication that comes out every few years, these changes can lead to confusion. We therefore changed the price points to a range with $ signs used as a code.

There is no single way to write a guidebook. You can approach it from the geographical point of view, or from the type of attraction. The advantage of categorizing by type of attraction is that someone who is interested in a particular sport or hobby can easily find what is available at a glance. If a teacher has a class in Revolutionary War history, a parent is looking for museums dedicated to children, or a newcomer to the state is looking for outlet shopping and flea markets, each can discover what is available immediately.

Some attractions are only seasonal and are simply not available all the times of the year. For example, the greenhouses at Duke Gardens are open only from October to May. The governor's mansion in Princeton is open only on Wednesdays from noon to 2 P.M. (and not at all in August). The unofficial summer season at the Shore starts on Memorial Day and ends on Labor Day (although many stretch the season through September). Mountain Creek is a ski area in the winter and a waterpark in the summer—with some bicycling and golf in between; that is why you will find it listed in the chapter on amusement parks as well as the chapter on outdoor life. You will find that some placements are purely arbitrary. When a particular place could belong to more than one category, we simply chose the one where it seemed to fit best.

There are quite a few new entries in this edition. To make room for all the new additions, we have deleted a few older listings. We have retained many nearby out-of-state entries, although not as many as before. There is always the problem of balance. We want to keep some interesting and sometimes newly discovered treasures in neighboring states in the book without allowing them to overshadow the many diverse attractions within our own state.

Ten Tips for Day Trippers

1. Always telephone first. Places may be closed unexpectedly, or they may change their public hours at any moment.

2. Check Websites when they are available. However, when it comes to hours and prices, they may not be as up to date as the recorded message. Websites are fine for "seeing the place" first and for travel directions.

3. Take along a full-sized map, drinks, snacks, flashlight, extra jacket, and other things you may need.

4. Do not show up during the last half-hour. Places that require guided tours often refuse admittance an hour before closing.

5. Use coupons and "two-fers." Most amusement parks have marketing arrangements with companies for two-for-one admissions with a can, coupon, or other promotion. Also check for discount coupons in brochures, flyers, and newspapers.

6. Go on free days or off-season. State parks, for example, are free off-season.

7. Buy season tickets. This makes sense if you live within close range. Or become a member of a local museum, garden, or zoo.

8. Use your corporate or organizational clout. When companies support institutions, their employees may get a free corporate day or a discount. Members of AAA or AARP often get discounts. Check with your town's recreation department; they may have discount tickets for attractions and events.

9. "Suggested Donation" means just that. If you are visiting for a short time or have a large family with you, you do not have to pay the full suggested donation, but you should pay something.

10. Watch out for extras, such as parking fees and sales tax. Always take along more money than you think you will need.

Prices, Abbreviations, and Hours

For this edition we are not including exact prices since they change so quickly from year to year. Instead we are using a simple range of prices with the following code:

$	=	up to $5
$$	=	$5.01 to $10
$$$	=	$10.01 to $15
$$$$	=	$15.01 to $25
$$$$$	=	$25.01 and above

ABBREVIATION: q.v. (which see) refers to another entry in the book.

HOURS

Hours of operation may change at any time. Readers are encouraged to telephone first, especially off-season. In most cases, for the sake of brevity, we have left out holiday closings. Unless the entry says "Open 365 days" you can assume that most sites, except public parks, are closed on Thanksgiving, Christmas, and New Year's Day. For other holiday closings, check first.

Hours noted within this book pertain to general public admission. There are often special hours and tours for groups and school classes. If you plan a group visit, always call ahead for group reservations, discounted prices, and possible lunchroom privileges.

New Jersey Day Trips

Unique Towns and Tours

Cape May's Victorian hotels and Bed & Breakfasts border the beachfront at the southern end of the state. *(Photo by Patrick Sarver)*

Princeton

Shades of F. Scott Fitzgerald! Golden lads and lasses walk the well-clipped paths between venerable university halls while russet leaves flutter overhead from rows of sturdy trees. Things have changed quite a bit, but still, for a trip to a true university town that combines history, culture, and typical collegiate Gothic architecture, nothing beats a visit to Princeton.

The best way to see the campus sights is to take the free tours offered by the Orange Key Guide Service—just go to the welcome desk at the Frist Center on campus during the school year. Tours leave at 10 A.M., 11 A.M., 1:30 P.M., and 3:30 P.M. weekdays and Saturdays. Sunday tours are 1:30 and 3:30 P.M. The telephone number for tours is 609-258-1766, and you can also get parking directions by calling. It is not necessary to reserve in advance. Although the Website says these tours are primarily for prospective students, they are for everybody and include history, culture, and a bit of gossip. Here are some of the campus sights included in the tour.

1. Nassau Hall: Built in 1756, this Georgian stone structure has survived pillage and fire (by the British, not the students) over the years. It served as a barracks and hospital for troops of both sides during the Revolutionary War. In 1783 Congress met here and drafted the Constitution while Princeton was the capital for a short period. It now serves as an administrative office for the university. A painting of Washington at the Battle of Trenton by Charles Willson Peale is to be found here.

2. Firestone Library: A beautiful two-million-volume library built in 1948, it is the embodiment of the collegiate Gothic style. Major collections include the papers of F. Scott Fitzgerald, Adlai E. Stevenson, John Foster Dulles, Woodrow Wilson, and other famous graduates. A changing exhibit of rare books is also on display.

3. Woodrow Wilson School of Public and International Affairs: Guides will show you the outside of this striking building, one of the few modern structures on campus. Designed by Minoru Yamasaki, it includes a reflecting pool and the Fountain of Freedom.

4. The University Chapel: Built in a Gothic design by Ralph Adams Cram in 1928, it is the third largest university chapel in the country, seating 1800. A sixteenth-century carved oak pulpit and some of the finest stained glass to be seen this side of the Atlantic Ocean makes the chapel an outstanding part of the Princeton trip.

5. The Putnam Sculptures: These are a series of massive metal and stone sculptures scattered around the campus as if a giant had decided to distribute his toys among the college buildings. Sir Henry Moore, Jacques Lipchitz, and Louise Nevelson are among the sculptors represented here.

6. Prospect House: A Tuscan villa built in 1949, it is now used as a Faculty Club and is not open to the public. However, the formally designed garden to the rear is open for browsing and is very pleasant.

Not included in the tour, but an important stop, is the Princeton University Art Museum. This is a first-rate museum, and wonder of wonders—it's free! Paintings include a generous sampling of Americana, Italian Renaissance, and French Baroque. You'll find a good collection of Chinese bronzes as well as artifacts from Central and South America. A top collection of prints, a statue of Diana, and a separate medieval room that includes part of the stained-glass window from the Cathedral at Chartres are also "must sees." Special changing exhibits are of high quality. Call 609-258-3788 for more information.

If you want to see an Ivy League football game, the new Princeton Stadium seats 6,000, and ticket prices are very reasonable. There is a special parking area for tailgaters only a short walk away.

Besides the university, Princeton has pleasant shopping along Nassau Street and Palmer Square, and many good restaurants (among them Lahiere's, the Nassau Inn, and the Alchemist and Barrister). You might also want to look at the Princeton Cemetery at Wiggins and Witherspoon, which holds the remains of Aaron Burr and Grover Cleveland among its many notables. The Princeton Battle Monument, a fifty-foot structure, stands imposingly at Nassau and Mercer Streets, and a walking tour of the area will take you past many lovely old houses. Albert Einstein's former home, at 112 Mercer St., is not open to the public. However, many people take a photograph of it as they pass by. A short drive down from the Einstein house is Princeton Battlefield Park, which has lots of greenery and a colonial house that is open on specific days.

Historic Morven, Drumthwacket (the present governor's residence), and Bainbridge House have separate listings in this book. Self-guided tour maps can be picked up at Bainbridge House, home of the Princeton Historical Society (158 Nassau St.). Anyone can join the walking tours on Sundays at 2 P.M.

The McCarter Theater on University Avenue runs a full program of professional plays, movies, ballets, and concerts. Call 609-258-ARTS for particulars. A good number of fairs and community events take place throughout the year, including a tour of private homes in December.

DIRECTIONS: Rts. 206 or 27 to Princeton. The university is on Nassau Street. **WEBSITE:** www.princeton.edu (university).

Lambertville, New Hope, and Lahaska

Lambertville: Once a poor relation to New Hope in Pennsylvania across the river, Lambertville has become a top destination for antique browsers. One reason is the growth of good restaurants, art galleries, funky clothing shops, and quaint townhouses along the banks of the Delaware.

Lambertville started life as a colonial village with a ferry that connected it to the town across the river. In fact, it was called Coryell's Ferry for many years, and a small contingent of the Continental Army crossed here from Pennsylvania on December 25, 1776, and met the larger group marching on Trenton. The town was also an important stagecoach stop on the New York–Philadelphia run.

In 1834 the Delaware & Raritan Canal opened alongside the Delaware River, and commerce thrived. The workers who had dug the canal rented simple rowhouses, much like the rowhouses one finds in English cities like Manchester. These were sturdy stone or brick homes, and they dotted the landscape of Lambertville.

The Marshall House (60 Bridge St.) is a small red brick building built in 1816, and it is one of the better townhouses in the city. John Marshall, who was born there, later discovered gold at Sutter's Mill

Lambertville has a bevy of quaint shops and restaurants.
(Photo by Lani Duffy)

in California. Unfortunately, he staked a claim too late and died broke, but the modest house that bears his name is now the headquarters of the Historical Society. The Society allows visitors on some Sundays and conducts tours of the town. **TELEPHONE:** 609-397-0770.

Although Lambertville remained a sleepy community for about a century, it was rediscovered in the 1980s. The Yuppies moved in. The old workers' houses were spiffed up and plastered over. New townhouses were put up along the river. The Lambertville railroad station was turned into a two-story restaurant-with-a-view, called, appropriately enough, the Lambertville Station. The Coryell Courtyard at the Pork Store (8 Coryell St.) features art galleries up a little alley. The yearly Shad Festival (the last week in April) began and still attracts thousands to town to savor the traditional shad while getting a glimpse of the revived town with lots of crafters and artists on its streets.

If you visit today, you'll find many shops and eateries clustered around Bridge Street (the main thoroughfare) and Union Street, which transects it, but there are plenty of alleyways and byways to duck into as well. Although antique shops are numerous, the prices here are pretty steep. Luckily, there are plenty of reproduction and collectible shops also. Some of the best restaurants are open for dinner only, but there are several coffee, brioche, and ice cream shops in town. A bevy of Bed & Breakfasts have opened up, along with two traditional inns, so if you want to sleep over there are plenty of accommodations.

If you go on a weekend, you can also drive south on Route 29 and go 2 miles past the town for a look at the Lambertville and Golden Nugget flea markets, which stand side by side on the left side of the road. There are lots of open tables on the hill and a few inside booths where dealers show "collectibles," junque, and doodads. Don't expect great finds here, but it's not a lot of white socks and T-shirts either, and you're out in the open air with a view of the old canal and the Delaware River beyond. For specific hours call: Golden Nugget (609-397-0811) or Lambertville Antique Market (609-397-0456).

DIRECTIONS TO LAMBERTVILLE: Rt. 287 to Rt. 202 south to Rt. 179, then right onto Bridge Street. **WEBSITE:** www.lambertville.org.

New Hope: There are a number of small towns in the United States that seem to survive simply by being picturesque. A combination of natural beauty, historical significance, and the establishment of an art colony (followed inevitably by a writer's colony and a rustic theater) creates that certain atmosphere that brings the tourists out in droves. Whether the original tourist impetus was the antiques in the historical part of town or the artworks in the art colony, the more people arrive, the more craft shops, antique stores, boutiques and charm-laden restaurants open.

New Hope, Pennsylvania, has long been the cultural and picturesque capital of Bucks County. On any fall weekend the narrow sidewalks of this sophisticated oasis set in Pennsylvania farm country are simply jammed. In the 1920s, landscape painters settled here, bringing with them the excitement of the creative world. By the thirties, Bucks County had become well known as a quiet weekend haven for novelists, poets, and playwrights. And in 1939, the Bucks County Playhouse opened in a former gristmill. It has been a stalwart of the summer theater circuit ever since. Since the theater offers family musicals and matinee performances it is one of New Hope's biggest draws. TELEPHONE: 215-862-0220.

Another warm-weather attraction is the New Hope Mule Drawn Barge Ride, which offers a one-hour ride down the old canal works. It is a slow and easy way to see the town. It departs from the barge landing at New Street, and usually several rides are offered during the afternoon. Call 215-862-2842 for details.

A popular pontoon ride is Coryell's Ferry, which offers scenic rides on the Delaware. It loads behind Gerensees Exotic Ice Cream Store, 22 S. Main St. during the summer season. TELEPHONE: 215-862-2050. Railroad enthusiasts will enjoy the New Hope and Ivyland Steam Railway, which operates between May and October. It leaves from a picturesque station at Stockton and W. Bridge Streets and steams through the Bucks County countryside. Call 215-862-2332 for information. Historic house lovers will enjoy the Parry Mansion at S. Main and Parry Streets. Guided tours are given seasonally. Call 215-862-5652 for additional information.

But even without these extras there is plenty to see in New Hope. Stroll along the leaf-strewn streets and visit the stores. There are plenty of shops featuring memorabilia, and if you collect old sheet music, military hats, or miniature dolls, you'll find much to pick from. Sometimes there are even horse-drawn carriage rides that leave from the Logan Inn. Art galleries can be found on Main Street, Mechanic Street, and on Route 202. Besides the standard landscape of Pennsylvania's red barn country, you can find modernistic sculpture and paintings. The kids will be more interested in the toy shops and the knick-knack and candy stores.

One of the charms of visiting a quaint riverside town is eating in a quaint, interesting restaurant, and there are plenty of them in New Hope, most of them along the main drag. Whether you opt for the casual Mother's, the glossy Hacienda, or the cutesy Picnic Basket, you will be satisfied. The better places fill up on weekends, though, so you'd better make reservations as soon as you hit town. There are a variety of nightspots and clubs that give the place a jazzier tone after 7 P.M.

Check the Information Center at 1 W. Mechanic St., or call 215-862-5880. **WEBSITE:** www.newhopepennsylvania.com.

Lahaska: If you drive out of New Hope onto Route 202 west you will eventually come to Lahaska just a few miles up the road. (Of course, you can also drive directly from New Jersey on Route 202.) On the way, there are a couple of antique shops along the road, but they are being replaced by the relentless developments of tract housing. Once in Lahaska the place to stop is **Peddler's Village**, a twentieth-century reconstruction of an eighteenth-century village filled with— what else—shops and restaurants. The landscaping here (by Derek Fell) is outstanding, and a giant waterwheel and floral beds lend the proper tone. In the fall there are scarecrow contests and apple dunking. The shops are mostly the country-store type, but there are several unique boutiques that feature everything from English teapots to Santa Fe windcatchers to special games and toys. Food can be found at the Colonial-style Cock and Bull Inn, Jenny's, and a few quick-stand places. The Golden Plough Inn offers good lunches and also has rooms for those who want to sleep over.

The atmosphere here is a little more child-friendly. Special weekend events include a Strawberry Festival, and a Teddy Bear Picnic. There is an indoor "entertainment center" called Giggleberry Fair that includes a restored 1922 carousel, several interactive play areas, and a corner for pizza and hot dogs.

On the other side of Route 202 is an outlet mall called **Penn's Purchase**. It features a constellation of discount and outlet stores designed to attract the bargain-minded crowd. You'll find Hanes, Bass, and Samsonite among the standards, and also a fast-food shop. **LOCATION:** Rts. 202 and 263, Lahaska, PA. **TELEPHONE:** 215-794-4000 (Peddler's Village). **WEBSITE:** www.peddlersvillage.com.

Atlantic City

Atlantic City keeps reinventing itself with new looks, new styles, and new owners, balancing between an old-fashioned New Jersey shore resort and a Las Vegas imitation. The new Convention Hall and a lighthouse replica now create a dramatic entrance into the city, and laser lights highlight the drama at night. There is new development at the Marina side, while on the boardwalk, casino-hotels are adding new facades and extensions every year.

But there are still amusement arcades, concession stands, and fudge shops around. Crowds of people, rolling chairs, and teenage rollerbladers pass by. The beach, now bumpy with sand dunes, is not used as much as it once was, but the city has added pleasant parks and courtyards to maintain a civilized air.

On the marina side, a newly constructed tunnel allows cars to proceed directly to this outpost of elegant hotels. While Harrah's and Trump Marina have long been tenants, the new Borgata Hotel/Casino dwarfs them in size.

Getting There: Bus tours are still the favorite way for most people to make a one-day visit. It costs around $19 from North Jersey, but the casinos give you a voucher for money and other freebies when you arrive. You must stay 6 hours if you take a bus tour. Casino-subsidized buses come from all points of New Jersey as well as Philadelphia and New York. Groups can charter their own buses. Regular buses and trains also service the town. A rail terminal, next to the Convention Center and Sheraton Hotel, has plenty of taxis available. If you come by car, most casinos allow free limited parking.

Transportation: The best way to get around town is to take the thirteen-passenger jitneys that operate along Pacific Avenue behind the hotels. They come frequently, cost $1.50, and travel as far as the inlet and marina. On the boardwalk you can walk on a nice day or take the push-along rolling chairs that cost about $5 for every six blocks. The slow but convenient tramcars that once traveled the boardwalk are long gone. Cabs are plentiful (at the hotel entrances) if you want to get away from the boardwalk area. And buses serve the length of the island 24 hours a day along Atlantic Avenue.

Hotels: Casino-hotels change their names more often than Hollywood stars change spouses. On the boardwalk they stretch from the Hilton (formerly Bally's Grand) to the Showboat at the north end. In between, a number of modestly priced chain hotels have popped up. Many large hotels now feature a dramatic theme. At Bally's Wild, Wild West you find a domed ceiling that simulates a real sky with sunsets and thunderstorms. Showboat has mechanical cats that play jazz (and live musicians as well). Caesar's Palace is now fitted out with marble atriums, fountains, and statues worthy of Augustus. The Tropicana is unveiling a new and grandiose annex (with perhaps a new Top of the Trop). And of course the Borgata aims to top them all.

Casinos: The days of evening dresses and tuxedos, leisurely gaming tables, and James Bond types floating around are long gone! This is supermarket gambling. Table games are placed side by side, and slot machines take up more space every year. High rollers are offered special rooms for Baccarat and other exotic games. Minimum bets are posted at each table, with $5 the cheapest and minimums rising as the day and evening wear on.

Casinos offer lots of variety, including Asian games at the tables and an ever-expanding variety of fruits, bells, pigs, cowboys, and whatnot on the slot machines. Slots now offer nickel and dime machines as well as the quarter, half-dollar, and dollar variety. They all take paper bills directly. To cash in a bucket full coins into dollars, you still must hike to the Coin Exchange. Frequent customers use a "club" card, which gives you back points every time you use the slot machines or tables. Eventually, if you spend enough money, you get enough "comps" to eat in the fancy restaurants, buy in the gift shops, or sleep in the hotel rooms.

Food: There are plenty of first-class restaurants, both in the casinos and the streets beyond. And every casino has a buffet. Some are elegant; some are simply cafeteria food at reasonable prices. But since they are often crowded, reserve your time as soon as you arrive. Then there are the theme restaurants: Planet Hollywood at Caesars, the Hard Rock Café, and the All-Star Cafe at the Taj Mahal are popular with families. Big Spenders go to the super-deluxe French, Italian, and Chinese restaurants that every hotel seems to have, but they are usually open only for dinner Wednesday through Sunday. Coffee shops and delis are available almost all the time, and there are a number of first-class restaurants in town, such as The Knife and Fork and Alberto's.

Entertainment: First-class shows, chorus girls, and big-name stars appear at the hotels, but the big names are usually weekend events. There are also piano lounges and comedy rooms. For large concerts, the centrally located Boardwalk Hall (the old convention center after a $90-million transformation) now serves as a sports and entertainment center, featuring such events as ice hockey teams, boxing matches, pop, rock, and classic concerts, and ballet.

On the boardwalk, during summer, the Steel Pier (across from the Taj Mahal) offers amusement rides that include roller-coasters, whirlwind rides, and interactive thrills. The usual hot dog stands and games of chance bring back the flavor of the "old" Atlantic City. The biggest indoor amusement is Ripley's Believe It Or Not Museum at New York Avenue. It features a tipsy building leaning over the boardwalk. Inside, there are displays of the world's tallest man, the double-eyed man from China, and a model of the Sydney Harbor

Casino hotels, old-fashioned arcades, the new Boardwalk Hall entertainment center, and crowds of people fill the boardwalk at Atlantic City. *(Photo courtesy Atlantic City Convention & Visitors Authority)*

Bridge made out of matchsticks. Try walking the swaying bridge in the mining tunnel (**ADMISSION: $$**). **TELEPHONE:** 609-347-2001.

At centrally located Kennedy Plaza there is a deluxe miniature golf course (during season) and a large courtyard for watching random entertainments. Video arcades for youngsters and teenagers are located in most hotels and at several boardwalk concessions.

History and Culture: For nostalgia buffs, there's a museum devoted to Atlantic City history, plus an art museum at the Garden Pier on the boardwalk north of the Showboat. The historical museum contains a vast amount of facts and displays everything from Miss America's tiara to a video of historical trends in seaside resorts. It's free and could use some customers. The art museum features changing exhibits.

Looking inland from the Garden Pier, you see Absecon Lighthouse (q.v.), the tallest such structure in New Jersey. The cute little lighthouse-keeper's cottage out front is free to visitors, but there's an admission charge to climb the 228 steps to the fine view of ocean and bay. Open Friday to Monday.

The New Jersey Korean War Memorial in front of the peaceful Brighton Park (next to Bally's Casino) is devoted to veterans of that conflict. Statues of soldiers emerge from a back wall engraved with the names of the 822 New Jerseyans who died in the war. Just a few blocks away, at Pacific Avenue and Dr. Martin Luther King Jr. Blvd. is the imposing Civil Rights Garden. It features a brick path through plants, flowers, and ginkgo trees that leads to eleven black granite columns etched with quotes. The central column has a large bronze bell that hovers over a reflecting pool.

On the inlet side, close to the large Farley Marina, Gardeners Basin is a nautically themed plaza with several points of interest. An aquarium called Ocean Life Center (q.v.) has helped stir up some interest. The nautical theme is reiterated in a restaurant called the Flying Cloud and a seashore-souvenir shack. You can also catch boat rides at the basin during season for dolphin-watching excursions, deep-sea fishing charters, or even a fast motorboat ride. The wide plaza here is the venue for a popular seafood festival and a jazz festival.

South of Atlantic City on Absecon Island is Lucy, the Margate Elephant, a 65-foot high, tin-plated Victorian architectural "folly." During the season, you can walk through its wooden interior (which is actually a museum) with a guided tour for a reasonable fee. You can even step outside onto the Howdah on top and view the surroundings. Lucy is at Decatur and Atlantic Avenues in Margate. **TELEPHONE:** 609-822-6519.

DIRECTIONS: (Atlantic City) Garden State Parkway to Exit 40 and Rt. 38 south, or N.J. Turnpike to Atlantic City Expressway. **TELEPHONE:** 800-BOARDWK, ext. 797. **WEBSITE:** www.atlanticcitynj.com.

Cape May

While Cape May has been a resort since the mid-1800s, it is only within the last thirty years that it has reached fame as a Bed & Breakfast town, rife with good restaurants and quaint shops. Architectural buffs have discovered the Victorian summer homes of Cape May and have converted them into inns. Gone are the dull, old-fashioned guesthouses whose porches always seemed to show peeling white paint. In their stead is a whole array of Victorian homes sporting the sprightly colors of pink, blue, and maroon. Gothic cottages, Italian villas, mansard and stick-style buildings have metamorphosed into charming, whimsical Bed & Breakfast homes, restaurants, antique stores, and art galleries. And the interest in this Victorian revitalization has led the town of Cape May to extend its season well beyond the summer.

One place to begin a visit is the Visitor Center (Lafayette and Bank Streets), which offers brochures on tours of Victorian Inns and whale-watching boats. They can recommend what's best to see if you have limited time. Depending on the season, you can take walking tours, house tours, trolley tours, and tulip tours on weekends from May through October. A special Victorian Week, held in October, features ten days of antiques, crafts, fashion shows, and tours. Another special event is the Christmas candlelight tours.

The group that runs many of these festivities is the Mid-Atlantic Center for the Arts, which operates out of the Emlen Physick Estate (1048 Washington St.). The Physick house itself is the scene of a popular, year-round tour. This sprawling 1881 stick-style home is typical of the late Victorian era, both in its brown exterior and its somewhat fussy furnishings and is said to have been built by architect Frank Furness. Tours may include costumed docents, and on certain days there is even an actor playing the part of Dr. Physick. There is also a charming Victorian tearoom and a gift shop here (open during season) in a separate building on the estate grounds.

A trolley car tour that leaves from the estate travels to the more colorful beachfront area, where houses trimmed in carpenter's lace, stores, and fancy restaurants await the visitor. The Washington Street Mall is a focal point for shoppers, and you can find any number of boutiques and outdoor cafes in this pleasant outdoor mall. (You can also book horse and carriage rides, trolley tours, and inn tours at the entrance to the mall.) The beachfront has a few modern motels and video game arcades along with the older hostelries. But the major ambience of the town is the restoration of its Victorian past. Inns like the Abbey and the Southern Mansion host afternoon tours of their public rooms at certain hours.

There is the beach, of course, which is easily accessible from the center of town, and you can rent chairs and umbrellas if you want to stay a few hours (beach badges are required during the summer). The depth of the beach seems to change each season depending on the winter storms, but the ocean is mild here. A few simple arcades dot the concrete boardwalk that borders the beach.

Cape May is also known as a restaurant town, and some of the better known eateries are the traditional Lobster House at Fisherman's Wharf near the entrance to town, the elegant dining room at Alexander's Inn (653 Washington St.), and the trendy 410 Bank Street (at that address). Of course there are plenty of less formal eating places, and for some, fried oysters at The Ugly Mug in Washington Mall is seafood heaven.

For information on tours contact the Mid-Atlantic Center for the Arts, P.O. Box 340, Cape May, NJ 08204 or telephone 800-275-4278. For other information call the Chamber of Commerce at 609-884-5508 or use the Websites below.

Another excursion is run by the Cape May Seashore Lines, an old-fashioned train ride that leaves from the depot with stops at the Cape May County Zoo and Historic Cold Spring Village during the summer months. Call 609-884-5300.

DIRECTIONS: Garden State Parkway to Exit 0; continue on Rt. 633 for 2 miles. **WEBSITES:** www.capemaymac.org; www.capemaychamber.com.

Newark

You don't have to be a foreign visitor to book a tour of Newark. Bus tours that give a mix of history, sociology, and architecture are available to groups. The tour includes the downtown area, the parks, the slums, and the grand old houses of the Forest Hills section. Did you know that Newark was founded by Puritans? Or that farmers insisted on a broad street so they could bring their cattle to market—the reason such thoroughfares are called Broad and Market?

The downtown tour includes the massive Federal Court Building and the Essex County Courthouse. The statue of Abraham Lincoln seated in front of the courthouse was created by famed sculptor Gutzon Borglum. Borglum also crafted the heroic statue glorifying the soldiers of American wars that stands in Military Park. Since Newark was a city of immigrants, each new group raised a church or synagogue as soon as it arrived. But it was the grandchildren of immigrants who built the magnificent Sacred Heart Cathedral, a huge Gothic-style cathedral situated on the edge of Branch Brook Park. The marble interior and three full rose windows are resplendent. The tour may also encompass a trip through the park (especially if the cherry blossoms are in bloom) and a glimpse of the little subway that takes riders from the Forest Hills section to downtown in seven minutes.

Whether you take a group tour or visit Newark on your own, you will probably end up in the Ironbound section, famed for its Spanish and Portuguese restaurants. The narrow streets here are filled with bakeries, groceries, and eateries. The Ironbound is so called because the train tracks and bridges form a triangle of iron that encloses the district. Tourists come for the Portuguese bakeries and the restaurants, such as Iberia, Fornos and Spain, that are known for their generous portions and reasonable prices. To book a tour, call 973-483-3348.

Greenwich

There are several "forgotten towns" in southwest Jersey—towns that reached their prime back in the eighteenth century when travel by water was more common than going by rough roads. The town of

Greenwich on the Cohansey River is such a place. It was started as a colony by John Fenwick, who welcomed Quakers, Baptists, and Presbyterians—groups that were not well tolerated in their previous home in Puritan Massachusetts.

Settlement began in 1683, and the town became the official port of entry to the Delaware River from 1695 to 1765. As such it was a bustling commercial port, and small townhouses in the English style grew up along the central street. In 1774, Greenwich had its own tea party in response to British taxes—the residents burned the English import which was being kept in a warehouse for safekeeping.

Today there is a monument to the Greenwich Tea Party—and many of the eighteenth-century houses along Ye Great Street still stand. The Cumberland County Historical Society makes its home at one of the oldest, the Gibbon House at 960 Ye Greate St. During open hours the society members conduct tours of the house, a well-furnished 1730 home that once belonged to the town's leading citizen (**HOURS**: Apr.–Dec., Tue.–Sun., 12–4).

Because Greenwich was dependent on maritime trade, a great interest in ships and shipping is apparent there. The John Dubois Maritime Museum (**HOURS**: Apr.–Dec., Sun., 1–4) has nautical maps, models of ships, tools, and tons of lore about coastal sailing. Other stops on the tour are the Prehistorical Museum and the Lummis Library, both with limited hours. The library is of particular interest to genealogists, since it is a fine resource for families who trace their ancestry back to early Protestant settlers.

Greenwich is not a tourist town. No arty shops or gourmet lunch spots are tucked into the townhouses. But it is a chance to see a quiet town from the past where the historical district is kept intact (even new buildings conform to the "look"). The Cumberland County Historical Society runs all the tours and goes out of its way to accommodate visitors—especially groups. Special yearly events include a juried Craft Faire (everything gets the old English spelling in this town). **TELEPHONE**: 609-455-4055. **WEBSITE**: www.cchs.org.

Stockton

Located a few miles north of Lambertville in Hunterdon County, this riverfront town is known for its "Small hotel with a wishing well"—the Stockton Inn, in the heart of town. A small but charming business area adds to the town's ambience, as does the handsome Woolverton Inn, a Bed & Breakfast on a hill not far from town.

The area is a popular weekend place for visitors who hike or bike the Delaware & Raritan Canal Path, which is part of the state park bordering the Delaware River. About a mile north of the town you'll find the picturesque Prallsville Mills on the left-hand side of Route 29. This complex includes a 1790 linseed oil mill, an 1877 gristmill, an 1850 sawmill, a grain silo, and a railroad trestle. Wickecheoke Creek feeds the canal at the mill complex, and there is a canal lock on the grounds. Although the grounds are open daily, the stripped-down interior of the gristmill is open only by appointment or on Sunday 1–4 when available. However, the gristmill hosts a well-known juried art show in April and many other events that are open to the public. The linseed mill houses an art gallery. All the buildings are operated by the Delaware River Mill Society. **TELE-PHONE:** 609-397-3586 for particulars. **WEBSITE:** www.dandrcanal.com/prallsville.

Nearby is another picture-taking favorite (especially in the fall): the Green Sergeant's Bridge, which is the pride and joy of the tiny town of Sergeantsville. This is the last remaining covered bridge in New Jersey, and it's white, not green. (It is named after a man called Green Sergeant.) The bridge crosses the Wickecheoke Creek, about 1.5 miles west of town. **DIRECTIONS:** From Rt. 29, take Rt. 523 to Rt. 604. **TELEPHONE:** 609-397-3240.

Bordentown

One of the oldest towns in New Jersey, Bordentown is no longer the thriving Quaker enclave it once was. Several famous citizens once lived here, among them Clara Barton, Thomas Paine, Francis Hopkinson (a Revolutionary notable), and Joseph Bonaparte, brother of Napoleon. Many eighteenth-century buildings are still standing, and the homes of the famous are here as well, although private. Today, the town is primarily working class, but it still possesses an aura of quaintness and history.

Self-guided walking tours begin with a brochure from the Historical Society, located in the Friends Meetinghouse, which houses a small museum. Unfortunately, it is open only by appointment, but brochures are available at the nearby UandI Bookstore on Farnsworth Avenue. None of the forty-five buildings listed are open to the public, but the history and architecture of each are nonetheless interesting. The Gilder House (closed for restoration) includes furnishings from Joseph Bonaparte's estate. Other houses on the self-guided tour are the Shippen House, Francis Hopkinson House, Thomas Paine House, and Joseph Borden House.

The Clara Barton Schoolhouse is a prime historical site in town. Miss Barton, who later founded the Red Cross, actually taught here for a very short time but made quite an impact. Until then, middle-class children went to private school, and public schools were considered to be for paupers. Barton had to persuade local school-children to attend. There was no fee, but each child was required to bring a stick of wood to keep the stove going. The small red brick building has benches and a raised platform where the teacher sat (in the back of the room, not the front). This also is open only for the reserved group-guided tour that the Historical Society offers. However, major sites are open for a Candlelight Tour in October and a Holiday Tour on the second Saturday in December. Contact: Bordentown Historical Society, 302 Farnsworth Ave., Bordentown (Burlington County). **TELEPHONE:** 609-298-1740.

Burlington

Another town that saw its heyday years ago when it was the capital of West Jersey and a stronghold of Quakerism is Burlington. Start with guided tours of the Burlington County Historical Society complex and a self-guided tour of the adjacent High Street area (hour-long audio tapes are available at society headquarters. Fee: $). The society's museum complex includes four houses. One was once rented by the family of America's first novelist, James Fenimore Cooper, although the writer spent only the first thirteen months of his life here.

The Captain James Lawrence House right next door is dedicated to pictures and memorabilia of the War of 1812 hero who is best known for his words, "Don't Give Up the Ship!" (During the tour you find out that the Americans actually did give up the ship and the British won the battle.) Although small, it is well furnished and very interesting. These houses are at 457 and 459 High Street. The rest of the complex includes the Bard-How House (453 High St.) and the Society's library and the museum gallery, located behind the historical houses. **ADMISSION:** $. Tue.–Sat., 1–5.

The complex is among more than forty historic sites in Burlington's mile-square historic district, which is covered in a walking-tour brochure from the Historical Society. Among the sites on the tour are views of Burlington Island (site of the first New Jersey settlement in 1624) from the riverfront, where you can enjoy an old-fashioned walk with a nice view.

Most houses on the walking tour are private, and these include the estate of William Franklin, Benjamin's son and New Jersey's last colonial governor. Other notable buildings are the 1785 Friends Meetinghouse, the 1685 Revell House, the 1856 Ulysses S. Grant House, and the Grubb Estate, a stop on the Underground Railroad, as well as several early day churches. For a brochure visit City Hall at 437 High St. **TELEPHONE:** 856-386-0200.

For information contact Burlington County Historical Society, 451 High St., Burlington. **TELEPHONE:** 609-386-4773. **WEBSITE:** www.tour-burlington.org.

Other Towns

Ocean Grove: A pleasant seaside town to visit for the beach or for the pretty Victorian buildings that now contain tea shops and restaurants, Ocean Grove began as a Methodist Camp Meeting summer colony. It was first filled with tents and then with the colorful stick-style cottages that remain to this day. Although the strict Methodist rules against driving and bicycling no longer apply, it is still a dry town (unlike Asbury Park next door). For those interested in history, there are guided tours that include an inside look at the Great Auditorium (q.v.) as well as an interior of a tent in the town's Tent Colony.

A well-known stop is the 1874 Centennial Cottage, which is furnished with Victorian antiques and has a garden with plants and flowers that were popular in the late nineteenth century. Some tours include a stop for tea and sweets at a local B&B. All tours start from the Historical Society's museum at 50 Pitman Ave. Telephone 732-774-1869 for hours and schedules. **WEBSITE:** www.oceangrovehistory.org.

Mount Holly: The Burlington County seat was another center of Quaker life in the early days. This quiet little town has several buildings of note on its walking tour. Among the noteworthy buildings are the Burlington County Prison Museum, designed by Robert Mills, architect of the Washington Monument; the Mill Street Hotel; the John Woolman Memorial; and a restored 1759 schoolhouse where Woolman, a famous Quaker abolitionist, once taught. Most of these are heavy old stone buildings that really set you back in time. Several other stops include the 1796 Old Courthouse Complex, a 1712 log cabin, and a Friends Meeting House used by the British in 1778 and the following year for meetings of the state legislature. A few miles outside of Mt. Holly is the historic mansion of Smithville (not to be confused with the historic town in Atlantic County). This large, columned house includes a museum of bicycles and is open for tours May–Oct. **TELEPHONE:** 609-261-3780. A pamphlet for the self-guided town tour is available from the town clerk at Township Hall, 23 Washington St. **TELEPHONE:** 609-267-8600, ext. 20. **WEBSITE:** www.mountholly.com.

Salem: Salem was an early Quaker settlement in West Jersey. Today, it is the home of a historic district (**TELEPHONE:** 856-935-5004) with a large number of Colonial and Victorian houses. Among important sights around town are the Old Court House, a reproduction of a 1640 Swedish cabin in John Prinz Park, and the Goodwin Sisters' House (an 1821 home that was an important stop on the Underground Railroad). Most famous is the historic Salem Oak in the Friends Burial Ground, said to be between 500 and 700 years old. Under its branches a peace treaty was signed with the Lenape Indians in the 1600s. The Salem County Historical Society headquarters is in the Alexander Grant House, 79-83 Market St., built in 1721. This nineteen-room museum displays Early American furniture and decorative arts as well as changing exhibits. Living rooms, bedrooms, featherbeds, rooms full of dolls, and much more are on view. Open Tue.–Fri., 12–4, plus the second Saturday of the month. Nominal fee. Here you can pick up the map for a walking tour of the local historic area. Once a year, on the first Saturday in May, Salem also hosts an Open House for its historic buildings. **TELEPHONE:** 856-935-5004. **WEBSITE:** www.salemcounty.com/schs.

Woodbury: The Gloucester County Historical Society's library at 17 Hunter St. is the place to pick up two tour maps. One is for a walking tour of Old Woodbury, a brochure and map to thirty-five historic, mostly private homes and businesses in town. There's also a driving tour map ($) of forty-eight historic buildings in the county, with a short history of each. Again, most buildings are privately owned. Of particular note is the historical society's headquarters, the 1765 Hunter-Lawrence-Jessup House at 58 North Broad St. Built in 1785 and altered during Victorian times, it was the home of the Reverend Andrew Hunter, a Colonial tea burner, and Captain James Lawrence of "Don't Give Up the Ship!" fame. Today, it serves as a twelve-room historical museum. Displays include military artifacts, antique toys, samplers, agricultural and architectural displays, and changing exhibits. Open Mon., Wed., & Fri., 1–4, and the last weekend of the month, 2–5. Small fee. **TELEPHONE:** Museum, 856-848-8531; Library, 856-845-4771.

Bridgeton: This town has New Jersey's largest historic district, with more than 2,200 homes and buildings from the Colonial, Federal, and Victorian eras—all in various stages of repair. The strongest ambience is Victorian, with many large homes found along the streets. The Cohansey River runs through town, and a pleasant riverfront plaza has been built to host concerts, fairs, and walking tours. Across the river is a large park, which includes the Nail Mill Museum, the Cohanzick Zoo (q.v.), the New Sweden Farmstead Museum (q.v.), and rhododendron and azalea gardens along the park drive. A walking tour allows one to see many historic homes and buildings. Stops open to visitors include Potter's Tavern, home of New Jersey's first newspaper (open weekends); South Jersey All Sports Museum in the Burt Avenue Recreation Center (Tue.–Sat., 10–12 and 1–3); and the George Woodruff Indian Museum in the library (Mon.–Fri., 1–4). Some boutiques have opened in the riverfront area, and the city is working to enhance its Victorian ambience. Maps, a film, and arrangements for self-guided audio tours as well as guided bus and walking tours are available at the Bridgeton-Cumberland Tourist Association, 50 E. Broad St., Bridgeton (Cumberland County). TELEPHONE: 856-451-4802. WEBSITE: www. historicbridgeton.com.

Haddonfield: Haddonfield Historic District encompasses almost 500 Colonial and Victorian houses, buildings, and sites along streets enhanced by trees, brick sidewalks, and gardens. Around 150 of the buildings have historical or architectural significance. Among the most notable are Indian King Tavern and Greenfield Hall (q.v.). Other sites around town include the Fire Company #1 Museum and the discovery site of the first complete dinosaur skeleton. There are also scores of galleries, boutiques, and antique shops. Stop by the Visitor Center (Mon.–Fri., 11 A.M. to 5 P.M.; Sat., 10 A.M.–4 P.M.) on Kings Court for a self-guided walking-tour brochure. The center also has a walking tour map of churches. There are also themed guided tours, included stained glass tours, history and architecture tours, and Haunted Haddonfield tours led by expert guides. Contact the Visitor Center, 114 Kings Hwy. East, Haddonfield (Camden County). TELEPHONE: 856-216-7253. WEBSITES: www.levins.com/haddon.html or www.haddonfieldnj.org.

Millville: The Glasstown Center Arts District along the Maurice River preserves buildings from the 1800s when Millville was a major glassmaking center. The district includes Riverwalk, a new landscaped walkway along the riverfront; a new marina; and the Riverfront Renaissance Center for the Arts, with works from more than one hundred artists. There is also a growing number of galleries in the adjacent business district. Two blocks east on Main Street is the Millville Historical Society and the Baracha Dunn House, built in 1798 (open Wed., Sun., 1–4). Glassmaking is also the theme at Wheaton Village (q.v.) north of the town. TELEPHONE: 856-825-6633. WEBSITE: www.glasstownartsdistrict.com.

Chester: This Morris County town dates back to pre-Revolutionary War times. The main thoroughfare of town still has a country air to it, even though the surrounding area is suburban. Main Street stores offer a mix of antiques, quilts, coverlets, and cookware. An English tea shoppe and shops that carry lavender and lace are nestled between antique stores with names like Aunt Pittypat's Parlour and the Spinning Wheel. The early 1800s Brick Hotel, now the Publick House, and the historic Larison's Country Inn are popular dining destinations. Lots of special weekend promotions can be found here, everything from Cabin Fever in late winter to large craft shows in spring and fall at Chubb Park. **LOCATION:** Rts. 124 and 206, Morris County. **TELEPHONE:** 908-879-4814. **WEBSITE:** www.chesternj.org.

A few miles east of Chester, the upscale community of **Mendham** reminds many of a quiet Connecticut town. A number of interesting antique shops as well as galleries and specialty shops are centered around the intersection of Route 124 and Hilltop Road, where you'll also find The Black Horse Inn, a mainstay of country dining. Mendham may have been the model for the country town in Philip Roth's *American Pastoral,* since a picture of the Brookside post office there was used on the original cover.

Hoboken: Known for its old-fashioned railroad terminal, Stevens Tech, Washington Street nightclubs, and, of course, Frank Sinatra, this is a town filled with art, music, and food celebrations. There are also many restored brownstones that make you feel like you're in an out-of-the-way corner of Manhattan—except when you can see the real skyline from Hoboken's riverfront walkways and Pier A, just north of the Hoboken Terminal. A nexus for the twenty and thirty-something crowd, Washington Street is the center of the action in Hoboken, where you'll find well-known nightclubs and restaurants, including Maxwell's and the Clam Broth House. Hoboken Historical Museum, at 1301 Hudson St. on the waterfront (201-656-2240; www.hobokenmuseum.org), features exhibits, lectures, and tours of homes, gardens, and historic sites (open Tue.–Thu., 5–9; weekends, 12–5). Seasonal guided walking tours include the Historical Museum; Elysian Field, the birthplace of baseball (at 10th and Hudson); Stevens Castle Room at Stevens Tech; the Erie Lackawanna Rail Terminal; and the Hoboken Police Museum.

The museum offers self-guided tour maps of the town as well as a Frank Sinatra tour. This includes the site of his boyhood home at 415 Monroe (now only a vacant lot behind a wall) and places where he performed. There's a one-room private museum next door to his home called "From Here to Eternity," which is more like a neighborhood bar with Sinatra memorabilia.

Hoboken also features a number of street festivals throughout the year, including the old-fashioned St. Ann's Festival in the summer (with Italian sausage and peppers) and a jazz/food festival that centers around the Terminal in September. **WEBSITES:** www.hoboken.com and www.hobokenmuseum.org.

Flemington: Known for its many Victorian homes, Main Street is the center of a historic district where 60 percent of the buildings are on the national register. These include the Hunterdon County Courthouse, where the Lindbergh baby kidnapping trial took place in 1935, and the historic Union Hotel across the street, where the famous reporters of the age stayed and reported on the trial. Other historic buildings of note include Fleming's Castle, built in 1756 (5 Bonnell St.); the 1846 Doric House, home of the Hunterdon County Historical Society (114 Main St.); and the Reading-Large House, an impressive home with massive columns built in 1847. There are also a number of Victorian B&Bs in the district. These buildings and houses are open for tours during the Flemington Comes Alive celebration, late Sept.–late Oct. (**TELEPHONE:** 908-782-2610), which includes a dramatic production of the Lindbergh trial at the courthouse (www.lindberghtrial.com). Flemington is also a center for outlets (q.v.), as well as specialty shops at Turntable Junction and along Main Street.

Hope: Guided walking tours of the Hope Historic District start at 10 A.M. on the first and second Saturdays of the month, June–Oct. The starting point is the Inn at Millrace Pond, a restored gristmill on Route 519 that is also a Bed & Breakfast and upscale restaurant. The 1½ hour tour ($$; under 12 free) of this historic Warren County village, which was founded in 1769 by Moravians, includes a community church (*Gemeinhaus*) and Moravian cemetery as well as the 1769 gristmill and other historic stops. Along the way, you pass antique and gift shops and many historic private homes. Stop by the Help Our Preservation Effort (H.O.P.E) historical library and exhibit center on Walnut Street. The historical society museum, which houses a small collection of local historic photos and artifacts, is around the corner on High Street (open Sunday afternoons, June–Oct.). For H.O.P.E. tours, call 908-459-9177.

Antique Towns

There are also a number of smaller towns scattered throughout the state that offer both old-fashioned charm and antique shops. Here are some of the more notable.

Mullica Hill: The Gloucester County village of Mullica Hill in South Jersey has long attracted buyers to its country-style antique stores. Antique dolls, books and ephemera, toys, furniture, together with collectibles and arts-and-crafts items can be found in a passel of stores. Antiques collectives include Kings Row Antiques, 46 N. Main St.; Old Mill Antique Mall, 1 S. Main St.; The Warehouse, 2 S. Main St.; and the Old Post Shoppes Antiques, 50 S. Main St. There are also numerous individual shops that include craft and doll repair specialties as well as antiques. Mullica Hill can be found at the junction of Routes 322 and 45. **WEBSITE:** www.mullicahill.com.

Hopewell: A colonial town known for its antiques and pleasant atmosphere lies a few miles west of Princeton in Mercer County. A number of antique shops along W. Broad Street plus the Tomato Factory (a group enterprise) makes this a nice destination for a country outing. The Hopewell Museum (q.v.), the Off-Broad-Street Theatre, and the Hopewell Valley Bistro & Inn and Failte Coffee House add character to this historic town.

Boonton Historic District: Boonton Historic Museum, 210 Main St. **HOURS:** Sat., 1–4. Walking tours of Main Street, Ironworks Hollow, and Ironworks Residential Historic District start at 10 A.M. on the boardwalk near 602 Main St. **TELEPHONE:** 973-402-8840. **WEBSITE:** www.boonton.org/historical. This Morris County town is also the site of the New Jersey Firemen's Home Museum, 565 Lathrop Ave. (973-334-0024), but it is probably better known as a browser's town, with more than twenty antique shops in operation.

Lafayette: A small country enclave on Rt. 15 in Sussex County is the home of the Mill Market, where a group of dealers run an antiques cooperative in a picturesque converted 1842 mill. The mill, open Fri.–Mon., is next to an old-fashioned General Store as well as a few other interesting antique shops. Not far away, the town of Andover is home to the Scranberry Coop (Rt. 206 south of town), which has 150 dealers under one roof and quite a variety of merchandise.

Clinton: The Red Mill Museum Village (q.v.) and Hunterdon Museum of Art (q.v.) on opposite banks of the South Branch of the Raritan River are the main draws in town, but the historic Main Street area offers a number of art galleries, antique stores, restaurants, and gift shops. Across the bridge is Clinton House, an inn dating back to 1743. The surrounding town has some interesting nineteenth-century homes. Take Rt. 78, Exit 15.

Red Bank: The Antique Center at Red Bank, which hosts about 150 dealers in three large buildings (195, 195A, and 226 W. Front St.), has been around for a long time. Usually open daily but best to telephone 732-842-4244 for hours. In recent years, this Monmouth County town has become more upscale, and the Broad and Front Streets area has evolved into an interesting collection of shops, coffeehouses, hip restaurants, and galleries. A nice place for walking and window shopping. The riverfront area is the scene for several music and family festivals.

Frenchtown: With four blocks of antique shops, galleries, and boutiques on Race and Bridge Streets leading to the old-fashioned Delaware River bridge, this small town on the banks of the Delaware provides an interesting stop in Hunterdon County. The Frenchtown Inn, Race St. Cafe, and Bridge Cafe also give this quaint small town more than its share of restaurants of note.

Allentown: Located on the far western edge of Monmouth County (just 10 miles east of Trenton) is a historic town that offers an old-fashioned historic district. The Shops at the Old Mill as well as antique and specialty shops along S. Main Street are popular draws. There's also an interesting nature trail along Doctors Creek in Heritage Park, next to the mill.

Mauricetown: A small nineteenth-century town south of Millville on the Maurice River features many interesting Victorian homes built by whaling captains. Stop by the historic society in the Edward Compton House on Front Street (open Sun., 1–3; call 856-785-1137). There are also a few antique shops around the Cumberland County town, and there are Chistmas house tours the second Sunday in December.

Where Washington Slept, Ate, and Fought

Washington headquartered at the well-appointed Ford Mansion during his two winters in Morristown. *(Photo courtesy Morris County Visitor Center)*

Jockey Hollow

The winter of 1779–1780 was the coldest in a century. On December 1, 1779, General George Washington entered Morristown and took up residence at the house of Mrs. Jacob Ford, Jr. Meanwhile, 4 miles away at Jockey Hollow, 10,000 men chopped down 600 acres of oak, walnut, and chestnut trees to build hundreds of huts along the slopes of the "hollow." Severe snowstorms hindered their work and delayed the supply of meat and bread they needed to survive. Starvation confronted the army, which also suffered from inadequate clothing, disease, and low morale. So terrible was the winter of the Morristown encampment that many troops finally mutinied. But the history books only tell you about Valley Forge. Why? Because New Jersey has simply never had a very good public relations person. Not until recently, anyway.

Today there are several reconstructed huts on the site, which is administered by the National Park Service. But first, go to the Visitor Center, which gives full information about the encampment. If you go beyond the main desk you find a mini-theater where an eleven-minute film begins at the touch of a button. The story of typical foot soldiers huddled in a simple hut waiting for the rations and money that took so long in coming is unfolded. After the film, you can move on to the mock-up of the soldiers' hut and see the straw beds, muskets, and clothing used at the time.

From the Information Center, proceed out the back door to the Wick Farm, where a Park Service employee is often in residence. The farmhouse was occupied by both the Wick family (owners of the farm that included Jockey Hollow) and General Arthur St. Clair and his aide. A vegetable and herb garden, a well, and a horse barn surround the wooden cottage. Inside the smoky cabin, a ranger dressed in colonial garb will be cooking, melting down candles or just answering questions. A tour through the house shows the little bedroom of Tempe Wick, the general's office, and his bedroom.

From the Wick house, you can drive to the open slopes of the winter encampment. You can visit the simple soldiers' huts on the hill or the various brigade lines. Altogether there are 27 miles of hiking trails within the park, so there's plenty of walking space. On special weekends there are often demonstrations, musters, or other doings both at the Wick Farm and near the reconstructed huts.

HOURS: Daily, 9–5. Closed major holidays. **ADMISSION:** Adults, $ (includes all of MNHP). Under 16 free. **LOCATION:** Take Rt. 287 to Rt. 202 to Tempe Wick Rd. (south of Morristown). Follow signs. **TELEPHONE:** 973-543-4030.

Washington's Headquarters

For another look at the details of the Morristown encampment go to Washington's Headquarters (the Ford Mansion and Museum), which is part of the overall site called Morristown National Historic Park. It's only a short drive away. You enter at a separate museum building where you will find dislays that emphasize the role of the citizens of Morristown and how they reacted to the soldiers in their town. Other exhibits include military paraphernalia, such as surgeon's tools, mess kits, muskets, cleaning rods, and uniforms. Two movies are shown periodically in the auditorium. The films were shot on location both here and in Jockey Hollow, and contrast the warmth and food available to officers at the mansion with the hungry, freezing men camped 4 miles away. A lively ball scene was filmed in the central hall of the Ford Mansion.

A park ranger, usually in period dress, will then take you on a tour of the Ford Mansion across the lawn. It's a solid frame Colonial house—by no means a mansion in the modern sense. As you enter the long central hallway, you notice how well such halls were suited for line dances such as the Virginia reel. The house was offered as headquarters to Washington by Mrs. Ford, a widow with four children. The Ford family lived in two rooms while the general and his staff occupied the rest of the house. The furnishings are authentic to the period and many are true Ford family pieces. Beds include the canopied master bed used by Washington. Highboys, chest-on-chests, wall maps, and lots of straw mattresses are all on display.

Despite the rigors of the Morristown encampment, the Ford Mansion looks like a warm, comparatively elegant abode for the chief of staff. From here, Alexander Hamilton (who was Washington's aide-de-camp at the time) courted Betsey Schuyler, who was staying at the nearby Schuyler-Hamilton house. The historic park also includes other sites such as Fort Nonsense. (*Note:* Future expansion of the Revolutionary War Museum is expected.)

HOURS: Daily, 9–5. Closed major holidays. **ADMISSION:** Adults, $ (includes all sites in MNHP). Under 16 free. **LOCATION:** Rt. 287 to exit 36 or 36A to Morris Ave. East, Morristown (Morris County). Follow signs to Washington's Headquarters. **TELEPHONE:** 973-539-2085. **WEBSITE:** www.nps.gov/MORR.

Dey Mansion

A solid Dutch farmhouse built in the early Georgian style, the Dey Mansion was Washington's headquarters for three months during the summer and fall of 1780. Here Washington was able to keep an eye on the British in New York, while staying close to food and forage for his army. Furnishings reflect the status of the Dey family, who were quite well-to-do (the father was a colonel in the militia). An unusual feature of this northern house is the separate kitchen. (There is a breezeway between it and the main house for use during the colder months.) According to the guide, the separate kitchen was practical, for if the hearth caught on fire, it would not take the rest of the house with it.

After an inspection of the well-stocked kitchen, you may tour the house with its two floors of well-kept furnishings and many family portraits. You can also see Washington's office, where he tended to his heavy correspondence.

Outside there are picnic facilities, a replica blacksmith shop, and other outbuildings. The house is actually part of Preakness Valley Park (part of the Passaic County Park System), and a golf course is quite close to the historic mansion. The Bergen County Militia offers special reenactments on the front lawn on special occasions.

HOURS: Wed.–Fri., 1–4:30; Sat. & Sun., 10–12 & 1–4:30. **ADMISSION:** $.
LOCATION: 199 Totowa Rd., Wayne (Passaic County). **TELEPHONE:**
973-696-1776.

The Wallace House

During the winter of 1778, the well-provisioned British army stayed in New York City, while the American army camped out in the Watchung Mountains in Middlebrook (now part of Green Brook). The winter of 1778–1779 was rather mild, much more pleasant than those at Valley Forge or Morristown. The soldiers lived in tents and later built log cabins, but General Washington stayed 4 miles away at the best house in the area. It was owned by John Wallace, a wealthy Philadelphian who had built a twelve-room Colonial out in rural Somerville to get out of harm's way. Washington rented out only four rooms for himself and his staff at a price of $1,000, while the Wallace family used the rest of the home.

The Wallace House is a solidly built wood structure with wide plank floors and painted walls. Guides take you through the parlors, dining room, and bedrooms, which have been refurbished to reflect the Wallace family lifestyle of the 1780s. However, the room where Washington slept is kept in "headquarters style," with a canopied four-poster bed, military trunk, and typical toiletry articles on the dresser. The formal parlor does not look large, but it is said up to thirty people ate there when General and Mrs. Washington entertained.

Because a new, larger parking lot has been put in place at the back of the building, you now have to walk around to the front door to gain entrance.

HOURS: Wed.–Sat., 10–12 & 1–4. Sun., 1–4. **ADMISSION:** Free.
LOCATION: 71 Somerset St., Somerville (Somerset County).
TELEPHONE: 908-725-1015.

The Old Dutch Parsonage

From the front yard of the Wallace House you can cross the street diagonally to the red brick house known as the Old Dutch Parsonage. (There may be a guide for each house, or one guide may have to do duty for both places.) This was the dwelling place of Pastor Frelinghuysen, minister of the Dutch Reformed Church. Later it became the home of the Reverend Jacob Hardenburgh, who married Frelinghuysen's widow. Hardenburgh was one of the "Fighting Pastors" of the Revolutionary War who condemned the British from the pulpit and was quite a hero. However, he is best known as the founder of Queens College, which began as a small theological school in the house and later grew into Rutgers University. Hardenburgh was a frequent host to General and Mrs. Washington when they lived close by in the Wallace House. (The parsonage was moved to its present location some years ago.)

The displays at the parsonage are meant to reflect the life and times of this Dutch pastor so you will find many period pieces, especially of Dutch style, such as a Kas, on display. One large front room is kept as a social hall for lectures, meetings, and open houses throughout the year. Featured are flute playing, singing, and even colonial dances.

HOURS, LOCATION: Same as Wallace House. **ADMISSION:** Free.

The Old Barracks

Set in the midst of bustling downtown Trenton, the Old Barracks, with its red-painted porches, is an authentic reminder of the past. This is the only standing barracks of the type used by the British to house foreign troops in colonial America. It is also the place where Washington and his troops surprised the Hessian soldiers after he crossed the Delaware on Christmas night in 1776 and turned the tide of the Revolution.

This U-shaped fieldstone building has quite a history. Just before it was saved from demolition, the rooms were being used as a "Home for the Relief of Respectable, Aged and Indigent Widows and Single Women." The Barracks were originally built in 1758 during the French and Indian War because American colonists objected to the billeting of British troops in private homes. In 1776, the British and Hessian mercenaries used it until the Americans gained control, after which it became a hospital for the wounded. After the war, the building went through a series of ups and downs until the Old Barracks Association saved it in 1899.

A full restoration has opened up plenty of space in the building. The long barracks room, complete with bunk beds, an officer's apartment, and a room dedicated to General Washington's triumphant return to Trenton are all on view. Nowadays, interpretative history, with costumed guides, is emphasized. In different rooms, you will see docents act out various "characters," such as a farm woman, a volunteer soldier, or a Hessian mercenary. They will tell you their stories or show you how to load a musket or care for the wounded. There are also maps, mock-ups, and displays in a museum room.

The Barracks hosts an annual recreation of the Battle of Trenton on the weekend after December 26, with lots of cannons and re-enactors in the streets.

HOURS: Tue.–Sat., 11–5; Sun., 1–5. Closed major holidays. **ADMISSION:** $$. Discounts: Seniors, children. Under 5 free. **LOCATION:** Barracks St. at West Front St., Trenton (Mercer County). Take Willow St. exit from Rt. 29 south. **TELEPHONE:** 609-396-1776. **WEBSITE:** www.barracks.org.

Washington Crossing State Park (New Jersey)

This popular park covers 991 acres stretching from the banks of the Delaware in Titusville and commemorates the crossing that led to the most important victory of the war's early years. On Christmas Night 1776, General Washington crossed the icy Delaware from Pennsylvania with 2,400 men, plus artillery and supplies. The crossing took nine hours, and the men and officers converged on this spot on the Jersey side. The ensuing surprise attack gave a sweet taste of victory to the discouraged American troops.

The Visitor Center is filled with information on this and other early battles of the Revolutionary War, plus the uniforms and muskets of the time. There are a variety of exhibits and audiovisuals, including the extensive Swan collection of eighteenth-century armaments.

Outside there are open fields for Frisbee throwing, an excellent nature center, and an open-air amphitheater featuring summer shows. There are many picturesque picnic groves here as well. Near the Delaware River sits a monument marking the spot where the troops disembarked, and two historic houses are set in the greenery. One of these, the Johnson Ferry House, a refurbished inn, offers guided tours at specific times (call 609-737-2515). Nearby, the Nelson House is even closer to the river. A separate group administers the guided tours there.

HOURS: Visitor Center, Wed.–Sun., 9–4:30. Shorter winter hours. Park open dawn to dusk. **ADMISSION:** Free, but there is a parking fee ($) on summer weekends. **LOCATION:** Rts. 29 & 546, Titusville (Mercer County). **TELEPHONE:** Park, 609-737-0623; Visitor Center, 609-737-9303.

Washington Crossing Historic Park (Pennsylvania)

Across the river, the site of the embarkation is the focus for a large park that stretches up the Delaware River and includes several sections. In the first section, a modern Visitor Center offers brochures, a theater for a film about the crossing, and tickets for the historical buildings within the park. Some of these buildings are within easy walking distance. The first is the McKonkey Ferry Inn, where Washington and his staff met and ate just before the crossing. It is fixed up as a travelers' inn with tables set with pewter and a bar and grill. In this section of the park there are two other historic houses plus replicas of the longboats that were used for the crossing. Traveling north you come upon another section of the park that includes a wildflower preserve, the high observation tower on Bowman's Hill, and the Thompson-Neely House (which is an original structure built of Delaware River ledgestone, looking as authentic as all get-out). Tickets for all historic houses are reasonably priced, and of course you get a guided tour through each.

You'll find lots of picnic pavilions, walking paths, and driving roads throughout the park, and in the autumn the foliage is perfect. The Visitor Center, movie, and self-guided walking tour are free. An annual re-creation of the crossing takes place every Christmas Day, when the general and his contingent row over to Titusville on the other side, weather permitting.

HOURS: Tue.–Sat., 9–5; Sun., 12–5. ADMISSION: Guided tour, $.
Discounts: Seniors, children. Under 6 free. LOCATION: Across Delaware River bridge from Titusville. North on PA Rt. 32 for other sections of park. TELEPHONE: 215-493-4076.

Fort Lee Historic Park

Set in scenic Palisades Interstate Park with a view of the Hudson, the George Washington Bridge, and Manhattan, Fort Lee commemorates a defeat, not a victory. The park is only 33 acres but contains a modern Visitor Center, meandering paved paths, a picnic area, reconstructed gun batteries and earthworks, and an authentic eighteenth-century soldiers' hut. The park is actually a quarter mile east of the original Fort Lee, named after General Charles Lee, who helped defend New York City.

Washington planned Fort Lee as a bulwark against the British navy's control of the Hudson River. With forts on both sides of the river and sunken ships in the river channel, Washington felt he could keep British ships at bay. However, General Howe forced the Americans out of Long Island and then New York City. In November 1776, when General Cornwallis ferried 6,000 men across the Hudson north of the fort, Washington ordered an immediate retreat. Weapons and other military supplies had to be left behind. It was a devastating blow that led to the darkest days of the Revolution, inspiring Thomas Paine's "The American Crisis" and his famous line "These are the times that try men's souls."

Today, you can see replicas of the abandoned cannon in the park and view the story on Plexiglas panels in the Visitor Center. A short film and displays of muskets are also on view. Down at the soldiers' hut, costumed guides interpret colonial life on summer weekends and for school groups. As part of the larger interstate park, good hiking trails and scenic overlooks are found nearby.

Also nearby is the Fort Lee Museum at the Judge Moore House. Operated by the Fort Lee Historical Society, this museum and adjacent Monument Park also offer exhibits on local Revolutionary history. The museum grounds served as an encampment area for Washington's troops. Open weekends, 12–4. **LOCATION:** 1588 Palisade Ave. **TELEPHONE:** 201-592-3580. **WEBSITE:** www.fortleenj.org/departments/museum.html.

Farther north, the Kearney House, along the Hudson at the Alpine Boat Basin, was long thought to have served as Cornwallis's overnight headquarters. Later research cast doubt on this notion and placed the British general's landing a mile or so to the south. But the belief did lead to the preservation of the four-room house as the nation's only historic site dedicated to a wartime enemy. Three rooms are furnished in nineteenth-century style and one contains exhibits of the Palisades Interstate Park in the 1920s. Open weekends and holidays, May–Oct., 12–5. **LOCATION:** Alpine Approach Rd., Alpine. **TELEPHONE:** 201-768-1360. **WEBSITE:** www.njpalisades.org/house.htm.

HOURS: Visitor Center: Mar.-Dec., Wed.–Sun., 10–5. **ADMISSION:** $ parking fee. **LOCATION:** Hudson Terrace, Fort Lee (Bergen County). Take last exit before George Washington Bridge. Turn left off Hudson Terrace. **TELEPHONE:** 201-461-1776. **WEBSITE:** www.njpalisades.org/historic.htm#Fort.

Monmouth Battlefield State Park

Although not a complete victory, the Battle of Monmouth on June 28, 1778, proved that American troops, honed by Von Steuben's training at Valley Forge, could win against the British. Today's park covers the scene of that hot day's artillery battle in which General Charles Lee ordered a retreat (later reprimanded by Washington), and a legendary lady named "Molly Pitcher" (whose real name was Mary Hays) became a heroine.

The rolling fields, woodlands, and orchards at Monmouth Battlefield are now peaceful, with several miles of nature trails. A large Visitor Center provides information and displays, including relief maps of the battle and videos of a reenactment of the fight as well as battle artifacts recovered from the area. Here you can pick up a map of the battlefield and nearby historic sites. Picnic facilities are nearby. In the park you will find the Craig House (off Rt. 9 South at Schiabanoff Rd.; open Sun., 12:30–4, Apr.–Oct.), which was occupied by the British and where the wounded were tended during the fight. The site of Molly Pitcher's well has not been precisely located, but it was near the Continental Army's artillery line on Perrine Ridge. A small sign along Route 522 indicates that it was at a farmhouse nearby. On the last weekend in June, you can see an annual reenactment of the battle.

> **HOURS:** Park, open daily, 8–4:30; spring & fall, 8–6; Memorial–Labor Day, 8–8:30. Visitor Center, daily, 9–4. **ADMISSION:** Free. **LOCATION:** Rt. 9 or Rt. 33 to Bus. Rt. 33 (Freehold Rd.), Manalapan (Monmouth County). One mile west of Rt. 9. **TELEPHONE:** 732-462-9616. **WEBSITE:** www.state.nj.us/dep/forestry/parks/monbat.htm.

Red Bank Battlefield

A small but decisive battle to defend Fort Mercer took place here on October 19, 1777. The Hessian army was soundly beaten by the Continentals, which, up until that point, had known mostly defeat. The fort, along with Fort Mifflin on the Pennsylvania side, guarded the Delaware River and prevented British ships from reaching occupied Philadelphia, so the defense of Fort Mercer was quite important. Although British ships got through after Fort Mifflin was lost, the victory at Red Bank, along with one at Saratoga, New York, three days earlier, convinced France to aid America's fight against the British. The picturesque park contains old cannons and monuments and some earthworks of Fort Mercer. Admission to the 1748 Whitall House, where the wounded were cared for, is free. Inside, there is a parlor, re-created field hospital, kitchen, an exhibit room, and an archeology office with a video on the park and historic artifacts that have been recovered there. The annual 18th Century Field Day, with a battle reenactment and other events, is held the third weekend in October, and candlelight holiday tours are held the second Friday and Saturday in December. Visitors can also enjoy Delaware Riverfront pathways and pier as well as an adjacent picnic area.

> **HOURS:** Grounds, daily, dawn–dusk. House, year-round, Wed.–Fri., 9–12 & 1–4. Also weekends, 1–4, Apr.–Oct. **ADMISSION:** Free. **LOCATION:** 100 Hessian Ave., National Park (Gloucester County).

TELEPHONE: 856-853-5120.
WEBSITE: www.co.gloucester.nj.us/parks/red.htm.

Indian King Tavern

Set in the town of Haddonfield, which looks as if it stepped out of the past, this public house, or tavern, was the site where the council and general assembly of the New Jersey legislature officially declared New Jersey a state in 1776. Among the many military visitors were General Anthony Wayne, Count Kasimir Pulaski, and the Marquis de Lafayette. The rooms shown by the guide include the keeping room (where food was brought in from a separate outside kitchen), bar room, assembly room, and the legislative council/public bedroom.

HOURS: Wed.–Sat., 10–12 & 1–4; Sun., 1–4. Closed major holidays and Wed. after holidays. **ADMISSION:** Free. Groups by appointment only. Children under 12 must be accompanied by an adult. Guided tours are ongoing; just wait at the door for the next tour. **LOCATION:** 233 Kings Highway, Haddonfield (Camden County). **TELEPHONE:** 856-429-6792. **WEBSITE:** www.levins.com/tavern.html.

Historic New Bridge Landing

Historic New Bridge Landing, known for the wooden bridge that allowed the Continental Army from Fort Lee to escape Cornwallis in 1776, is an 18-acre park that includes a number of historic buildings.

The Steuben House, built in 1752, with a further addition in 1765, is an example of early Dutch Colonial architecture. The house was confiscated during the Revolutionary War because the owners, the Zabriskie family, were loyal to the British. Its position on the Hackensack River made it a strategic prize for both sides, and it was the site of several skirmishes during the Revolution. Washington headquartered here in September 1780. The house was presented to Baron von Steuben in 1781 for his service in training the troops during the war. Noticeable in the furnishings here is the emphasis on local craftsmen and on the Dutch influence in Bergen County. Some fine specimens of the local colonial craft include a New Brunswick kas and an old settle.

The Campbell-Christie House was built in 1774 by Jacob Campbell in New Milford, and it served as a tavern in the late 1700s after it was bought by John Christie. The inventor J. Walter Christie, born in the house in 1865, worked on pioneer submarines, developed front-wheel drive for cars and trucks, and is the father of the modern tank. The house, moved here in 1977, serves as the headquarters of the Bergen County Historical Society and houses the society's collection of furniture and historic objects. It is open and staffed for special events only. **TELEPHONE:** 201-343-9492. **WEBSITE:** www.carrol. com/bchs.

The Demarest House Museum (J. Paulison Homestead), a Bergen Dutch sandstone cottage with two rooms built in the 1790s, was moved behind the Steuben House from nearby River Road in 1956. At the time, it was believed to be a home of the family of early pioneer Samuel Demarest. It is open and staffed only during special events. **TELEPHONE:** 201-261-0012.

> **HOURS:** Steuben House, Wed.–Sat., 10–12 & 1–5; Sun., 2–5. **ADMISSION:** Free. **LOCATION:** 1209 Main St., River Edge (Bergen County). Take River Edge exit from Rt. 4. **TELEPHONE:** 201-487-1739. **WEBSITE:** www.carroll.com/bchs.

Covenhoven House

One of the four historic houses administered by the Monmouth County Historical Association, it is significant for its role in the Battle of Monmouth. Henry Clinton, commander of the British troops at the battle, stayed at the home from Friday, June 26, until Sunday, June 28, 1778. After the battle, he and his troops left Freehold and returned to New York.

The main section of the home is in Georgian style and is furnished according to a 1790 inventory of William A. Covenhoven, the well-to-do farmer who owned the property. A mural depicting a sea battle and walls decorated in a blue-and white Delft pattern were discovered in one bedroom during the restoration of the house. Extremely authentic and well done—an interesting house to visit.

> **HOURS:** May–Sept., Tue., Thu., Sun., 1–4; Sat., 10–4. **ADMISSION:** $. Discounts: Seniors, children. Under 6 free. **LOCATION:** 150 West Main St., Freehold (Monmouth County). **TELEPHONE:** 732-462-1466.

Proprietary House

This mansion is a true Palladian villa, known as High Georgian in America. It was built in 1763 for the last royal governor of New Jersey (who was Benjamin Franklin's "natural" son, William). However, Franklin did not move in until 1774. When the Revolutionary War began, he was arrested—for, unlike his famous father, he chose the Tory side. Benjamin Franklin made two visits in 1775 but could not talk his son into switching allegiance.

The house suffered much damage during the war and succumbed to fire in 1792. After that it had as many ups and downs as a soap opera heroine. It was a popular seaside hotel, and then was sold at a sheriff s auction. There were "rich" years as a merchant's abode, and then a downward slide. The house became in turn a widow and orphans' home, an apartment house, and a rooming house. Restoration began some years ago and is still ongoing. Special exhibits are on view throughout the year.

Although the house is sparsely furnished, during a tour one can get a feel for its dimensions. The true Palladian windows, the high ceilings, and the Adamesque fireplace are evident. The governor's drawing room, also called the "Great Parlour," is dramatic. The fully restored upstairs bedroom features a housekeeper's typical furniture. The most charming room in the building is the downstairs vaulted wine cellar constructed of red brick.

> **HOURS:** Wed., 10–4; Sun. by appt. **ADMISSION:** $. Under 12 free.
> **LOCATION:** 149 Kearny Ave., Perth Amboy (Middlesex County).
> **TELEPHONE:** 732-826-5527.

Boxwood Hall

Also known as the Boudinot Mansion, this very nicely furnished colonial house is not far from the main drag in Elizabeth. Built in 1750, it was the home, during the Revolution, of Elias Boudinot, president of the Continental Congress. George Washington had lunch here on the day he embarked for New York and his inauguration as president. House furnishings include both the Colonial and later Empire style. State Historic Site.

> **HOURS:** Mon.–Sat., 9–12 & 1–5. **ADMISSION:** Free. **LOCATION:** 1073 East
> Jersey St., Elizabeth (Union County). Off Rts. 1 and 9. **TELEPHONE:**
> 973-648-4540. Call first.

Buccleuch Mansion

This is a handsome Georgian mansion with outstanding decoration. The surrounding gardens are very impressive. The house is set inside Buccleuch Park on a tree-lined street that is practically part of the Rutgers University campus in New Brunswick. Originally built in 1763, White House Farm, as it was then known, was sold to an English army officer in 1774.

The house was confiscated by the Americans in 1776, but by December the British troops had reoccupied New Brunswick. The banister still retains the marks of the soldiers' musket barrels from the time of this occupation, which lasted until 1777. After the war, Colonel Charles Stewart, Commissary General of the Revolutionary Army, became the owner. At this time, White House Farm was visited by George Washington, John Hancock, and Alexander Hamilton, all of whom loved the setting.

Much of Buccleuch Mansion's furnishings today are of nineteenth-century origin. Of particular note is the striking wallpaper in the downstairs and upstairs hallways. Rooms include a Victorian parlor and a drawing room with Queen Anne pieces. You can also inspect the bedrooms (including the one where Washington slept), a toy room, and a craft room with spinning wheel.

HOURS: June–Oct., Sun., 2–4. Group tours by appointment. Although visiting hours are limited, the surrounding park and well-tended gardens are always open. **ADMISSION:** Free (donations accepted). **LOCATION:** Easton Ave. to Buccleuch Park, New Brunswick (Middlesex County). **TELEPHONE:** 732-745-5094.

Rockingham

Washington lived in this house when it was in Rocky Hill in 1783 while the Constitution was being hammered out at nearby Princeton. Actually, both George and Martha stayed here and entertained extensively. It is best known as the house where the "Farewell Address to the Armies" was composed. The story that Washington read the farewell to assembled troops from the porch has not been substantiated.

A handsome, medium-sized two-story colonial with front porch, the house was once part of a fine estate of 350 acres with barns, coach house, and granary. It was removed from its original site (because of dynamiting in a nearby quarry) and set on Route 518. Then it was removed again in 2001 and sent to a Kingston Township location very close to its previous location.

Rockingham's furnishings include such period pieces as Chippendale sets, burnished bureaus, canopied beds, and an antique tea service. The study where the Farewell Address was composed is shown with the ink stand and green cloth on the table. This setting will all be re-created at the new site. New outbuildings and a kitchen garden are planned for the ample lot. Details for hours were not available at press time. **TELEPHONE:** 609-921-8835.

Other Revolutionary War Sites

Princeton Battlefield State Park: A short decisive battle was fought here on January 3, 1777, just a week after the famous crossing of the Delaware. General Hugh Mercer was mortally wounded during this battle. Within the park, you can visit the Thomas Clarke House, a refurbished colonial home used as a hospital following the battle, when it is open. Free. **HOURS:** 9 A.M. to dusk. **LOCATION:** 500 Mercer St., Princeton. **TELEPHONE:** 609-921-0074.

Washington Rock Park: This huge outcropping at the top of Watchung Mountain offers a 30-mile panorama that includes New York City. Washington used it in 1777 during the Middlebrook encampment to track the movements of the British army. It was used more recently to view the sad events of 9/11. A makeshift memorial to the victims made up of flowers, flags, and other tributes grew up around it. The park has limited parking space but there are picnic tables. Green Brook (Somerset County). Free.

Drake House: During the battle of the Watchung Mountains, Washington used this house as his command headquarters. Although there is a colonial bedroom where he is supposed to have rested, the house was later remodeled. It now reflects the Empire and Victorian styles as well as the basic Colonial. **HOURS:** Sun., 2–4. **ADMISSION:** $. **LOCATION:** 602 W. Front St., Plainfield (Union County). **TELEPHONE:** 908-755-5831.

Schuyler-Hamilton House: This nice little Colonial home is squeezed into a cul-de-sac along with a cluster of other buildings in downtown Morristown. This is where Alexander Hamilton courted Betsey Schuyler when he was aide-de-camp to Washington at the nearby Ford Mansion. **ADMISSION:** $. **LOCATION:** 5 Olyphant Place, Morristown (Morris County). **TELEPHONE:** 973-267-4039. Call for hours.

Allen House: Since this 1750 house was operated as the Blue Ball Tavern during the Revolutionary War, two major rooms here have been furnished in that manner. Tables are set with pewter, there is a bar and grill with whiskey jugs, and so forth. It was a meeting place for local revolutionaries. Upstairs, there are changing exhibits. **HOURS:** May–Sept., Tue., Thu., Sun., 1–4; Sat., 10–4. **ADMISSION:** $. Under 6 free. **LOCATION:** Rt. 35 & Sycamore Ave., Shrewsbury (Monmouth County). **TELEPHONE:** 732-462-1466.

Hancock House: In a raid on March 21, 1778, nine Continental soldiers and Judge William Hancock were killed here and twenty others were wounded. This 1734 house has five rooms filled with period furnishings. There's also a Swedish Colonial cabin on the site, salvaged from another area home, where it was discovered encased in later construction. Wed.–Sat., 10–2 & 1–4, Sun., 1–4. Free. **LOCATION:** Rt. 49 at Hancock's Bridge, 5 miles south of Salem (Salem County). **TELEPHONE:** 856-935-4373.

Van Horne House: During the battle of Bound Brook in 1777, British troops captured three American cannons on the front lawn. The house was used by American generals Lincoln, Stirling, and Lee and

British general Cornwallis during the war. Exhibits. Special events. **ADMISSION:** $. Open on weekends; call for hours. **LOCATION:** 941 E. Main St., Bridgewater (Somerset County). Across the street from Commerce Bank Ballpark. **TELEPHONE:** 732-356-8856. **WEBSITE:** www. heritagetrail.org.

Cannon Ball House: Built in 1740, this house was used as a hospital during the Battle of Springfield in 1780. During the battle, the house was struck by a cannonball, which is now on display. One of only four structures standing after the British burned the town, today the house has been renovated to its original appearance and is the Springfield Historical Society headquarters. It has five Revolution-ary-era rooms, some Civil War items, early tools, a battle diorama, and a colonial garden. Open for four special events during the year and by appointment. **LOCATION:** 126 Morris Ave., Springfield (Union County). **TELEPHONE:** 973-912-4464.

Osborn Cannonball House Museum: This colonial saltbox farmhouse run by the Scotch Plains-Fanwood Historical Society was built around 1760. It features a restored kitchen and three rooms deco-rated to reflect its original Colonial style plus one depicting the Vic-torian period. Outside, you can enjoy a colonial herb and flower garden noted for its historical accuracy. The house received its name from a cannonball fired at the British in 1777 that hit the house instead. **LOCATION:** 1840 Front Street, Scotch Plains (Union County). Costumed docents lead tours 2–4, the first Sun. of each month and on special holidays, except Jan.–Feb. **TELEPHONE:** 908-322-6700, ext. 230.

NEARBY OUT-OF-STATE SITE

Valley Forge National Historic Park

It is known as "The Crucible of Victory" because the 10,000 men who emerged from the harsh winter had coalesced into an efficient, well-trained fighting force. The encampment lasted from December 19, 1777, to June 19, 1778. It is now commemorated in a 3,466-acre park, which is so big you must start with a map or a bus tour. The modern Welcome Center offers an 18-minute film and a small exhibit of Revolutionary military equipment. This is where you can board buses, which operate in warm weather, for a tour that stops at key sites and features a taped narration along the way. Or you can rent or buy a tape to use when you drive the tour route yourself. Among the important sites on the scenic drive are the National Memorial Arch, earthen fortifications, the parade ground where

Von Steuben trained and reviewed the troops, soldiers' huts, Artillery Park, and headquarters of several of Washington's generals.

When you get to Washington's Headquarters, costumed soldiers are on hand to welcome you. There is a small additional admission fee here in season. There are often costumed personnel at the soldiers' huts as well who point out the hardships Revolutionary soldiers endured here. The park also has picnic grounds, bicycle trails, a snack bar, a souvenir shop, and lots of beautiful scenery. There is a small entrance fee April through November, and there is a fee for bus tours, tapes, and entry to some historic houses.

HOURS: Open daily except Christmas, grounds open sunrise to sunset, Washington's Headquarters, 9–5. For buses, warm weather only.
LOCATION: Visitor Center, Junction of PA 23 & N. Gulph Rd., Valley Forge, PA. Take Exit 326 from Pennsylvania Turnpike. **TELEPHONE:** 610-783-1077. **WEBSITE:** www.nps.gov/vafo.

Historic Homes
of the Rich and Famous

Skylands is a Tudor-style mansion that presides over terraces and gardens at the Skylands section of Ringwood State Park. *(Photo by Patrick Sarver)*

Lambert Castle

Situated on a hillside below the cliffs of the Garret Mountain Reservation on the border of Paterson and Clifton, Lambert Castle is impressive inside and out. Designed and built by silk manufacturer Catholina Lambert in nineteenth-century opulence, it was inspired by castles he saw during his childhood in England. This 1892 sandstone and granite mansion stands like a medieval castle with rounded towers and crenelated turrets, recalling images of long-bow archers repelling invaders.

It wasn't invading hordes that undid Lambert, however, but the silk strike of 1913 and a decline in the American silk trade. Many of Lambert's prized European paintings and fine furnishings had to be sold to pay his debts. He retained the house, though, until his death in 1923. Soon after, it became part of the Passaic County park system, along with Garret Mountain Reservation, which encompasses hundreds of acres of woods, picnic grounds, and an impressive overlook atop the cliffs behind the castle. Lambert's hilltop observation tower still stands there and is currently undergoing restoration. The view from the castle also remains impressive, encompassing the city of Paterson and the New York skyline to the east.

The castle today is the home of the Passaic County Historical Society, and its first-floor rooms (dining room, music room, breakfast room, front hall, Lambert's office, and private art court) contain a number of Lambert's possessions, including artwork and a 13½-foot-high clock made for the 1867 Paris Exhibition. On the second floor you'll find numerous paintings and artifacts related to local history. The third floor contains changing exhibits. Also of note is a stained-glass window above the stairway memorializing Lambert's daughter Florence, who died in her early twenties. Volunteers provide on-going tours, and the castle also has a small gift shop. Note: From early November to early December, furnishings are removed to accommodate a Holiday Craft Fair fundraiser.

> **HOURS:** Wed.–Sun., 1–4. **ADMISSION:** $. Discounts: Seniors, students.
> Under 12 free. **LOCATION:** Valley Rd., Paterson (Passaic County).
> Exit 57 off Rts. 80 and 19. **TELEPHONE:** 973-881-2761. **WEBSITES:** Castle,
> www.lambertcastle.com; Historical Society, www.geocities.com/pchslc.

Walt Whitman House

A narrow row house in Camden contains the rooms where the poet who sang of America lived out the last eight years of his life. This national historic landmark offers a glimpse into the life of the poet. Whitman's original letters, personal belongings, the bed in which he died, and the death notice that was nailed to the front door in 1892 have all been preserved. There is also a collection of rare nineteenth-century photos, including the earliest known image of Whitman taken in 1848. (Whitman was the most photographed person in America in his time.)

Accumulations of furniture (much of it the housekeeper's, which she brought with her when she took over the job), books, pipes, and other memorabilia are here. Whitman had a paralytic stroke, and some of the house's contents were given to him by friends during his disabled period. A bathtub kept in the bedroom is typical of the many gifts his friends collected for him. A settee there was for his visitors.

Surprisingly, this house has only a few rooms on each floor. Whitman spent the money collected by friends on an elaborate mausoleum in a cemetery 2 miles away. The house has been returned to its original look, with mustard-colored walls, wallpaper, and fading furniture. A guide will show you displays of books, manuscripts, and photographs. The house is close to the Camden waterfront area and the Benjamin Franklin Bridge.

> **HOURS:** Wed.–Sat., 10–12 & 1–4; Sun., 1–4. Call first. **ADMISSION:** Free. **LOCATION:** 328 Mickle Blvd., Camden (Camden County). Two blocks from waterfront attractions. **TELEPHONE:** 856-964-5383.

Edison National Historic Site

This National Park site consists of the Edison Laboratory Complex in downtown West Orange, and Glenmont, Thomas Edison's home, a mile away in the private enclave of Lewellyn Park. The laboratory section includes a Visitors Center with exhibits of Edison's inventions, a separate chemistry lab, a huge storage section of elephant ears and other unusual resources, and a replica of the "invention factory." Also on the grounds is a replica of the original "Black Maria," where early films were shot.

Although ongoing renovation keeps the labs closed, they may open for short periods before the official 2005 reopening date. There will be structural changes, but one thing that will remain the same is Edison's golden oak library, where his cot, desk, and 10,000 volumes of books still stand. The huge clock on the wall is stopped at 3:27—the time on October 18, 1931, when Edison died.

As for Glenmont, the rambling Queen Anne–style house where Edison lived with his second wife, Minna, is a warm family home filled with carved oak woodwork, oriental rugs, and mementos from world visitors. The house and surrounding gardens (including the gravesite) will also be closed until the renovation is finished. Check the Website for updates.

> **HOURS:** The site is closed for renovation until mid-2005. **LOCATION:** Main St. & Lakeside Ave., West Orange (Essex County). **TELEPHONE:** 973-736-0550. **WEBSITE:** www.nps.gov/edis.

Historic Morven

This gracious Georgian Colonial mansion has been the home of five governors, two senators, and at least one millionaire. Richard Stockton, a leading colonial attorney and later a signer of the Declaration of Independence, built this historic Princeton residence in

1758. His wife, poet Annis Boudinot Stockton, named it "Morven" after the mythical kingdom in a popular epic poem. The house was occupied by British troops for a time during the Revolutionary War when Richard was taken prisoner. After he died in 1781, Annis remained there. She hosted members of the Continental Congress during their Princeton stay in 1783, when they convened in Nassau Hall to hammer out the Constitution. (The president of the Congress, Elias Boudinot, was her brother.) Descendants of the Stockton family (for whom both Stockton, New Jersey, and Stockton, California, are named) kept ownership of the house for many years. Later, Robert Wood Johnson of the Johnson & Johnson pharmaceutical firm purchased the house and added a pool and modern conveniences.

In 1945, Governor Walter Edge bought the house and later deeded it to the state to be used either as an official residence for governors or a museum. After years as a governors' abode, the mansion and surrounding 5-acre garden became too small for official functions. The official residence was moved in the 1980s, and Morven returned to museum status. Since then, Morven has been opened, closed, its gardens dug up, and its furnishings and paintings squabbled over. Now the gardens will be replanted to their original colonial look, and the house will become partly a museum for decorative arts and partly a restored eighteenth-century mansion. The reopening of the gardens and mansion will take place in steps.

HOURS: TBA. **LOCATION:** 55 Stockton St. (Rt. 206), Princeton (Mercer County). **TELEPHONE:** 609-683-4495. **WEBSITE:** www.morven.org.

Grover Cleveland Birthplace

Grover Cleveland, the only U.S. president born in New Jersey, spent his early childhood in this pleasant manse. The clapboard house was built in 1832 for the pastor of the First Presbyterian Society. Two years later, the Reverend Richard F. Cleveland obtained that position. Grover was born here in 1837, but four years later the pastor moved his family to Buffalo.

The house, which is a state historic site, includes a museum area and a restored house area. The open-hearth kitchen reflects the earlier 1830 period, when life in the country was fairly simple. However, a number of later pieces from Cleveland's presidency reflect the richer, more ornate world of the 1880s. A large chair from his White House term plus several other pieces show both Cleveland's girth and his station in life. A picture of Mrs. Frances Cleveland, a beautiful young woman whom he married when she was 21 and he was 49, adorns the house. Frances was Grover's ward, and she turned down his marriage proposal several times before she finally said yes. She was the youngest First Lady ever, and their marriage was the first to take place in the White House. Their baby, Ruth, was a media icon and became the namesake of a still-popular candy bar. Much memorabilia and photographs of Cleveland and his administration can be found here. Cleveland was the only president to be elected to two nonconsecutive terms and is best remembered in trivia books for that distinction. However, he was president during the Gilded Age, and the memorabilia here reflect that.

After his second term, Cleveland retired to Princeton, where he served as lecturer and trustee. He became friends with Woodrow Wilson, who was president of the university at that time. Cleveland is buried, incidentally, in the Princeton Cemetery. The manse is set on a busy street in Caldwell. Although it is not large, there is a nice garden out back and ample parking space.

HOURS: Wed.–Sat., 9–12 & 1–5; Sun., 1–6. Call first. **ADMISSION:** Free.
LOCATION: 207 Bloomfield Ave., Caldwell (Essex County).
TELEPHONE: 973-226-0001.

Ballantine House

One of the pleasures of visiting the Newark Museum is touring the Ballantine House next door. You enter this opulent late Victorian townhouse from an interior passageway in the museum proper. This corridor is filled with Belleek pieces and other decorative china. Inside, a foyer depicts the history of the Victorian home as a haven from the outside world. In fact, you get a short course in cultural history before you enter the actual house. The Ballantines were a Scottish family who rose from poor immigrants to wealthy beer barons within the span of two generations. They built this house in fashionable Washington Park when they had "arrived." But this three-story Renaissance Revival townhouse is shown not only as a family home but also as an emblem of the Victorian upper class of the 1880s, with their manners and aspirations.

A hallway leads you to the public rooms on the first floor—the library, dining room, reception room, and parlor. While you cannot go completely into the rooms, you can see everything perfectly from behind the room barriers. It is a marvelous job of restoration, with the colors brighter and the furniture cleaner than it probably ever was in its heyday. In the high Victorian period the term "interior decoration" was taken literally and every inch of space was covered, plastered, paneled, draped, or otherwise prettified. The dining room, for instance, features oak and cherry parquet floors, mahogany woodwork, a ceiling of molded papier mache panels

The ornate dining room of the Ballantine House, Newark.
(Photo courtesy Newark Museum)

between painted plaster beams, and walls of leather-looking paper. Add to that a brick and wood fireplace, small stained glass windows, tapestried chairs, and a table sparkling with white linen, and you get a scene of solid bourgeois luxury that was meant to impress the guests. Other rooms include the delicate French-style parlor and the somber reception room where visitors would wait while their calling cards were brought to the family. A magnificent stained glass window with its rising sun presides over the stairwell. On the second floor the family bedrooms and exhibits of china and silver are on view. The silver includes some niceties of formal dining, such as pickle forks and place-card holders. The Ballantine House provides not only insights into Victorian living, but its legacy of manners and mores as well.

HOURS: Wed., Sun., 12–5. **ADMISSION:** Free. **LOCATION:** 49 Washington St., Newark. Enter through Newark Museum. **TELEPHONE:** 973-596-6550. **WEBSITE:** www.newarkmuseum.org.

Bainbridge House

This small brick building wedged between businesses on Princeton's busy Nassau Street stands opposite the iron gates of Princeton University. Built in 1766 by Job Stockton, cousin of Declaration of Independence signer Richard Stockton, the house was the birthplace of Captain William Bainbridge, a hero of the War of 1812 and commander of the U.S.S. *Constitution*. British general William Howe reputedly used the house as his headquarters in late 1776, and it may have provided housing for Congress when it met in Princeton in 1783. Today it serves as headquarters for the Historical Society of Princeton, which has restored the house to its eighteenth-century appearance. Luckily, the historical society keeps its house open to the public much longer than most. A typical small home of a well-to-do family of the late eighteenth century, it features exhibits on Princeton history but mostly displays changing exhibits on detailed topics. There's also a small museum shop, and the society conducts tours of Princeton from here. Anyone can join the 2 P.M. Sunday walking tour. Self-guided maps are also available.

> **HOURS:** Tue.–Sun., 12–4. Closed Jan., Feb. except weekends.
> **LOCATION:** 158 Nassau Street, Princeton (Mercer County).
> **TELEPHONE:** 609-921-6748. **WEBSITE:** www.princetonhistory.org.

Ringwood Manor

If they ever film a Chekhov play in New Jersey, Ringwood Manor would make a perfect setting. This rambling manor house set on a rise overlooking a small lake where ducks paddle about is a prime example of the Victorian country house. Actually, the house goes back to colonial days, when it was the residence of Martin Ryerson, an ironmaster during the Revolutionary War.

One side of the house has been restored to reflect that period, with the gracious colonial dining room and foyer part of the tour. Relics of the old iron forge days dot the landscape. Short cannons and iron chains are placed near the entrance as a salute to the heavy artillery that was forged in this area. But it is the expanded manor with a porte cochere designed by Stanford White that gives Ringwood its high Victorian look. In 1854, it became the country home of Peter Cooper, the industrialist and philanthropist who founded not only Cooper Union but also the short-lived Greenback Party. Then his son-in-law, Abram S. Hewitt, took over. Ringwood was enlarged and modernized to nineteenth-century taste. It became a pleasant haven filled with antiques and cottage furniture. The Victorian rooms open to the public include bedrooms with lace curtains, parlors filled with paintings, a heavy oak stairway, and bronze chandeliers.

Outside on the grassy lawn and beyond, visitors picnic or meander around the wide grounds with their gardens. The manor presides over one corner of a huge state park in the Ramapo Mountains. Each section of the park has its own tollgate and parking fee (during the summer season). Shepherd's Lake has a lovely swimming, canoeing, and picnic area and therefore is by far the most popular area of the park, filling up early on weekends.

> **HOURS:** Park, daily, dawn–dusk. Manor House, Memorial Day to Labor Day, Wed.–Sun., 10–4. **ADMISSION:** Summer parking fees, $. **LOCATION:** 1304 Sloatsburg Rd., Ringwood (Passaic County). Rt. 287 to Exit 57, then follow signs. **TELEPHONE:** 973-962-7031. **WEBSITES:** www.ringwoodmanor.com, or www.state.nj.us/dep/forestry/parks/ringwood.htm.

Skylands Manor

In another section of Ringwood State Park you can find Skylands, a 44-room mansion in the Tudor style that looks like an English castle. Skylands is best known for the state botanical gardens (q.v.), but the first-floor rooms of the mansion are open for limited Sunday afternoon tours and one weekend in December, when it is decked out for Christmas.

The house as it appears now was built in 1922 by architect John Russell Pope for investment banker and garden connoisseur Clarence Mackenzie Lewis. The interior has sparse furnishings but features stained glass medallions in its leaded windows and a huge marble mantle. The stone terrace with its view of flowering trees and statuary is quite romantic. The whole house has the look of an English baron's esate. At one time the holdings covered almost 2,000 acres, but the present house and gardens comprise around 96 acres. While the gardens and trails are part of the state park and open all the time, tours of the mansion are handled by the Skylands Association. A private catering company handles weddings and corporate functions inside the mansion. Group tours were allowed on weekdays in the past. Check with the Skylands Association on this; the situation changes over time.

> **HOURS:** First Sun. of month except Jan. & Feb., 1–4. **ADMISSION:** Summer parking fee, $. **LOCATION:** Morris Rd., Ringwood (Passaic County). Rt. 287 to Exit 57, then follow signs. **TELEPHONE:** 973-962-7031. **WEBSITES:** www.njbg.org, or www.state.nj.us/dep/forestry/parks/ringwood.htm.

Liberty Hall Museum

When you drive through towns like Livingston and Caldwell or pass Kean University, do you ever wonder about the people behind those names? Liberty Hall, an estate on the Essex/Union county border, was the enclave of two illustrious families. It has been converted into a "living history" museum and can be found tucked behind corporate buildings across from Kean University.

William Livingston built the original colonial homestead in 1772. A member of the Constitutional Convention, Livingston became the first elected governor of New Jersey. When the governor's daughter married John Kean, the two families became entwined. The house is full of history. John Jay, the first Chief Justice of the Supreme Court, married Livingston's daughter Sarah in the front hall. When he was a teenager, Alexander Hamilton lived in one of the upstairs bedrooms for a year. And in 1780, during the Revolutionary War, British soldiers invaded the home—the hatch marks of their sabers are still evident on the banisters. They fled when they thought they saw the ghost of Hannah Caldwell, a minister's wife who had been killed in the nearby Battle of Springfield, on the staircase.

Since the Kean family lived in Liberty Hall until the 1970s, furnishings represent all the eras the house encompasses: Colonial, Victorian, Edwardian, art deco, and modern. Many people still remember the elegant lifestyle of the last of the Kean family to inhabit the house. Reminiscent of that lifestyle is the Afternoon Tea,

Alexander Hamilton's bedroom at Liberty Hall Museum, where he stayed while attending boarding school "up north." *(Photo courtesy Liberty Hall Museum)*

available on Wednesdays. It is served as it would have been in the 1930s with scones, jam, tea sandwiches, and white glove service. (Reservations required/separate fee.) Regular tours include the Visitor Center, outbuildings, and the surrounding gardens (a formal English parterre, a rose garden, fruit trees, and a large horse chestnut planted in 1772). Special events, such as an 1890s baseball game, are also featured on particular weekends.

> **HOURS:** Wed.–Sat., 10–4; Sun., 12–4. Closed Jan–Mar. **ADMISSION:** $$$.
> Under 6 free. **LOCATION:** 1003 Morris Ave., Union. **TELEPHONE:**
> 908-527-0400. **WEBSITE:** www.libertyhallnj.org.

MacCulloch Hall

This 1908 Federal-style structure has furnishings that are quite handsome. These include oriental rugs, huge crystal chandeliers brought over from the Twombly estate in Madison (now a Fairleigh Dickinson campus), and an original portrait of Washington by Rembrandt Peale. There is no attempt to furnish each room according to a specific period, but you will see quality cupboards, china, and crystal of the eighteenth and nineteenth century throughout. Besides its eclectic collections, MacCulloch Hall is a museum dedicated primarily to the decorative arts. Temporary exhibits vary, so anything from a cache of English teapots to quilts to vases might be shown in the museum rooms. A permanent gallery is dedicated to Thomas Nast, the famous cartoonist whose vitriolic drawings helped topple the corrupt Boss Tweed in New York. (Nast's house, a private residence, is diagonally across the street). His depictions of Santa Claus created the classic image we now know. Nast also created the donkey and elephant as symbols of the political parties. The house is open for limited hours, but you may wander through the English garden behind it daily. The mansion is tastefully decorated for Christmas tours and offers special exhibits at other times of the year.

> **HOURS:** Wed., Thu., & Sun., 1–4. **ADMISSION:** $. Under 12 free.
> **LOCATION:** 45 MacCulloch Ave., Morristown (Morris County).
> 2 blocks south of South St. (Rt. 124). **TELEPHONE:** 973-538-2404.
> **WEBSITE:** www.machall.org.

Drumthwacket

On any Wednesday you can visit Drumthwacket, the governor's mansion in Princeton, for a tour of the gracious Greek Revival building that has been refurbished to the hilt. The governor will not be in, of course. For two hours, this white-columned house belongs to those who pay for its maintenance, namely New Jersey residents.

Drumthwacket, the governor's mansion in Princeton, is open to the public on Wednesday afternoons. *(Photo by Barbara Hudgins)*

With its two-story Ionic columns and wide veranda, Drumthwacket will remind many of the plantation houses of the Deep South. Indeed, Charles Olden, who built it in 1835, had spent nine years in New Orleans and was impressed by southern architecture.

The entrance hallway includes several historic paintings. A docent explains the history of the building as you move from room to room. Moses Taylor Pyne bought the estate from Olden's widow in 1893. Pyne named the house Drumthwacket, which is Celtic for "wooded hill." He added two wings, one of which includes a striking wood-paneled library with a Gothic Revival stone fireplace mantel worthy of a Dracula film. You can also visit the Governor's Study, which features an unusual two-sided desk.

The dining room is most impressive. The extra-long table is often set with sterling silver candelabra, an ornate punchbowl, and gold-trimmed Lenox china with the green seal of New Jersey. Across the hall in a comfortably furnished living room, a special exhibit of New Jersey porcelains from the studios of Cybis and Boehm are displayed. Many paintings and furnishings have been donated; others are on loan from museums. Outside, you can wander through the lovely formal terraced gardens behind the house that have been restored.

HOURS: Wed., 12–2. Reservations needed. **ADMISSION:** Free.
LOCATION: 354 Stockton St., Princeton (Mercer County).
TELEPHONE: 609-683-0057. **WEBSITE:** www.drumthwacket.org.

William Trent House

The founder of Trenton—so to speak, because his house and property were known as Trent's Town—William Trent built his stately home in 1719. It was later the residence of four governors. "A genteel brick dwelling house, three stories high, with a large, handsome staircase and entry," according to an early observer, it is one of the best restorations in New Jersey. It is built in the Georgian style with eighteenth-century English furniture and many early American pieces. Some of the William and Mary and Queen Anne furnishings here are equal to what you would find in Colonial Williamsburg.

Guided tours are run by knowledgeable volunteers who give out many tidbits of information. They will point out teacups without handles, which were early imports from China, and the front parlor chandelier with removable "arms" (candleholders that were used to light the way to bed). In the master bedroom is a trundle bed for the children that pulled out from the main, canopied bed. Although this was a wealthy colonial household, it was not unusual for children to sleep in the same room as their parents. The downstairs kitchen, with its wealth of old-fashioned gadgets, is alone worth the tour. A visitor center in an adjacent carriage house includes a gift shop.

HOURS: Daily, 12:30–4. **ADMISSION:** $. Discounts: Students, children.
LOCATION: 15 Market St., Trenton. **TELEPHONE:** 609-989-3027.
WEBSITE: www.williamtrenthouse.org.

Kuser Farm Mansion

The country home of the Kusers was built in 1882 as both a vacation home and a working farm. The family had financial interests in hotels, beer, cars, and more, but is best known for its connection with 20th Century Fox movie studio. The elder Kuser had helped William Fox start his motion picture company with a $200,000 loan. The connection continued for years, with the Kusers showing movies at a specially constructed screen in their dining room well into the 1960s. While the house is not a place of super luxury (it was meant for casual summer entertaining and family get-togethers), it is of meticulous craftsmanship. Specially trained German craftsmen worked on the ornately carved mantelpieces throughout the house. Double floors, heavy woodwork, stained glass windows, and a bedroom featuring a Delft tile fireplace are among the notable details.

The 45-foot dining room features a heavily ornate table and chairs that were the hallmark of the Victorian age.

The Kuser Mansion and surrounding farm were sold to Hamilton Township in the late 1970s to be used as a public park. The outdoor area includes a gazebo and many picnic tables and has a pleasant, quiet atmosphere. Last tour begins half an hour before closing.

HOURS: (House) May–Nov., Thu.–Sun., 11–3. **ADMISSION:** Free. Christmas open house and other special events. **LOCATION:** 390 Newkirk Ave., Hamilton Twp. (Mercer County). Take Kuser Rd. exit from Rt. 295. **TELEPHONE:** 609-890-3630.

Craftsman Farms

No, it's not a farm. And there usually are no craftsmen. This is the home of Gustav Stickley, a well-known furniture designer of the early twentieth century. He was also the foremost American spokesman for the Arts and Crafts movement. His large, wooden, somewhat chunky furniture is often referred to as "Mission" style. Stickley also published a journal called *The Craftsman* (hence the name of the farm), which printed his house designs. Although he was not a trained architect, his plans appealed to those who disliked the overly ornate houses of the Victorian age. Since local builders used these plans, there are many Craftsman-style houses in New Jersey. They are typically two-story, with large overhanging eaves, a porch supported by round, wooden columns, and windows that are grouped together. When styles changed and his furniture and house plans were no longer popular, Stickley went bankrupt. Nowadays, Stickley furniture is back in vogue.

Craftsman Farms was saved from developers a few years ago. There are 26 acres left of the original 650-acre tract. The main house—a large log cabin with a stone chimney—was originally intended as a clubhouse for a boys' farm. This explains the huge kitchen and the 50-foot-long living room and dining room. The home features rounded ceiling beams and hammered copper fireplace hoods and, of course, Stickley furniture. Tours take about an hour and include a short walk around the sloping acreage. An interesting gift shop sells books on the Arts and Crafts movement. Many special events, plus brown-bag Wednesday lectures, are features here.

HOURS: Apr.–mid-Nov., Wed.–Fri., 12–3; Sat., 10–4; Sun., 11–4. **ADMISSION:** $$. Discounts: Seniors, children. Under 6 free. **LOCATION:** Rt. 287 to Rt. 10 west to Powder Mill Estates, Parsipanny (Morris County). Follow signs. **TELEPHONE:** 973-540-1165. **WEBSITE:** www.stickleymuseum.org.

NEARBY OUT-OF-STATE HOMES
Nemours

The fabulous homes of the super-rich are America's equivalent of the palaces and castles of Europe. And no home is more palatial than Nemours, the former residence of Alfred I. DuPont, located outside Wilmington in the popular Brandywine Valley area. The mansion, built in 1909, is a modified Louis XVI French chateau. The landscaped gardens are in the French formal style and include marble statues, cascading fountains, and a series of terraces and stairways to please the eye. In fact, the hand of Louis XVI seems to be everywhere in Nemours, a tribute as much to the Gallic origins of the DuPonts as to the possibility that American millionaires in 1910 must have known the era of conspicuous consumption was about to end. A few years later the income tax and World War I helped destroy any notion of an American aristocracy.

Once you enter the chateau, you are led by a tour guide into a home of vast elegance. The gold and white dining room has ornate moldings on walls and ceilings, Rococo-style paintings, and a chandelier worthy of the Phantom of the Opera. The reception room, living room, and other public rooms are equally fabulous with inlaid ceilings, marble tiled floors, rich oriental rugs, and carved walls. Furniture includes both genuine antiques, such as George Washington's chair, as well as fine copies of Louis XVI furnishings.

You rarely see kitchens of great homes, but at Nemours there's a downstairs tour of a restaurant-sized cooking area with an empty pantry and huge pots. Also downstairs is a bowling alley, a billiard room (with a table the size of a bowling alley), and a furnace room (ingeniously set up by Alfred himself, an engineer). After the house tour you board a minibus for a garden tour. Fountains and pools, colonnades and balustrades, marble Cupids and Dianas, a reflecting pool and fountain, velvet lawns, and clipped hedges create a mini-Versailles. Nemours doesn't admit hordes of people; tours are limited and reservations highly suggested. No children under 16.

HOURS: May–Nov., tours Tue.–Sat. at 9, 11, 1, & 3; Sun. tours: 11, 1, & 3. **ADMISSION:** $$$. **LOCATION:** Rockland Rd., Wilmington, DE. Inside Alfred I. DuPont Institute. **TELEPHONE:** 302-651-6912. **WEBSITE:** www.nemours.org.

Winterthur

Henri DuPont, grandson of the founder of the DuPont empire, was a great collector of American decorative arts. Winterthur is his crowning achievement. Although he actually lived in this mansion, inherited from his family, he turned it into a veritable museum. Not only china and furniture but whole rooms were transported into the house. The main mansion contains 175 rooms, many of them decorated in a pre-1860 style. You will find dining rooms, kitchens (including walls, ceilings, and fireplaces) placed panel by panel inside the mansion. Several style periods are shown: seventeenth century, William and Mary, Queen Anne, Chippendale, Federal, Empire, and Victorian. Each piece is documented, so that the Duncan Phyfe room, for instance, had its architectural elements removed from a specific house in New York where Phyfe furniture was used. You can find a striking plantation dining room removed in its entirety from a South Carolina home, a New England kitchen, a Shaker bedroom, a New York parlor, and a flying staircase copied from an estate in North Carolina. One oft-photographed room features authentic eighteenth-century Chinese wallpaper that covers the walls as well as the ceilings.

After the guided tour, you can visit the museum galleries on the other side of the main building. These include displays of furniture, china, and silver and explanations of their social significance, plus a Touch-It Room for children. In the separate Dorrance Gallery, you will also find the wonderful collection of eighteenth-century tureens from the Campbell Soup Collection that was once in Camden.

Besides the museum, there are extensive gardens at Winterthur, 60 acres of greenery dotted with woods and copses. During spring, flowering displays include azaleas and dogwoods. A tram takes you through the gardens. It leaves from the main Visitor Center, where you can also buy tickets, pick up maps, eat at the cafeteria, or check out the extensive book and gift shop. For those who want to engage in serious shopping, there are rugs, chairs, and china for sale at the Gallery and Plant Shop. General admission includes the galleries, shops, and gardens but not the mansion tour.

HOURS: Mon.–Sat., 9–5; Sun., 12–5. Closed major holidays.
ADMISSION: Prices vary for different house tours, general and garden tours. **LOCATION:** N.J. Turnpike to Rt. 295 & Delaware Memorial Bridge, then north on I-95 to Rt. 52 (Exit 7), then left to Winterthur.
TELEPHONE: 800-448-3883. **WEBSITE:** www.winterthur.org.

Home of Franklin D. Roosevelt

For people who lived under Franklin Delano Roosevelt's administration, there is either a deep love for the man who dominated the White House from 1932 to 1945—or an abiding hatred. As president during the Great Depression and World War II, Roosevelt was both blamed and praised for cataclysmic changes in American life. And

Roosevelt's charming boyhood home has always been identified with the man.

Now a National Historic Site, the Hyde Park complex consists of the family home, the beautiful grounds on a high, green hill overlooking a clean Hudson River and the Roosevelt Library and Museum. You enter from a parking lot, which is lined with apple trees still bearing fruit. The white, classically proportioned country house called "Rosewood" is not overly large and can accommodate only a limited number of people at a time. Currently, access is by guided tour only.

Upon entering the main hall, you see the heavy furnishings that characterized a country home of the 1890s. Further on, the pretty Dresden Room is brightened by the colorful floral drapes and upholstery picked out by Sara Roosevelt in 1939 shortly before the king and queen of England visited. The whole house, in fact, shows much more the influence of Franklin's mother, Sara, than of his wife, Eleanor. The upstairs section contains FDR's boyhood bedroom and other family and guest rooms.

Next to the house is the FDR Library. The museum section contains gifts from foreign rulers, cartoons, photographs, and a passing picture of both the Depression and World War II. There are re-creations of rooms from the White House (such as the War Room) and sections of the Rosewood home (such as the dining room). This is a self-guided area. Outside on the quiet green lawn next to the rose garden are the graves of both FDR and Eleanor. And, in another section of the estate, Val-Kill, the Eleanor Roosevelt Historic Site, is open to viewers from a separate road. This is a smaller house that also requires a guided tour.

HOURS: Daily, 9–5. **ADMISSION:** Adults, $$$. Under 16 free.
LOCATION: Hyde Park, NY. Take Garden State Parkway to N.Y. Thruway to Exit 18. Cross Mid-Hudson Bridge, then Rt. 9 north for 7 miles. Follow signs. **TELEPHONE:** 854-229-9115, 800-967-2283 (advance registration). **WEBSITE:** www.nps.gov/hofr.

Vanderbilt Mansion

If the Roosevelt home radiates quiet wealth, the Vanderbilt Mansion exudes conspicuous consumption. A marble palace in the style of the Italian Renaissance, it is set on large estate grounds where swans paddle about in a meandering stream. Inside, the mansion's furnishings are closer to French Rococo than Italian Renaissance. The huge marble reception hall opens to both the dining room and drawing room. The dining room, which seated thirty, and the beautifully furnished drawing room were the scene of gala balls. A small side room called the Gold Room was the gathering place for guests to sip sherry before dinner. This room attracts tourists to its ceiling painting, which depicts scantily clad maidens floating in an azure sky.

If the downstairs chairs all look like thrones, then the upstairs bedrooms of Mr. and Mrs. Vanderbilt were certainly fit for a king and queen. Walls of embroidered silk and a bed with a marble gate around it are features copied from a French queen's bedroom to outfit the one Mrs. Vanderbilt used. As for Mr. Vanderbilt, he merely had a canopy with a crown above his bed and true Flemish tapestries hanging on the walls. It all goes to show what you could do if you had money in the pre-income tax days.

The mansion with its marble floors and the heavily treed grounds all help to re-create the splendor of a bygone era. Tours begin at the Visitor Center, where you can buy tickets and pick up brochures and postcards. A film about the estate is shown here. It's a short walk over to the mansion, which is open only by guided tour at this point. However, you can walk around the grounds yourself, and check out the view and the nearby formal gardens which are being restored. Advance registration during the popular foliage season is recommended.

HOURS: Daily, 9–5. Closed major holidays. **ADMISSION:** Adults, $$. Under 16 free. **LOCATION:** Use Hyde Park directions. **TELEPHONE:** 854-229-9115, 800-967-2283 (advance registration). **WEBSITE:** www.nps.gov/vama.

Kykuit

You may never be as rich as Rockefeller, but at least you can visit the family estate in Pocantico Hills, near Tarrytown, NY. The mansion was the country home of four generations of Rockefellers: John D.; his son, John D. Jr.; Nelson; and Nelson's children. The furnishings inside and the magnificent terraced grounds show the influence of the first three generations. John D. Rockefeller, who started the fortune, did not believe in conspicuous consumption. The original stone house, called "Kykuit," which is Dutch for "lookout," was not particularly ornate. It was later remodeled in the Renaissance Revival style.

Inside the house you'll find rooms decorated in various ways, including a beautiful Adamesque side room. The most spectacular is the two-floor music room (it once housed an organ) which now has graceful balconies rimming the oculus, an oval ceiling opening. Eighteenth- and nineteenth-century furniture along with Chinese vases from various dynasties are found in the first-floor rooms.

What makes Kykuit unique is the incorporation of modern paintings and sculptures into classic and Victorian surroundings.

Both Nelson Rockefeller and his mother, Abby Aldrich Rockefeller, were strong collectors of modern art. So you will see a modern work or folk art mixed in with traditional furnishings. However, most of the modern paintings, rugs and lithographs are found downstairs in a separate, air-conditioned art gallery. Kandinsky, Picasso, Motherwell, and a number of "Op Art" pieces from the 1960s are on display.

Once outside, you really get a feel for the opulence of the place. The magnificent gardens, originally landscaped by William Bosworth in the Italian Villa style, are built in a series of terraces that drop down the hill. The view of the rolling hills, the Hudson River, and the Palisades beyond is spectacular. The terraces include a stone teahouse, a rose garden, and a nine-hole golf course. And that' s not all. There are also all those modern sculptures placed around the greenery. Some blend in beautifully. Others may take you back a bit.

Last stop on the tour is the coach and carriage house, where the men can admire the 1916 Crane Simplex or the 1939 Cadillac convertible along with a number of pony carts, halters, and horse stalls.

The Visitors Center at Philipsburg Manor is where you begin the tour, run by Historic Hudson Valley. You watch an introductory film, then hop on the eighteen-person bus that takes you to the mansion. The guided tour takes about 2¼ hours. A separate tour, which concentrates only on the outside gardens and sculpture, is available on a limited basis. Tickets are sold on a first-come, first-served basis, but you can reserve a specific time beforehand (extra fee for this). Of course, if you take the New York Waterways ferry tour (first from N.J. then from the N.Y. pier) the price is included.

Not far from Kykuit is the Union Church of Pocantico Hills, a community church where the Rockefeller family worshiped. The small stone structure is famous for its stained-glass windows created by two modern masters. Henri Matisse designed the rose window above the altar, while the side windows and the huge Narthex panes were painted by Marc Chagall in strong colors and swirling images. Tours are conducted by Historic Hudson Valley also (use telephone number below). The church is located on Rt. 448, east of Rt. 9 in North Tarrytown.

HOURS: End of Apr.–first week of Nov., daily exc. Tue., 10–3; Sun., 10–4. **ADMISSION:** Adults, $$$$. Discounts: Seniors, students. **LOCATION:** Upper Mills, North Tarrytown. Take Tappan Zee Bridge, then Rt. 9 north for 2 miles. **TELEPHONE:** 914-631-8200. Day Cruises, 800-53-FERRY. **WEBSITE:** www.hudsonvalley.org.

Lyndhurst

Just a few minutes south of the Tappan Zee Bridge, this Gothic Revival "castle" was first built in 1838 by New York City mayor William Paulding. In 1880 it became the summer home of railroad tycoon Jay Gould. The crystal greenhouses were once the foremost indoor gardens in America. The house, with its turreted towers and manicured lawn, is often used in commercials as an example of the good life.

Today the estate is owned by the National Trust for Historic Preservation. Visitors are led through the home by tour guides (although you are also allowed to take a self-guided audio or brochure tour instead). Among the tour stops are an ornate dining room with enough carved woodwork to fill a Gothic church, the butler's pantry, an elegant parlor, and the art gallery—a huge drawing room filled with paintings, stained glass windows, and a view of the Hudson.

Upstairs, the tour includes living quarters, highlighted by the Duchess's guest bedroom. Much of the interior is wood or plaster painted to look like stone to enhance the medieval look—a common effect in Gothic Revival homes of the period. A short walk away, the renovated carriage house offers a lunch cafe. The gift shop and a museum gallery can be found in a separate carriage house. You can also walk around the sweeping lawns, with a view of the Hudson River, as well as the rose garden, perennial beds, and conservatory. Guided tours are held throughout the day.

HOURS: Mid-Apr.–Oct., Tue.-Sun. and Mon. holidays, 10–5; Nov.–Apr., weekends, 10–4. **ADMISSION:** Adults, $$. Discounts: Seniors, students. Under 12 free. **LOCATION:** 635 S. Broadway (Rt. 9), Tarrytown, NY, one-half mile south of Tappan Zee Bridge. **TELEPHONE:** 914-631-4481. **WEBSITE:** www.lyndhurst.org.

Sunnyside

Home of Washington Irving, America's first internationally famous author, Sunnyside was built in a whimsical manner to suit Irving's individual taste. The reconstructed house is a mélange of the Dutch, the Spanish, and the quaint, with wisteria growing up its walls. It was built on the banks of the Hudson with several acres of lovely grounds, including an icehouse and swan ponds. At the Visitors Center a charming film about the Legend of Sleepy Hollow is shown.

The house is shown by guided tour only, and because the rooms and hallways are small, the tour takes time. Docents costumed in top hats or hoop skirts take you through the canopied bedchamber, the parlor, and up and down the stairs to the other household rooms. It is modestly furnished in early nineteenth-century style, but hosted many a famous visitor. Irving's sister and her children lived in the house and maintained the household for him. Since Irving lived abroad for seventeen years, he acquired a taste for the English romantic garden, which he translated to the acreage at Sunnyside. Picnicking is allowed on the grounds, and there is a cafe for light bites on weekends. The Sleepy Hollow Church and graveyard are nearby.

> **HOURS:** Apr.–Oct. 10–5; Nov., Dec. 10–4. Daily except Tue. Weekends in March. **ADMISSION:** Adults, $$. Discount: Seniors, children. Under 5 free. **LOCATION:** Tappan Zee Bridge to Tarrytown, NY, then Rt. 9 south to Sunnyside Lane. **TELEPHONE:** 914-631-8200, 914-591-8763. **WEBSITE:** www.hudsonvalley.org.

Boscobel

A stately Federal mansion set on the banks of the Hudson River (it was moved 15 miles from its original location), Boscobel was begun by Morris Dyckman in 1804. Dyckman, who made his money as an arms dealer, was able to afford the best furnishings. Although he died before the house was finished, his wife moved in and furnished it most elegantly. The house is completely restored and refurbished (in fact, it was refurbished twice) and reflects an authenticity of period.

A large central hall, sweeping stairway, patterned wallpaper, Duncan Phyfe furniture, china, glass, silver, and a bevy of whale-oil lamps reflect an era of early and gracious wealth. The wide lawns, the elegant rose garden, and the view of West Point across the river all add to the air of quiet gentility. Guides take you through the home, but you may peruse the outdoor vistas, including the belvedere overlook, on your own. A small gift shop is located in a separate building.

> **HOURS:** Apr.–Oct., daily except Tue. Tours: 9:30–5; Nov. & Dec., 9:30–4. Closed Jan.–Mar. **ADMISSION:** Adults, $$. Discounts: Seniors, children. **LOCATION:** 1601 Rt. 9D, Garrison, NY, 8 miles north of Bear Mountain Bridge. **TELEPHONE:** 845-265-3638. **WEBSITE:** www.boscobel.org.

Pennsbury Manor

Here is a complete re-creation, on the original site, of the beautiful Manor House built by William Penn on the banks of the Delaware. Located 25 miles above Philadelphia in what was then a wilderness, the estate includes many outbuildings such as a bake and brew house, a smoke house, icehouse, and stable. Although everything was built from scratch in the 1930s, great care was taken to follow the letters and journals of Penn regarding this self-sufficient estate.

There are two striking things about Pennsbury Manor. One is the earliness of the period. The house was built in the late seventeenth century (Penn lived there only from 1699 to 1701), so the furnishings reflect the heavy Jacobean hand. The other is the surprising elegance of this Quaker household. Although nothing is lavish, the furnishings are richer than one would expect of a Quaker leader.

As the guide points out, although William Penn was a great believer in the equality of men, he was still the Proprietor, entitled to receive an annual fee from each settler for each parcel of land sold. He had, after all, received the charter of Pennsylvania from King Charles II. He also came from a wealthy background and apparently relished good furniture.

After a tour through the bedrooms, parlors, and counting rooms of the manor, a tour through the grounds is in order: first to the barge landing, then the herb garden, the barnyard with its peacocks and hens, and the orchards. A brew/bake house where great vats of ale were mixed and where huge ovens baked loaves of bread is also on the estate. There are regularly scheduled tours (usually two or three, depending on the season) a day. However, you can tour the grounds yourself.

> **HOURS:** Mid-Mar.–Nov., Tue.–Sat., 9–5; Sun., 12–5. Call for winter hours and special Christmas hours. **ADMISSION:** Adults, $$. Under 6 free. **LOCATION:** 400 Pennsbury Memorial Rd., Morrisville, PA. **TELEPHONE:** 215-946-0400. **WEBSITE:** www.pennsburymanor.org.

Andalusia

Nicholas Biddle was one of America's first millionaires, and the Biddle name still connotes a sense of grace, polish, and old money in the Philadelphia area. Andalusia came to him through marriage. He transformed it in 1834 from a Regency mansion to its present form as one of the outstanding examples of Greek Revival architecture in the Northeast. Indeed, its facade of startling white pillars and "Greek temple" architrave will remind you of many antebellum Southern mansions built in the same style.

The house faces the Delaware River, and its large sloping green lawn runs down to the edge of the water. On this lawn you will find both a billiard room and a Gothic "ruin." The "ruin," a crumbling tower, was built that way. This was not uncommon in the 1830s, when the romantic novels of Sir Walter Scott and tales of excavations in the Middle East had Americans crazy over anything medieval, Greek, Turkish, or Egyptian.

Inside the mansion, furniture varies from polished Regency buffets to odd-shaped Greek-style chairs and other American Empire designs. The music room, with its delicate pianoforte and whale-oil lamps, brings visions of genteel ladies offering an evening musicale to an assemblage of local gentry.

Outside, there are extensive grounds, which include a hedge walk, a grape arbor, and another huge house, which is not open to visitors. Tours of Andalusia are for groups only, but one can go through with a minimum of seven people for a set price.

HOURS: By reserved tour only. **LOCATION:** Bensalem Twp., Bucks County, PA. **TELEPHONE:** 215-245-5479. **WEBSITE:** www.andalusiahousemuseum.org.

Pearl S. Buck Home

Bucks County, Pennsylvania, was a haven for writers in the 1930s. Most of the literary celebrities of that time moved on to other pastures. But Pearl S. Buck, who reached the zenith of her fame during the pre–World War II period (she won the Nobel Prize in 1938), remained here in her lovely country home until her death in 1963. The stone and wood house seems to typify the Hollywood picture of a writer's country retreat: a huge floor-to-ceiling brick fireplace, great expanses of polished wood flooring, overstuffed sofas, and walls lined with books. Add to this a collection of Oriental lamps and tables, screens, and sculptures, and you get a picture of Pearl S. Buck, author and admirer of Chinese culture. At one point there were also nine adopted Amerasian children in the house, which explains the generous dimensions and open spaces of the home.

Visits to the home are by guided tour only. The tour includes a look at the room where her awards and prizes are displayed and the study where Ms. Buck wrote her works (sitting in a most uncomfortable-looking straight-backed Chinese chair). Outside there is a lovely old-fashioned patio, lots of green rolling hills, and a separate shop where you may purchase Oriental pieces and other souvenirs. The Pearl S. Buck Foundation, dedicated to helping Amerasian children abandoned by their fathers, is located in the big red barn not far from the house. A film about the foundation often precedes the tour. Chinese luncheon available for groups of twenty-five or more.

HOURS: Tours: Tue.–Sat., 11, 1, & 2; Sun., 1 & 2, Mar.–Dec. Closed Jan. & Feb. **ADMISSION:** Adults, $$. Discounts: Seniors, students. Under 6 free. **LOCATION:** 520 Dublin Rd., Perkasie, PA. Rt. 202 south to Rt. 313 west to Dublin, PA. Turn left on Maple Ave., which becomes Dublin, then go one mile. **TELEPHONE:** 215-249-0100. **WEBSITE:** www.pearl-s-buck.org.

Restored and Reconstructed Historic Villages, Farms, Mills, and Homes

Two young apprentices demonstrate tin punching at Historic Cold Spring Village in Cape May County. *(Photo by Barbara Hudgins/Courtesy Historic Cold Spring Village)*

Waterloo Village

With thirty historic structures, this is the largest restoration in New Jersey, offering homes and mills scattered along a scenic wooded terrain beside the Musconetcong River. The village complex covers over 5,000 acres and includes buildings ranging from a 1760s inn to an 1870 Victorian mansion. Since Waterloo prospered during the Revolutionary War as an iron works and also during the nineteenth-century period of the Morris Canal and Sussex Railroad, the buildings reflect Colonial, Federal, and Victorian styles.

Guides are dressed according to the period. A blacksmith and a potter are usually on hand at their workplaces and will answer questions. Docents are in each house. The hostess in the Canal House, for instance, demonstrates a clockwork weasel that was used to draw the wool yarn into a skein. At the gristmill, you can watch the guide upstairs pour corn kernels between two huge grinding stones. Then you troop downstairs where the waterwheel is turning and discover cornmeal pouring out the spout, while another guide explains the process.

There's a lot of walking to do here, with several homes and inns, a general store, a sawmill, blacksmith shop, and the Canal Museum to visit. The 1859 Methodist church looks like it came straight out of Vermont. A long walk up a hill takes you to the separate Lenape Indian village, which looks as it would have in the 1600s. A longhouse, animal skins drying on a pole, and the accoutrements of tribal life are here, together with a guide who explains the customs.

Food is available at the Pavilion Cafe or Towpath Tavern, or you can bring your own for a picnic. There's also a museum store. Horse-drawn carriages are available weekdays in summer and nonfestival weekends all season. There's also a tented amphitheater for classical and folk music events. The larger pop and rock concerts take place in a field a mile outside the village proper.

HOURS: Late May–early Sept., Wed., 12–4; Thu., Fri., 11–4; weekends, 11–5. **ADMISSION:** $$. Discounts: Seniors, children. Under 6 free. **LOCATION:** Byram Twp. (Sussex County). I-80 to Exit 25 to Rt. 206 north, left on Waterloo Rd. **TELEPHONE:** 973-347-0900. **WEBSITE:** www.waterloovillage.org.

Red Mill Museum Village

An old red mill with a churning waterwheel sits by a 200-foot-wide waterfall to create the picturesque environment for this museum village. In fact, the red mill is one of the most photographed structures in New Jersey. This mill is the hub of a village that includes smaller buildings scattered along the banks of the South Branch of the Raritan River. There's a log cabin, little red schoolhouse, general store/post office, blacksmith shop, quarry with stone crusher, and an information center in the small complex.

The 1810 mill offers several floors of exhibits. The agricultural development of the region is followed with a series of displays of tools and country life. Everything from barrels to baskets is shown, with the whoosh of the water "buckets" from the wheel always within earshot. The gift shop has a pleasant country store ambience. The museum also runs a series of specials to attract the crowds. These include Revolutionary and Civil War encampments, spring and fall antique shows, summer concerts, craft days, a harvest jubilee, and the Haunted House for Halloween weekend. (Extra fee for events.)

HOURS: April to mid-Oct., Tue.–Sat., 10–4; Sun., 12–5.
ADMISSION: $. Discounts: Seniors, children. Under 6 free.
LOCATION: 56 Main St., Clinton (Hunterdon County). Exit 15 off Rt. 78.
TELEPHONE: 908-735-4101. **WEBSITE:** www.theredmill.org.

Batsto Village

Once a self-contained community in the heart of the Pinelands, this village is now part of Wharton State Forest, the largest parkland in the state. Pine, oak, and cedar woods; open lowlands; and a sparkling lake provide a scenic backdrop for a place that preserves the lifestyle of bygone days in the South Jersey pines. Founded in 1766, Batsto was once the center of the bog iron industry in New Jersey, and its iron provided armaments for the Revolution. Later, in the 1800s, glass was manufactured here, then lumbering and cranberry farming were tried. As you approach, you find a handsome farm surrounded by split-rail fences with horses and ducks in view.

William Richards bought the iron works in 1784, and it remained in his family's hands for ninety-two years. The Richards Mansion has an eight-story mansard-roofed tower rising from its center. The rooms inside are filled with the furniture of the well-to-do families who lived there, and the wall-to-wall library of Joseph Wharton, the financier who bought the complex in 1876, is most impressive.

The first stop at Batsto is the Visitor Center. If you want the mansion tour, buy your tickets immediately, for only fifteen people are admitted at a time. The tour takes 45 minutes and is very comprehensive. (The mansion was closed for refurbishing at press time. Call before you go.) There is also a walk-through museum at the Visitor Center that features old-time tools and plenty of information about the region.

Except for the mansion tour, you can peruse the village on your own. Among the structures are the General Store, a post office (where you can have your postcard stamped), a barn with farm animals, and a few workers' houses. During the summer, the houses usually have some craftsmen inside—a weaver or a potter at work.

The working sawmill is usually open only Sunday afternoons in summer.

The farm with its unusual main house, surrounding barns, and wide-swept fields all in the middle of the untouched Pine Barrens has the true look of a place from another time. A nature center, a full nature trail, a picnic area, and a large lake where fishing is allowed are all part of the grounds.

HOURS: Grounds, daily, dawn to dusk. Village, daily, 9–4:30.
ADMISSION: Mansion, $. Discounts: Children. Under 6 free. Parking fee summer weekends. **LOCATION:** Rt. 542, Wharton State Forest (Burlington County). Rt. 9 to Rt. 542 west. Garden State Parkway to New Gretna exit to Rt. 9 south to Rt. 542. **TELEPHONE:** 609-561-3262.
WEBSITE: www.batstovillage.org.

Historic Allaire Village

Set inside the greenery of Allaire State Park, this complex was an active workers' community during the nineteenth century. The huge brick blast furnace is left over from the bog iron days when James P. Allaire bought the ironworks in 1822 and sought to establish a sort of ideal, self-contained community. Since this was the age of Utopian communities, such a workers' paradise did not seem unusual. In fact, as long as the ironworks transformed local bog into pig iron, everyone prospered. But after 25 years, competition from high-grade iron ore brought economic ruin to the region. A well-documented display on the ironworks can be found in the Visitor Center.

During warm-weather weekends (including Fridays) you will find docents, dressed in 1830s costumes, in the various buildings. They talk about village life, and perhaps a blacksmith or pattern maker will be about. You can also view the church, which has a unique feature—its steeple was erected on the wrong end. There's a pond, a bakery with fresh bread, and a gift shop (open Wed.–Sun.), plus several other houses. During the week, when the docents may not be around, you may walk around the grounds and take pictures. Groups can reserve tours. On summer and fall weekends there are always lots of activities, including crafts and antiques fairs while lantern tours are held in October and December. These are run by the nonprofit organization that administers the village.

While at Allaire, be sure to ride the Pine Creek Railroad, a narrow-gauge rail line that runs a short trip on both diesel and steam locomotives. It is close to the parking lot. For information call 732-938-5524. The park also offers nature trails, bicycle trails and picnic areas. During the summer, there may be a hot dog and ice cream concession open next to the Visitor Center.

HOURS: Park, dawn–dusk. Buildings, summer, Wed.–Sun., 11–5; Sept.–Nov., 10–4. Visitor Center, weekends, 10–4; daily in summer, 10–4. **ADMISSION:** $ for parking on summer weekends. **LOCATION:** Allaire State Park, Rt. 524, Wall Twp. (Monmouth County). Garden State Parkway to Exit 98; go 2 miles west. **TELEPHONE:** 732-938-2371 (park); 732-919-3500 (village). **WEBSITE:** www.allairevillage.org.

Millbrook Village

One of New Jersey's best-kept secrets is this nineteenth-century village set in the Kittatinny Mountains. It is run by the National Park Service as part of the Delaware Water Gap National Recreation Area. On weekends from May to October, guides dressed in period costumes of the 1860–1880 era lead tours and demonstrate various crafts at some of the buildings. During Millbrook Days, the first full weekend in October, more than one hundred volunteers demonstrate crafts from last century. At other times, you may walk around the village yourself, although the houses may not be open.

The original Millbrook Village was a small enclave of houses and stores clustered around a gristmill that opened in 1832 beside Van Campens Brook. Since the mill served grain farmers in the surrounding countryside, the town became the social and commercial center of the community. A hotel with taproom, a smithy, a general store and a simple white-steepled church are among the buildings that surrounded the original mill.

Millbrook reached its zenith around 1875. The village declined after 1900 and by mid-century only a blacksmith remained. What you see here now is a recreation of Millbrook at its height. Today, the village has two dozen well-kept homes, school, blacksmith and woodworking shops, barns, general store and a church within walking distance.

HOURS: Grounds, daily, dawn to dusk. Buildings, weekends, Memorial Day to early Oct., 9–5. **ADMISSION:** Free. **LOCATION:** Warren County. Rt. 80 west to last exit in N.J. (Millbrook exit). Turn right, follow Old Mine Road 12 miles north. **TELEPHONE:** 908-841-9531. **WEBSITE:** www.nps.gov/dewa/pphtml/facilities.htm.

Tuckerton Seaport

Do you know what a sneakbox is? If you don't, you can find out about the duck hunters, clammers, and fishermen who worked the bays and tidal creeks along the Jersey shore at this seaport village. Hunting for waterfowl, dredging for oysters, building boats, and carving decoys was a way of life that has just about disappeared. Tuckerton Seaport is a memorial to these baymen and a tourist destination at the same time.

The cornerstone of the village is the reconstructed Tucker's Island Lighthouse, now used as a museum. Exhibits on lighthouses, pirates (Captain Kidd and others), and buried treasure are found along with examples of duck decoys and life-saving lore.

Outside, about fifteen wooden buildings (some no larger than shacks) line the edge of Tuckerton Creek. Wooden walkways take you from one structure to the next. These include a decoy carving shop, the Perrine Boat Works, a sawmill, and an instructional clam house. At the Boat Works a docent describes sneakboxes and their role in the economy. In another house, a decoy maker, painting a duck, explains how he hollows out the inside and places the head in various positions.

Although decoys are considered to be an icon of folk art, they began as a simple utilitarian object for duck hunters. Decoys were put in the water to entice ducks on the wing to come down and settle beside the "sitting ducks." Duck hunting was once a viable occupation for Tuckerton residents, but so many regulations curtailed both waterfowl hunting and bay fishing that this way of life has practically come to an end.

The Yacht Club building emphasizes marine ecology and offers several interactive exhibits for the kids, along with a gift shop and a Lenni-Lenape exhibit. And since you can't have a seaport without serving seafood, Skeeters, a replica of a local summer cottage, serves fried clams, fried oysters, French fries, and even hamburgers.

The seaport is about 15 miles south of Long Beach Island (across from Lake Pohatcong) and is a welcome stop for those driving down to the shore. Lots of special events here include a boat parade and a big gun and decoy show in September.

HOURS: Daily, 10–5. **ADMISSION:** $$. Discounts: Seniors, children. Under 5 free. **DIRECTIONS:** Garden State Parkway to Exit 58. Take Rt. 539 south to Rt. 9 traffic light (Main Street). Turn right, go 1,500 feet. **TELEPHONE:** 609-296-8868. **WEBSITE:** www.tuckertonseaport.org.

Historic Cold Spring Village

A delightful little restored village can be found among the pine trees on a quiet stretch of road not far from the hubbub of the Wildwood motels. Historic Cold Spring Village has much charm. It's not so large as to be exhausting, nor so small that it might disappoint.

The buildings are set around a village green that has a mid-nineteenth-century look to it. Most of them have been moved here from elsewhere. They range from an ancient Colonial to the large Grange Hall, which dates back to 1897. Inside the various structures, you'll find a printer at his shop or an 1820s schoolhouse complete with resident schoolmistress, or a tinsmith punching holes in tin. These are docents and craftspeople who explain what they are doing while they work. Workers at the rope-twisting shop even let onlookers add their own twist to the newly wound coils.

There are bits of country nostalgia here such as an old-fashioned water pump (the water is undoubtedly from the cold spring), a farm enclosure with sheep and other animals, and walkways made out of crushed clamshells. A horse-drawn carriage, on hand the day we visited, was a big hit with the children.

In the large Visitor Center, a Marine Museum offers displays on the whaling industry and other regional interests. For those who get hungry, the village offers an ice cream store and bakery. Full meals are available at the Grange Hall where superior American fare is featured. Weekends there are often special events such as singers at the gazebo on the green, contests and so forth. A special excursion train at the adjacent Cold Spring Station to and from Cape May is available in summer.

HOURS: Father's Day to Labor Day, Tue.–Sun., 10–4:30; June & Sept., weekends. **ADMISSION:** $$. Under 5 free. **LOCATION:** 720 Rt. 9, Cold Spring (Cape May County). Garden State Parkway to Exit 4A to Rt. 9 south. **TELEPHONE:** 609-898-2300. **WEBSITE:** www.hcsv.org.

Wheaton Village

Set around a green, with buildings styled in 1888 gingerbread, Wheaton Village is a nice, clean spot in the middle of a small industrial town called Millville, about 35 miles west of Atlantic City. The village is dedicated to the glass industry that still flourishes in this corner of New Jersey, and one of its main attractions is the Museum of American Glass.

The museum is housed in an elegant Victorian building and includes glass items that go back to Jamestown, Virginia, and even earlier. Collectors will probably enjoy the world's largest bottle, plus paperweights, medicine bottles, and exhibits of contemporary glass. You'll learn everything you ever wanted to know about bottles, Sandwich glass, and cut and pressed glass.

Another attraction is the glass factory where visitors can watch from a gallery above while gaffers plunge their rods into the blazing furnaces and then shape them into wine glasses, bottles, and paperweights. At these "shows" an announcer with a mike explains just what the gaffer is doing. This is hot work, and even from the gallery you can feel the intensity of the furnace.

Nowadays, Wheaton Village allows visitors to make their own paperweights. For a fee, you and a qualified gaffer can make an individual creation. Call to reserve for this offer. The village has also become a center for glass "sculptors" who specialize in glass art.

Other buildings on the green include a craft bulding where you can see weavers, potters, and others go about their work. The craftsman's handiwork plus the art glasswork can be purchased in the stores on the village green. The Down Jersey Folklife Center exhibits the diverse ethnic crafts of the region such as Japanese origami, Puerto Rican music, or Ukrainian embroidery. For kids there's a small play area on the green, an 1876 schoolhouse to peek at, and an 1897 train station with a miniature train ride (extra fee).

The General Store sells penny candy from an old-fashioned glass jar, but for real food go to the restaurants outside the gates. Special-event weekends feature everything from art glass demonstrations to fire engine musters and Civil War reenactments.

> **HOURS:** Daily, 10–5. Reduced schedule Jan.–Mar. **ADMISSION:** $$.
> Under 5 free. Reduced winter rates. **LOCATION:** 1501 Glasstown Rd.,
> Millville (Cumberland County). Exit 26 off Rt. 55. **TELEPHONE:**
> 609-825-6800. **WEBSITE:** www.wheatonvillage.org.

East Jersey Olde Towne

This is a collection of restored and/or reconstructed colonial houses set around a pretty 12-acre village green in Johnson Park, Piscataway. Many buildings were moved here from other localities in central Jersey. Although it was started years ago by a professor interested in preserving the heritage of the Raritan Valley, the village was ignored for a long time. Now a large money grant has renewed the place. Several of the buildings are open for guided tours on specific days. One is the Smalleytown Schoolhouse, where students learned their lessons in the mid-1800s or faced wearing a dunce cap or, even worse, corporal punishment with a paddle.

Another is the FitzRandolph house, which represents a typical farmhouse of the Raritan Valley. The Vanderveer house, on the other hand, with more elegant furnishings, reflects a wealthy landowner. Guides take you up and down the narrow stairs of these early homes.

The Church of the Three Mile Run is a typical Dutch structure with a pyramid roof and an interesting history—it is an exact reproduction of an earlier church and can be used for weddings. A brick tavern and a barracks building are partially open or are used for administration. The whole village has a pretty look with white picket fences, brick pathways, and an authentic kitchen garden behind one of the houses.

The village is administered by the Middlesex County Cultural and Heritage Commission, and while you can walk around the green and take pictures, you can only enter the buildings (except for the Visitor Center) during the limited guided-tour hours. And yes, it's closed on Saturdays.

HOURS: Tue.–Fri. & Sun., 8:30–4:30. Tours at 1:30. **ADMISSION:** Free.
LOCATION: 1050 River Rd. (Rt. 18) at Hoes Lane, Piscataway (Middlesex County). Rt. 287, Exit 9, to River Rd. **TELEPHONE:** 732-745-3030; Middlesex County C&H Commission, 732-745-4489.

Longstreet Farm

For those who want to recapture the sights and smells of farm life a century ago, a visit to Longstreet Farm fills the bill. Although the farm is kept to the 1890s era, the machinery here was used well into the 1920s and may bring back memories to those born on a farm. Old-fashioned combines and tractors, an apple corer, and other antique contraptions are kept in a series of barns and sheds. Animals are present, although not in profusion. There are pigs lying in the mud as well as horses, cows, and chickens. Open-slatted corncribs that allow the air to circulate are on view. The milking shed is fitted out in the old way, with slots for the cow's head and buckets for hand milking. The carriage house contains a variety of buckboards.

Since Longstreet is a living historical farm, the workers dress in casual 1890s clothes as they go about their farm chores. During summer there is a historical camp for children in which the kids help out. The main farmhouse offers tours on weekends and holidays. It contains the furniture and artifacts of a late Victorian home.

Longstreet is part of beautiful Holmdel Park, which provides much lovely scenery. Across the street, a sheltered picnic area offers tables and a snack bar. In a hollow below the shelter, a pond allows ducks to swim by gracefully. And beyond the pond, a cultivated arboretum presents a colorful view of flowering crabapples, rhododendrons, and hundreds of shade trees. The park also provides nature trails that wind among the beech, oak, and hickory trees. Wildflowers and blueberry bushes are other pluses at this abundant county park.

HOURS: 10–4 daily, summer 9–5. Farmhouse: Mar.–Dec., 12–3:30.
ADMISSION: Free. **LOCATION:** Longstreet Road, Holmdel (Monmouth County). Garden State Parkway to Garden State Arts Center exit, follow Keyport Rd., look for signs. Off Holmdel Rd. **TELEPHONE:** 732-946-3758.
WEBSITE: www.monmouthcountyparks.com/parks/longstreet.html.

Howell Living History Farm

This active farm in Mercer County is set in the turn-of-the-century style. Various stages of mechanization are shown: the reaper reaps and binds mechanically, but it does not thresh. The wheat is bound by machine, but the machine is pulled by a plodding draft horse. The wagon that picks up the bound sheaves is also available for hayrides.

There's plenty of acreage at the farm, and you feel the bucolic atmosphere from the moment you leave the parking lot and walk down the dirt road to the farmhouse. You pass sheep, pigs, and geese—all safely behind fences. A renovated barn serves as the visitor center. The early 1800s farmhouse itself is a simple one, with a furnished parlor, antique kitchen, and gift shop. School groups are welcome here to take part in seasonal activities. On Saturdays, a professional farmer is on hand to guide the draft horse in plowing, sowing, and reaping. Several Saturdays are devoted to such things as a Spring Market and a Fall Festival. Special events, such as a maze in a cornfield, are held in season. Visitors are invited to help plant, cultivate, and harvest crops, care for animals, or make soap, butter, and ice cream.

> **HOURS:** Apr.–Nov., Tue.–Sat., 10–4; Sun., 12–4. Programs, Sat., 11–3. **ADMISSION:** Free. Fee for children's crafts and maze. **LOCATION:** Valley Rd., Howell Twp. (Mercer County). Rt. 29 to Belle Mountain Ski Area turnoff (Valley Rd.), then 2 miles east. **TELEPHONE:** 609-737-3299. **WEBSITE:** www.howellfarm.org.

The Hermitage

Known primarily as an outstanding example of nineteenth-century Gothic Revival architecture, the original Hermitage was a two-story brownstone erected in 1750. During the late eighteenth century it was owned by Lt. Colonel Prevost and his charming wife, Theodosia. At that time, the house was host to James Monroe, Alexander Hamilton, Marquis de Lafayette, and Aaron Burr, among others. When Colonel Prevost died, Burr wooed his widow. In 1782, Burr and Theodosia married in the parlor of the Hermitage.

Twenty-five years later Dr. Elijah Rosencrantz bought the house (which his family retained for 163 years). In 1847 the structure was remodeled into a picturesque Gothic Revival home. Steep gabled roofs trimmed with carpenter's lace and diamond-paned windows give it the Victorian look we often associate with Charles Dickens. In fact, one of the several programs given at the house is a performance of *A Christmas Carol*. The Hermitage portrays the upper middle-class life of the late Victorian period, including furnishings, personal items, and papers of the Rosencrantz family. There are also changing exhibits based on the museum's large collection of antique clothing (448 women's gowns alone), which includes fans, handbags, and handmade lace. Special events include a costume exhibition and two craft boutiques that last four weeks during fall and spring. Special prices for these.

> **HOURS:** Wed. & Sun., 1–4. Last tour, 3:15. **ADMISSION:** $.
> Discounts: Children 6–12. Under 6 free. **LOCATION:** 335 N. Franklin
> Tpk., Ho-Ho-Kus (Bergen County). **TELEPHONE:** 201-445-8311.
> **WEBSITE:** www.thehermitage.org.

Whitesbog Village

Unlike strawberries, blueberries were cultivated rather recently—in 1916 to be exact. That's when Elizabeth White, together with a researcher, found the best blueberry bushes in Pemberton Township and cultivated them on the family farm. She also figured out how to package them. Elizabeth was the daughter of J. J. White, who owned the largest cranberry bogs in the state (hence the name Whitesbog). Like most cranberry growers he used hundreds of migrant workers to harvest the dry crop and had about forty full-time workers on site. The workers (and the management) lived in a company town with small homes, a general store, post office, school, pay office, barrel factory, and cranberry-processing buildings. The blueberries, by the way, were a means to raise a crop in June and July, since cranberries aren't harvested until September.

This abandoned company town, deep in the Pinelands, is slowly being restored by the Whitesbog Preservation Trust. The General Store is now the Visitor Center, and a few other buildings display agricultural tools and antique engines. Pictures of immigrant workers from Philadelphia handpicking the berries in the early 1900s are part of the museum. There are picnic tables here and a kiosk with maps for walking and driving tours, so even if the village isn't open you can explore the surrounding forest. There are also numerous cranberry bogs at this 3,000-acre site. Events include a Blueberry Festival in late June and Cranberry Harvest Tours in the fall.

> **HOURS:** Grounds, dawn to dusk; Visitor Center, Apr.–Nov., Sat. & Sun.,
> 10–4. **ADMISSION:** Free. **LOCATION:** Brendan T. Byrne (formerly
> Lebanon) State Forest, Pemberton Twp. (Burlington County). Rt. 70
> to Rt. 530; 4 miles east of Browns Mills. **TELEPHONE:** 609-893-4646.
> **WEBSITE:** www.whitesbog.org.

Historic Speedwell

Every nineteenth-century technological breakthrough led to further inventions. And Historic Speedwell in Morristown is the scene of one of the most important American achievements. It was here that Samuel Morse and Alfred Vail spent years perfecting the electromagnetic telegraph. And that invention gave rise to the later inventions of radio and television. One thing you learn from a visit to this green and pleasant village compound: you do not have to be a scientist to be an inventor. Samuel Morse was a portrait painter by profession. At the Vail House (the main building of the complex), you can see the portraits Morse painted of the senior Mr. and Mrs. Vail. Other rooms in the house show a modest early Victorian lifestyle.

The original Vail money came from their iron works. One of the buildings is devoted to an exhibit concerning the making and molding of iron machinery and to the ironworkers themselves. The foundry was best known for its early steam engines. In fact, the first transatlantic steamship was built here.

At the factory building, originally built for cotton weaving, you will find an exhibit about the telegraph. Vail and Morse held the first public demonstration of this new wonder here in 1838. An exhibit of documents, models, and instruments illustrates the invention and development of the telegraph. Other historic buildings on the site include several colonial buildings (such as the well-furnished L'Hommedieux house), which were moved here to avoid destruction.

Historic Speedwell is situated on the old homestead of the Vail family across from a picturesque dam where a Vail factory once stood. Special Christmas events and summer history camp available.

> **HOURS:** May–Oct., Thu. & Sun., 1–5. **ADMISSION:** $$. **LOCATION:** 333 Speedwell Ave. (Rt. 202) at Cory Rd., 1 mile north of Morristown. **TELEPHONE:** 973-540-0211. **WEBSITE:** www.speedwell.org.

Historic Smithville

Set around Lake Meone, and only 12 miles from Atlantic City, this "towne" started out as a colonial village that featured the authentic eighteenth-century Smithville Inn together with a mix of boutique shops. Built up by Fred and Ethel Noyes, there were costumed "colonials" spinning yarn in tiny restored houses on one side of the lake, and charming stores on the other. The Noyeses sold the complex and donated much of their money to the nearby Noyes Museum (q.v.).

Now, both sides of the lake are devoted to shopping and eating—no more colonial spinners! Still, this is a pleasant spot and parking is free. An old mill, a quaint bridge and brick walkways give an old-time ambience to the village, which is dubbed Historic Smithville on one side of the lake, and the Village Greene on the other. A bakery, an ice cream shop, the Smithville Inn, and other eateries along with a potpourri of specialty shops are on the site. In season there are miniature-train rides, a carousel and paddleboats on the lake, puppet shows for children, and an occasional buckboard ride around town.

LOCATION: Rt. 9 at Moss Mill Rd., Smithville (Atlantic County).
TELEPHONE: 609-652-7777.

Fosterfields

Another old-fashioned farm that dates from the turn of the century in American agriculture, Fosterfields is run by the Morris County Park Commission. The large farm has many farm implements on display and a variety of farm animals, including horses and cows, visible in barns and enclosures. There is also a large plowing field and many outbuildings as you walk along the road from the visitor center toward the house on the hill.

The main house, The Willows, has been faithfully restored. It is a handsome Gothic Revival farmhouse built in the 1850s (for a descendant of Paul Revere) with many original furnishings intact. The farm was later owned by the Fosters, and tours of the house

Fosterfields is a working farm restored to its early twentieth-century condition. *(Photo by Barbara Hudgins)*

reflect the life of a young woman growing up in the early twentieth century, as Caroline Foster did. These tours are given only on specific days and cost a bit extra.

On weekends, from the spring to fall season, there are demonstrations of farm tasks such as ploughing, sowing seed, or threshing. Perhaps the women at the farmhouse will be washing clothes and setting them out to dry, or someone will milk a cow. Often, the visitors are allowed to get involved in such jobs as butter-churning and other farm chores.

The Visitor Center has farm displays and also offers a short film on the history of Fosterfields. Here is where you can pick up brochures, book tours of The Willows, and get information on special activities—whether it's a Fourth of July picnic or a Saturday devoted to hay racking.

HOURS: Apr.–Oct., Wed.–Sat., 10–5; Sun., 12–5. Call for house tour hours. **ADMISSION:** $. Under 6 free. **LOCATION:** Rts. 124/510 & Kahdena Rd., Morris Twp. (Morris County). **TELEPHONE:** 973-326-7645. **WEBSITE:** http://parks.morris.NJ.US/parks/ffmain.htm.

Barclay Farmstead

Down the road behind a typical Cherry Hill strip mall, you'll find this peaceful 32-acre parcel of greenery which features a Federal-style, three-story red brick farmhouse. The house, with its central hall and staircase, connecting parlors, seven fireplaces, and period furnishings reflects the life of the early nineteenth century. It also reflects the Quaker heritage of this part of southern New Jersey. The one-time farm includes several outbuildings, such as a working blacksmith shop, a corn crib, and a spring house. There is also a well-kept kitchen garden outside. Costumed docents interpret life circa 1816, when the Thorn family inhabited the farmstead, but only at specific times.

The farmstead is also kept as a recreational area for the town, so there is a community garden, a picnic area, and a small playground on site. There are several nature trails and a foot bridge that goes through a woodlands path to the north branch of Cooper Creek.

HOURS: Tue.–Fri., 9–4; Sun., 1–4. **ADMISSION:** Free for Cherry Hill residents. Others: $. **LOCATION:** 209 Barclay Lane, Cherry Hill (Camden County). Off Rt. 70 east. **TELEPHONE:** 856-795-6225.

Merchants and Drovers Tavern

Built around 1795, this four-story Federal-style structure served as an early public meeting place for merchants, politicians, and farmers as well as a stagecoach stop for travelers. Owned by the same family from 1798 to 1971 and operated continuously as an inn until the 1930s, this hotel has remained largely unchanged over the years. Two parlors, a taproom, kitchen, long room, twelve bedrooms, and servant quarters have recently been carefully restored to an 1820s appearance and furnished with period antiques and reproductions. Interpretive exhibits on early tavern life and stagecoach transportation are being created for the long room. The tavern also hosts special events, including evening candlelight tours. Also on the property is the Terrill Tavern, which houses a museum shop.

> **HOURS:** Thu., Fri., and first & third Sat., 10–4. Second and fourth Sun., 1–4. Tue. by appointment. **ADMISSION:** $. Discounts: Seniors, students. **LOCATION:** Rt. 27 and Westfield Ave., Rahway (Union County). **TELEPHONE:** 732-381-0441. **WEBSITE:** www.merchantsanddrovers.org.

Israel Crane House

A handsome house built in the Federal period and then remodeled in the Greek Revival style, the Crane House was moved from its original site to the present location by the Montclair Historical Society. Costumed docents give guided tours throughout the three-story building with its furnishings in the Federal and Empire styles. Behind the main house is a two-story kitchen building reconstructed to resemble the 1840 kitchen that once existed. One unique feature of the Crane House is that the docents do allow you to sample the cooking. Just a tiny piece, but you can taste bread from the beehive oven, while the chicken simmers over the open hearth. Docents are quite good at explaining about the cooking utensils (such as the lazy-back that eased cooking chores for wives).

Beyond the kitchen building is a pleasant backyard planted with flowers and herbs in eighteenth-century fashion. And beyond that, the Country Store. Although most of the items in the store are just wooden models and not for sale, you do get the sense of an old-fashioned post office/store as the social center for a town. A few books and gifts are available for purchase.

> **HOURS:** Mid-Sept. to mid-June, Sun., 2–5. **ADMISSION:** $. Discounts: Children. **LOCATION:** 110 Orange Rd., Montclair (Essex County). Off Bloomfield Ave. **TELEPHONE:** 973-744-1796.

Miller-Cory House

Every Sunday during the school season, volunteers cook, spin, or perform seasonal tasks in and around this 1740 farmhouse. The everyday, humdrum tasks of colonial life—from soap making to herb drying—are emphasized here. The house, the adjacent Visitors Center, and a separate kitchen comprise a small enclave of colonial life.

In pleasant weather, wool spinners and other workers may be found outside. The separate kitchen is the scene of soup and bread making by volunteers who use an open hearth and beehive oven.

Guided tours of the house proper take about half an hour. The tour is most thorough and includes everything from how to tighten the rope springs on a bed to how to make utensils from a cow's horn. Schoolchildren and adults will find the house tour highly educational, while preschoolers may be content to simply mosey around the grounds. They can tour the herb garden, visit the museum shop, or watch the outdoor volunteers at work. There is a special Sheep-to-Shawl festival in the spring.

HOURS: Sept.–June, Sun., 2–5; Jan.–Mar., Sun., 2–4. **ADMISSION:** $.
LOCATION: 614 Mountain Ave., Westfield (Union County).
TELEPHONE: 908-232-1776.

Peter Mott House

The underground railroad was a pre–Civil War phenomenon: a series of "safe houses" where runaway slaves, escaping from the plantations of the South, could find food, shelter, and guidance to the next stop. Many of these railroad "stations" were run by white Quaker farmers. But there were free black men in the north who also took on this task. Since it was illegal, some of these homes had secret cellars where the fugitives could hide. But a house in the middle of a free black community was pretty safe from the incursions of the bounty hunters, who had the legal right to seize runaways during the 1850s.

Such a place was the Peter Mott House, which stands in Lawnside, the only historically African American incorporated community in the northern states. This two-story, white clapboard house, a regular stop on the Underground Railroad, was restored and dedicated as a museum in 2001. Built by Mott, a free black man, it was saved from real estate developers by local citizens (primarily Clarence Stiles, a descendant of a UGRR "conductor"). Now it stands as a sometime stop on the African-American Heritage Tour and a learning center for school and church groups and individuals.

The house is shown as a typical "house museum," but occasionally there may be temporary exhibits on the story of "the middle passage" (the importation of slaves from Africa under terrible conditions), the Underground Railroad, and the Jim Crow era.

HOURS: Sat., 12–3. Groups by appointment. **ADMISSION:** $.
LOCATION: 26 Kings Ct., Lawnside (Camden County), Rt. 295, Exit 30, south on Warwick, right on Gloucester Ave., then left on Moore to Kings Ct. **TELEPHONE:** 856-546-8850.

Other New Jersey Historic Sites

Long Pond Ironworks: Founded in 1766 by a German ironmaster who brought five hundred ironworkers and their families to build an ironworks along the upper Wanaque River, the area originally contained a blast furnace and a large forge. Operations ceased in 1882 when the industry converted to anthracite furnaces. What is left consists of a few buildings and the remnants of iron-making structures such as furnaces, casting house ruins, ice houses, and large waterwheels. At this time, the only building open to the public is the old Country Store, which houses a museum full of displays, artifacts, and relics of life here. **HOURS:** Tours of the furnace area and village at 10, 12, and 2 on the second Sat. of the month and at 1 and 3 on the second Sun., Apr.–Nov. The museum is open weekends, 11–5, Mar.–Nov. The village is adjacent to Monksville Reservoir, a popular fishing area. **LOCATION:** W. Milford Twp. (Passaic County), Rt. 511, 2 miles east of Greenwood Lake. **TELEPHONE:** 973-657-1688 (Friends of Long Pond Ironworks). **WEBSITE:** www.longpondironworks.org.

Historic Walnford: This 36-acre historic district in Crosswick Creek Park is a former country estate and mill village. The Georgian-style Waln House, built in 1773, is the largest pre-Revolutionary residence in Monmouth County. It has been restored to an early twentieth-century appearance, preserving the various changes made by five generations of the Waln family and their descendants. The picturesque nineteenth-century gristmill on Crosswicks Creek was powered by turbine rather than a water wheel—the peak of stone gristmill design when it was rebuilt in 1872. An 1879 carriage house, along with a caretaker's cottage, barn, wagon house, and other outbuildings and farm structures preserve this atmosphere of this historic farm village. Free. **HOURS:** Daily, 8–4:30. **LOCATION:** Walnford Rd., Upper Freehold Twp. (Monmouth County). Off Rt. 539, south of Allentown. **TELEPHONE:** 609-259-6275. **WEBSITE:** www.monmouthcountyparks.com/parks/walnford.html.

Belcher-Ogden Mansion: This house originally belonged to John Ogden Jr., one of the first settlers in Elizabeth, and was built between 1680 and 1722. Later, from 1751 to 1757, Royal Governor Jonathan Belcher lived in this historic Georgian residence. Tours by appointment only. **LOCATION:** 1046 E. Jersey Ave., Elizabeth (Union County). **TELEPHONE:** 908-351-2500.

Greenfield Hall: This well-furnished, handsome Georgian building built in 1841 includes early-American furniture, china, tools, a doll collection, and spinning wheels. The hall, which is the headquarters of the historical society of Haddonfield, also has changing exhibits on local history as well as a museum shop. **LOCATION:** 343 King Highway East, Haddonfield (Camden County). **HOURS:** Wed.–Fri. and first Sun. of the month, 1–4. **TELEPHONE:** 856-429-7375. Special events are also held throughout the year. Next door is the Samuel Mickle House, built in the 1730s, which houses the society's library, including photos, maps, old books, and genealogical records. Tue. & Thu., 9:30–11:30, and 1–3 the first Sun. of each month.

Township of Lebanon Museum: A white 1825 schoolhouse restored with all its desks, textbooks, and inkwells in place. Reserved school tours are booked and classes taught. The second floor offers exhibits displaying a permanent Lenape Indian collection plus special exhibits. **HOURS:** Tue., Thu., 9:30–5; Sat., 1–5. Free. **LOCATION:** 57 Musconetcong River Rd., Hampton (Hunterdon County). **TELEPHONE:** 908-537-6464.

Double Trouble Village: This village in Double Trouble State Park contains fourteen original structures from the late nineteenth and early twentieth centuries associated with the Double Trouble (Cranberry) Company, including a general store, a schoolhouse, and cottages. There's also a restored sawmill and a cranberry sorting and packing house. A trail leads alongside several cranberry bogs. Call for tour information. **LOCATION:** Double Trouble Rd., Berkeley Twp. (Ocean County). Off Garden State Parkway, Exit 74. **TELEPHONE:** 732-341-6662. **WEBSITE:** www.state.nj.us/dep/forestry/parks/double.htm.

Holcombe-Jimison Farmstead: The farmstead features the oldest remaining stone house in Hunterdon County, built in 1711, as well as several other buildings and an herb garden. The bank barn is used as a museum of rural life and displays early plows and other farming tools, sleighs, meat grinders, bottles, and assorted implements. Visitors are surprised to find a complete dentist/doctor's office on the second floor. The wagon shed outdoors shelters a printing press and a blacksmith shop. Special events include a celebration of farming (second weekend in Sept.). **LOCATION:** Rt. 29, Lambertville. **ADMISSION:** $. Discounts: Students. Under 5 free. **HOURS:** May–Oct., Sun., 1–4, and Wed., 9–12. **TELEPHONE:** 609-397-2752.

New Sweden Farmstead Museum: Seven log structures commemorate the 350th anniversary of the first Swedish settlement in America in the Delaware Valley in 1638. Opened formally by the king and queen of Sweden in 1988, this small settlement includes a blacksmith shop, storehouse, threshing barn, stable, residence, barn, sauna, and smokehouse. A Swedish team supervised the construction to assure authenticity, and many of the buildings contain authentic artifacts on permanent loan from Sweden. Tours of the seventeenth-century farmstead present the lifestyle and contributions of early Swedish settlers, who introduced the log cabin to America. **ADMISSION:** $. Discounts: Seniors, children, students. Under 6 free. **HOURS:** Sat., 11–5; Sun., 12–5 mid-May through Sept. **LOCATION:** City Park, Bridgeton (Cumberland County). **TELEPHONE:** 856-451-9785.

Fort Mott State Park: Fort Mott was part of a coastal defense system designed for the Delaware River in the late 1800s that included Fort Delaware on Pea Patch Island and Fort DuPont across the river. The fortifications seen today at Fort Mott were erected in 1896 in anticipation of the Spanish-American War. Today, you can see maritime history exhibits at the Welcome Center and wander through the old batteries following interpretive signs. **HOURS:** Daily, 8–8 in summer and Sept. weekends; 8–6 in spring and fall; 8–4 in winter. **LOCATION:** 454 Fort Mott Rd., Pennsville (Salem County). Off Rt. 49. **TELEPHONE:** 856-935-3218. **WEBSITE:** www.state.nj.us/dep/forestry/parks/fortmot. htm.

From Fort Mott, Three Forts Ferry carries visitors to the other two forts (seasonal operation; for ferry information, call 302-832-7708). Fort Delaware on Pea Patch Island was built in 1847 and served as a major Union military prison during the Civil War. Tours and exhibits at the fort re-create that era.

Just outside Fort Mott at Finn's Point is the site of a 115-foot lighthouse, built with an unusual metal exoskeleton. Open for visitors 12–4 the third Sun. of the month, Apr.–Oct. Also nearby is Finn's Point National Cemetery, where most of the 2,700 soldiers who died on Pea Patch Island during the Civil War are buried.

Church Landing Farm: This three-story farmhouse museum on the Delaware features rooms furnished as they were between 1840 and 1860. Guided tours relate the area's history, including the days when a ferry carried worshippers to church across the river to Wilmington and New Castle. The grounds include flower and herb gardens, as well as outbuildings containing a one-room maritime museum, Riverview Beach Park memorabilia, and an 1880 wash house. The riverfront at the farm includes a scenic view of the Delaware Memorial Bridge. A Day at the Farm is held every spring, featuring early farm crafts as well as a Civil War encampment. **ADMISSION:** $. Discounts: Seniors. **HOURS:** Wed. & Sun., 12–4. **LOCATION:** 86 Church Landing Rd., Pennsville (Salem County). Off Rt. 49, half mile south of Rt. 295. **TELEPHONE:** 856-678-4453.

D.A.R. Van Bunschooten Museum: This 1787 Dutch Colonial house was the home of the Reverend Elias Van Bunschooten, who served the Dutch Reformed Church in northwestern New Jersey for forty years. Operated by the Daughters of the American Revolution, the house is furnished with an impressive collection of early American antiques, all original furnishings. Outside there is a huge barn, ice house, and privy. The guided tour includes the Wagon House, where carriage and farm implements await. Two special events each year, with crafters and demonstrations. **HOURS:** May 15 to Oct. 15, Thu. & Sat., 1–4. **ADMISSION:** $. Discounts: Children. **LOCATION:** Rt. 23, 4 miles north of Sussex (Sussex County). **TELEPHONE:** 973-875-5335.

Old Millstone Forge Museum: The longest-operating blacksmith shop in America, it was used from the mid-1700s until 1959. Demonstrations and displays show the history of blacksmithing. Upstairs, blacksmith and wheelwright items are on display. Donation. **HOURS:** Sun., 1–4, Apr.–June, mid-Sept.–Nov. **LOCATION:** N. River St., Millstone Borough (Somerset). **TELEPHONE:** 732-873-2803.

Barnegat Heritage Village and Museum: Several historic structures with period furnishings from other sites include the Lippincott-Faulkinburgh House, built in the 1700s; Edwards House, built by a Revolutionary War soldier; an 1900 barber shop; and a butcher shop, built with lumber from the storm-wrecked Barnegat lightkeeper's house. Some buildings contain exhibits. The village also hosts occasional special programs. **HOURS:** Sat., 1–4, Memorial–Labor Day. Barnegat Historical Society, 575 E. Bay Ave., Barnegat (Ocean County). Garden State Parkway, exit 67. Follow Bay Ave. east through town. **TELEPHONE:** 609-698-5284. **WEBSITE:** www.barnegathistoricalsoc.com.

Cooper Mill: At this 1826 mill you can see corn ground into meal before your eyes. Guided tours are available upon request and for groups. **HOURS:** July & Aug., Fri.–Tue., 10–5. May, June, Sept., & Oct., weekends only. Located on Rt. 513/124, Chester (Morris County). One mile west of Rt. 206. **TELEPHONE:** 908-879-5463.

Kearny Cottage: This picturesque 1781 four-room cottage near Raritan Bay was once the home of poet Elizabeth Lawrence Kearny (half-sister of James Lawrence, the War of 1812 hero). It is now used as a house museum. **HOURS:** Tue. & Thu. afternoons (but call first). **LOCATION:** 63 Catalpa St., Perth Amboy. **TELEPHONE:** 732-826-1826.

Shippen Manor: Part of the Oxford Furnace Historic District, this Georgian mansion is constructed of stone walls 2 feet thick and features three immense chimneys. Built by the well-known Philadelphia

Shippen family in 1754, the house was a center for an iron manufacturing area. Original iron firebacks in chimneys, period furniture and cellar kitchen are featured. Tours are given by costumed docents. The front lawn is used for many special events. **HOURS:** Sun., 1–4. **LOCATION:** 8 Belvidere Ave., Oxford (Warren County). **TELEPHONE:** 908-453-4381.

Van Riper–Hopper House: This Dutch Colonial farmhouse contains period furnishings, a local history display, and an herb garden. Open Sat., Sun., 1–4. Small admission fee. **LOCATION:** 533 Berdan Ave., Wayne (Passaic County). **TELEPHONE:** 973-694-7192.

Somers Mansion: The oldest house in Atlantic County, it has an unusual roof shaped like an upside-down ship's hull and contains nice furniture and local memorabilia. Tours at this state historic site are given by docents from the Historical Society next door. Call for hours. **LOCATION:** Rt. 52 to Shore Rd., Somers Point. **TELEPHONE:** 609-927-2212.

Acorn Hall: A fine example of a Mid-Victorian home in the Italianate style, this house features original furnishings in its two parlors, dining room, and foyer and displays children's toys and gadgets. It has a well-kept lawn with huge red oak and Victorian garden with gazebo. Tours by docent only. **HOURS:** Mon. & Thu., 10–4; Sun., 1–4. **ADMISSION:** $. **LOCATION:** 68 Morris Ave., Morristown (Morris County). **TELEPHONE:** 973-267-3465.

Dr. William Robinson Plantation: This restored 1690 farmhouse contains artifacts, maps, and pictures in its museum section. Guided tours are by costumed docents. **HOURS:** Apr.–Dec., first Sun. of month, 1–4. **LOCATION:** 593 Madison Hill Rd., Clark (Union County). **TELEPHONE:** 732-381-3081.

NEARBY OUT-OF-STATE SITES
Van Cortlandt Manor

Set on a rise overlooking both the Hudson and Croton Rivers, Van Cortlandt Manor is a prime example of the strong influence of the Dutch in the New York–New Jersey area. At one time in the late 1700s, the estate extended as far as Connecticut. The Manor House is now one of the better colonial restorations in the area, and is one of several sites run by Historic Hudson Valley.

Tours begin at the reception center, where accurately costumed guides take groups of people through several buildings. Our group stopped first at the Ferry House. The ferry once plied the Croton River, and travelers would stop here for food, drink, and lodging.

The building is not large, but travelers would sleep three or four to a bed, so they all managed.

At the other end of a long brick walk, lined with rows of tulips, is the Manor House itself. While not as elegant as Southern Colonial mansions, it is impressive for this area—three stories high with a two-story porch wrapped around it. A heavy Dutch door opens to the main floor, where the atmosphere is one of burnished wood and quiet elegance. Delft tiles line the fireplaces. Chippendale and Queen Anne furniture fill the rooms, and English china rests in the practical Dutch cupboards whose doors could be closed at night.

In the ground-floor kitchen the guide shows a true Dutch oven (a heavy iron kettle with a closed lid), a beehive oven in the back of the fireplace, and a gridiron for baking steaks. The property also includes a smokehouse, icehouse, tenant house, and a blacksmith forge, and there is a picnic area available.

> **HOURS:** Apr.–Oct., daily except Tue., 10–4. Nov. & Dec., weekends only. **ADMISSION:** $$. Under 6 free. **LOCATION:** Croton-on-the-Hudson, NY. Take Tappan Zee Bridge to Rt. 9 north to Croton Pond Ave., one block east to South Riverside Ave., turn right and go a quarter-mile to entrance. **TELEPHONE:** 914-631-8200. **WEBSITE:** www.hudsonvalley.org.

Philipsburg Manor

A large farm and gristmill, a wood-planked bridge that spans a tranquil stream, an old stone manor house, and a huge modern reception center filled with exhibits are all a part of this Historic Hudson Valley restoration. The estate is set up as it would have been from 1680 to 1750, with authentic furnishings and authentically garbed guides. You begin with a movie about the Philipse family, who once managed 90,000 acres and shipped flour and meal down the Hudson. Unfortunately, they backed the losing side during the Revolutionary War and lost their holdings as a result.

Guided tours of the manor, a demonstration of the gristmill, and a walk around the large property and through the barn are part of the outing. You can see sheep and lambs gamboling about as you traverse the property. The Visitor Center includes a large, well-stocked gift shop and a glass enclosed cafe that offers light lunches (closed on Tuesdays). This is also the embarkation point, in season, for tours of the Rockefeller estate, Kykuit.

> **HOURS:** Apr.–Dec., daily except Tue., 10–4. Weekends only in March. **ADMISSION:** $$. Discounts: Seniors, students. Under 6 free. **LOCATION:** Upper Mills, North Tarrytown, NY. Take Tappan Zee Bridge, then Rt. 9 north for 2 miles. Follow signs. **TELEPHONE:** 914-631-8200. **WEBSITE:** www.hudsonvalley.org.

Museums of All Kinds

Statue at the New Jersey Vietnam Veteran's Memorial in Holmdel. Behind the memorial is the beautifully structured Vietnam Era Educational Center. *(Photo courtesy NJVVMF, Inc.)*

ART AND SCIENCE MUSEUMS

Newark Museum

Newark Museum is twice the size it was a few years ago; it is open, airy, and convenient—a truly first-class museum. There is room to show off the collection—American paintings, Tibetan statues, African masks—plus plenty of space for the special exhibits that come and go. The center court is open for light lunches and teas, and there's a museum shop nearby. There's also a separate Science Shop in the museum.

The Asian Galleries on the third floor not only include the museum's fine Tibetan collection but also Indian, Chinese, and

Korean treasures. As in the other galleries, the exhibits are well mounted and the explanatory material is easy to read.

The American Art Galleries covers two floors on the North Wing, tracing the development of art in the United States from colonial works to contemporary painting. Works from major artists are displayed in separate galleries according to time period and theme.

The newly opened Dynamic Earth, in the Victoria Hall of Science, adds a strong natural science angle to the museum's collections. It features seven galleries that cover forces shaping the natural world, an exploration of the world's ecosystems, and a look at New Jersey's natural setting. Hands-on activities are mixed with traditional exhibits to explore volcanoes, earthquakes, and survival of the fittest. There's a Discover Field Station, where kids can do their own scientific investigations. You'll also find a real mastodon skeleton uncovered in a "dig," ancient insects trapped in amber, fluorescent minerals from New Jersey, and fossils in a re-created New Jersey cave. Science workshops and other programs are often held on weekend afternoons. Also of interest to families is the Junior Gallery and minizoo with terrariums and aquariums. Nearby, the Native American Gallery offers costumes and artifacts. There is also a program hall for the school classes that come to the museum.

The fifty-seat Dreyfuss Planetarium is near the garden entrance. This facility offers sky shows to the general public on weekends and holidays (there's an extra fee). The museum also includes a pleasant garden complete with several modern sculptures. A tiny one-room schoolhouse that dates to 1784 and a Fire Museum are also part of the garden scene.

Attended parking is available in an adjacent lot (corner of Central and Washington Aves.). Have your ticket stamped at the Information Desk, where you can also pick up floor plans. The Ballantine House (q.v.) is also accessible through the museum.

HOURS: 12–5, Wed.–Sun. Closed major holidays. **ADMISSION:** Free, with donations welcomed. **LOCATION:** 49 Washington St., Newark (facing Washington Park). **TELEPHONE:** 973-596-6550; planetarium, 973-596-6609. **WEBSITE:** www.newarkmuseum.org.

Montclair Art Museum

A true art museum nestled in a town that was once an artists' center, the Montclair Art Museum reflects a high level of community support. Built in the early twentieth century, this is a solid, neoclassical stone edifice dedicated to painting and sculpture, with a permanent collection of more than 15,000 works.

The collection consists entirely of American art, covering a period of three centuries. Many familiar names such as Hopper, Cassatt, Sargent, Whistler, Eakins, Copley, and Currier & Ives are represented here, along with many other prominent American artists. One gallery is dedicated to the work of George Inness, the Hudson River School painter who did much of his work in Montclair. The museum is also a repository for the works and papers of Morgan Russell, originator of Synchromism, the first American modernist art movement. The paintings in the permanent collection are often used as the basis for constantly changing exhibits, which are themed for a certain point of view.

Kids are likely to find the permanent Native American collection most interesting, but the collection is also used for adult-oriented exhibits. Costumes and artifacts highlight the Plains and Southwest Indians, including interesting displays of Sioux and Navajo dress. Froom time to time the museum shows works by contemporary Native American artists. This is an active museum, with classes, children's programs, and lectures supporting current exhibitions as well as gallery tours. Many traveling exhibits are shown throughout the year, all focusing on American art. A gift store and free parking lot behind the museum help make a visit a pleasant experience.

HOURS: Tue.–Sun., 11–5. Free tours Sat. at 12 and 1 or by appointment. **ADMISSION:** $$. Discounts: Seniors, students. Under 12 free. Free, Fri., 11–1. **LOCATION:** S. Mountain and Bloomfield Aves., Montclair (Essex County). **TELEPHONE:** 973-746-5555. **WEBSITE:** www.montclair-art.org.

Zimmerli Art Museum

The Jane Voorhees Zimmerli Art Museum, on the Rutgers Campus in New Brunswick, keeps growing all the time. Once a small collection, there are now over 60,000 works (paintings, lithographs, drawings, photographs) in this museum. The lobby level is home to American Art, a large Russian Art collection, children's book illustrations, Soviet nonconformist art, and the museum store. Upstairs, on the mezzanine level, is the home of American prints and an environmental sculpture gallery. A spiral ramp leads to the lower level, where a maze of walls presents ancient art, modernist European and American art, Japonisme, European art, special exhibition galleries, and additional Soviet nonconformist works.

The American Art collection includes paintings and sculpture from the late eighteenth century to today, including nineteenth-century portraits and landscapes and American art influenced by surrealism and abstraction. Other American collections cover women artists, original illustrations for children's literature, and a regional stained-glass design. Kids will enjoy the Learning Center, which has computers and interactive learning materials on art for the entire family.

The Riabov Collection of Russian Art contains a wide variety of periods and media, including folk prints, sculpture, religious icons, landscapes, and stage designs, as well as Russian émigré art. The Dodge Collection of Non-conformist Art from the Soviet Union is the largest collection of its kind in the world, encompassing more than 17,000 works by dissidents.

The Zimmerli also has a large graphic arts collection from the nineteenth century. European modernism is represented through the graphic arts, displayed in the twentieth-century galleries. There is a small teaching collection of European paintings from the fifteenth to nineteenth centuries.

A Japonisme room also displays a permanent collection of European and American works on paper and ceramics—a selection that reflects the strong influence of Japan on Western art in the late 1800s and early 1900s. Plus, the museum features a number of traveling exhibits throughout the year.

HOURS: Tue.–Fri., 10–4:30; weekends, 12–5. Closed major holidays and Aug. **ADMISSION:** $. Under 18 free. Free the first Sun. of each month. **LOCATION:** 71 Hamilton St., New Brunswick (Middlesex County). At corner of George St. **TELEPHONE:** 732-932-7237. **WEBSITE:** www.zimmerlimuseum.rutgers.edu.

Grounds for Sculpture

For those who like to stroll on lush lawns and inspect large works of sculpture at leisure, this is the only major venue in New Jersey. Located on the former grounds of the New Jersey State Fair, the 35-acre site includes two large buildings dedicated to indoor exhibitions and an expanse of well-tended greenery that serves as a backdrop for the large sculptures. Although there are many abstract pieces, you will also find "lifelike" forms by such artists as J. Seward Johnson who specialize in renditions of real people. Overall, dozens of artists' works in all manner of media are displayed at this art park. Special exhibits are offered several times a year.

Walkways throughout the site are made of concrete and pebble, but there is no prohibition against walking on the grass. A large lake serves as backdrop for the grounds. One of the pleasant aspects of this place is the number of benches and Adirondack chairs where you can sit and contemplate the lawn, ornamental trees, and heroic-sized sculptures. In fact, the grounds have so many plants and flowering bushes, it is as attractive to garden groups as it is to art lovers.

The Domestic Arts Building includes large spaces for rotating exhibits, a small cafe, and a museum shop. The cafe also offers an outdoor courtyard where you can sit at a bistro-style table next to bamboo trees and a three-dimensional rendition of a French cafe scene. A formal Water Garden, which features reflecting pools, concrete walkways, plantings, and outdoor "rooms" of sculpture, is on the far side of the building. At the far side of the grounds is the Toad Hall shop and gallery and an upscale restaurant called Rats (open for lunch and dinner), which is accessible on foot or via a separate entrance.

> **HOURS:** Tue.–Sun., 10–9. Tours Sat. at 11, Sun. at 2, late May–Oct. Closed major holidays. **ADMISSION:** $$ ($ on Tue.–Thu.) Discounts: Seniors, students. Under 12 free Tue.–Thu. **LOCATION:** 18 Fairgrounds Road, Hamilton Twp. (Mercer County). Rt. 295, Exit 65B. Follow signs. **TELEPHONE:** 609-586-0616. **WEBSITE:** www.groundsforsculpture.org.

Princeton Art Museum

One of the leading university art museums in the United States, the Princeton Art Museum is beautifully laid out with a modern, well-lit interior. The collection of 60,000 works range from ancient to contemporary, with concentrations on the Mediterranean, Western Europe, China, the U.S. and Latin America.

The museum's greatest strengths are its collections of Greek and Roman antiquities from the university's excavations in Antioch, as well as Chinese and pre-Columbian art, most notably Olmec, Maya and Aztec items. Medieval European works include sculpture, metalwork and stained glass. Western European paintings encompass important examples from the early Renaissance through the nineteenth century, with a growing collection of twentieth-century and contemporary art. The American Gallery includes works by such artists as Copley, Peale, Eakins, Homer and Sargent, while the Nineteenth-Century Gallery features works by Impressonist notables like Cezanne, Degas, Gaugin, Van Gogh, and Monet. The museum also has many old master prints and drawings as well as a wide collection of original photographs. Special exhibits show portions of these collections on a rotating basis. You'll also find a nice museum shop here.

> **HOURS:** Tue.–Sat., 10–5; Sun., 1–5. Closed major holidays. Several adult group tours are available; call 609-258-3043 for options. **ADMISSION:** Free. **LOCATION:** Princeton University Campus, Nassau and Witherspoon Sts., Princeton (Mercer County). From Nassau St., walk past the left side of Nassau Hall. Museum is straight ahead. **TELEPHONE:** 609-258-3788. **WEBSITE:** www.princetonartmuseum.org.

Liberty Science Center

Perhaps you've seen the gleaming white building with its campanile style tower and spherical hump as you pass Exit 14B on the N.J. Turnpike. That's the science and technology museum in the forefront of the interactive, get-the-kids-to-like-science centers. Set in the middle of Liberty State Park, the modern building is surrounded by grasslands and a nature center and offers a view of New York Harbor from its outside deck.

As you enter the building, the first thing that strikes your eye is the aluminum Hoberman Sphere which expands and contracts as it hangs in the 90-foot atrium in the center of the building. This fascinating ball lets you know you have come to a place where technology is king.

Exhibits are housed on the three levels that circle the atrium. There are distinct areas: Environment, Health, and Invention. This covers everything from fish tanks on the top floor to pink-toed tarantulas over at the bug zoo, to the playful doodads on the bottom floor. There are always interesting traveling exhibits (which often outshine the permanent ones).

Some of the permanent attractions are a virtual reality basketball game where you play "hoops" against a video "pro"; a large touch tunnel where children navigate a pitch-black maze using only their tactile senses; and a mini-wall for rock climbing. Down on the Invention Floor there are plenty of goodies, including a sound booth where you can mix high-tech electronics to compose music, and the Discovery Room where guests can build their own structures assisted by staff members.

As for the IMAX Theater—it is housed in a geodesic dome (which helps give the Science Center its unique appearance) and features an eight-story curved screen. Movies produced in the Imax format are twice as large as feature films and use a six-channel sound system. This gives an all-surround feel to the films (and vertigo to some). Nature films are popular here—best to reserve when you come in (or even ahead of time). Two or three different movies may be shown on a single day.

Although the 3-D shows are in a separate theater and are an extra expense, they are usually very good. There is a large gift shop on the middle floor, and the Laser Lights Cafe offers sandwiches and salads and a very nice view of the harbor.

HOURS: Tue.–Sun., 9:30–5:30. Extended summer hours.
ADMISSION: Adults, $$$. Discounts: Seniors, children. Combination fee for IMAX & 3-D show available. **LOCATION:** Exit 14B, N.J. Turnpike,

turn left, follow Liberty State Park signs, take Burma Road to the Science Center. **TELEPHONE:** 201-200-1000. **WEBSITE:** www.lsc.org.

New Jersey State Museum

It stands in Trenton, pristine and white against the backdrop of the Delaware River, the very model of a modern, well-kept museum. There is no admission charge. The adjacent Museum Theater offers a well-proportioned stage and comfortable seating. The planetarium, housed in its own section, seats 150 people. The restrooms are well maintained and plentiful. The State Museum seems to have everything (although it could use more visitors).

Set up as a family museum, with exhibits to interest both children and adults, the museum offers a balance between its art and science sections. On the upper-floor galleries, paintings and decorative arts range from seventeenth-century urns to twentieth-century cubist canvasses. The natural science section offers an excellent collection of stuffed animals posed within their natural habitats. Another large display is devoted to life around the seashore, with relief dioramas depicting the chain of tidal life from worms to higher life. There are also exhibits on insects, minerals, and the solar system. The first floor is devoted to changing exhibits of art and sculpture. As for the planetarium, public shows are given on weekends and also weekdays during summer. Check for appro-

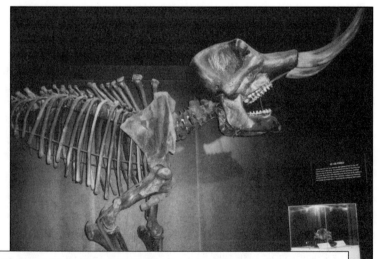

The New Jersey State Museum balances exhibits on nature, science, and art. *(Photo by Barbara Hudgins)*

priate shows for children. The seats are comfortable and the simulated sky has great depth once the stars start moving around. Laser concerts, scheduled on Friday and Saturday nights, are highly popular with teenagers. There is a gift shop outside the planetarium with science items. Another gift shop upstairs has a larger selection. And the first floor museum cafe offers quick lunch items.

For people living within easy driving distance of the museum, this is a bargain not to be missed. For those farther away, it is a worthwhile stop when you are in the area.

> **HOURS:** Tue.–Sat., 9–4:45; Sun., 12–5. **ADMISSION:** Planetarium, $. Otherwise free. **LOCATION:** 205 W. State St., Trenton. Use Rt. 29 along Delaware River or Rt. 1 into State St. **TELEPHONE:** 609-292-6464. **WEBSITE:** www.newjerseystatemuseum.org.

Morris Museum

On rainy days, empty weekends or just any day, there's nothing like a quick trip to a local bastion of culture to uplift the spirit, educate, and get the kids out of the house all in one fell swoop. The Morris Museum of Arts and Sciences is one of these dependable bastions. Housed in a lovely old mansion surrounded by great trees, it is small enough not to be to exhausting to young kids, but varied enough to appeal to all ages.

One popular area is the rock and mineral exhibit (it comes complete with a darkroom for viewing fluorescent rocks). Another is the natural science section with its glass-encased exhibits of stuffed animals in their natural environments. And since it is called a museum of arts and sciences, there is always at least one art exhibit on display that is changed every few months. In recent years, major traveling exhibits have taken over much of the first floor. Sometimes, they are interactive and continue onto the outside deck. Permanent exhibits include a good size dollhouse and a collection of Victorian dolls, a model railroad, and a tiny dinosaur room. The gracious Dodge Room is kept as a reception room with some excellent paintings and decorative arts shown in a domestic atmosphere.

Planned expansion may change some of the settings and allow for greater display of the museum's large costume collection. Also on site is the comfortable 300-seat Bickford Theater, which is the setting for both adult and children's shows, and a gift shop with an interesting range of gifts.

> **HOURS:** Tue.–Sat., 10–5; Sun., 1–5; Thu. until 8. **ADMISSION:** $$. Thu., 1–8, free. **LOCATION:** 6 Normandy Heights Rd., Morristown (Morris County). Off Columbia Tpk. **TELEPHONE:** 973-971-3700. **WEBSITE:** www.morrismuseum.org.

The Paterson Museum

Located a block from Paterson's Great Falls, in the one-time factory building of the Rogers Locomotive Company, the Paterson Museum takes up the huge first floor of the imposing red brick building. The museum contains a fascinating compilation of photographs, factory machines, old posters, and early inventions. Among other things, you'll find the great wheels that spun silk thread and ribbons, or the jacquard-style punch-hole machines. There is also a collection of Colt pistols and other armaments (the Colt factory in Paterson first manufactured sails). Although primarily a historical museum, there are other exhibits as well, including one on minerals, a model train set for children, and rotating art shows.

Paterson seems to be the only community in New Jersey that does not equate the historical with the quaint. The great weaving machines and the metal shell of the first submarine all testify to the fact that the dominant thrust of the nineteenth century was the industrial revolution. The two Rogers locomotives that stand outside the building are symbols of the Iron Horse that opened up the plains.

For more on Paterson's history, walk up the hill to the overlook next to the Great Falls. A Visitors Center there offers a 20-minute film and lots of literature. A stop at the point overlooking the Great Falls to take a picture is de rigeur. These falls are quite majestic, and if Alexander Hamilton hadn't decided to harness their power for a new industrial city, they might have been a great tourist attraction. In fact, there's a group in Paterson that is trying to do just that.

HOURS: Tue.–Fri., 10–4; Sat., Sun., 12:3–4:30. **ADMISSION:** Adults, $.
LOCATION: 2 Market St., Paterson (Passaic County).
TELEPHONE: 973-881-3874.

Hiram Blauvelt Art Museum

Founded in 1957, this was the first museum in New Jersey concentrating solely on wildlife art. Mini-galleries on the main floor feature one of seventeen remaining original 1830s Audubon folios in the United States as well as extinct birds and an ivory collection. The permanent gallery presents works of wildlife art masters and contemporary artists. Upstairs in this 1893 shingle and turret-style carriage house, the emphasis is on natural history, with exhibits promoting the conservation of big game species, including a diorama of the African Water Hole Group as well as preserved North American animals. Outdoors, you'll find a pleasant sculpture garden featuring ten large bronzes. The museum offers programs on art and natural history for schools, and an artist-in-residence presents painting demonstrations from time to time.

HOURS: Wed.–Fri., 10–4; Sat. & Sun., 2–5. Closed holidays.
ADMISSION: Free. **LOCATION:** 705 Kinderkamack Rd., Oradell
(Bergen County). Garden State Parkway exit 165 to Oradell Ave., then
left on Kinderkamack. On-site parking. **TELEPHONE:** 201-261-0012.
WEBSITE: www.blauveltmuseum.com.

Other Art and Science Museums

The Tenafly Museum of African Art: Run by the Society of African
Missions (SMA) fathers and set inside a church complex, this
museum highlights West African art and artifacts. Its permanent
collections, exhibited on a rotating basis, offer a chance to see sub-
Saharan sculpture, painting, costumes, textiles, and decorative arts
as well as religion and folklore. On display are such items as masks,
beadwork, sculpture, and religious symbols from throughout Africa.
Tours for school groups. Surrounded by 5 acres of beautifully landscaped grounds. Free. **HOURS:** Daily, 9–5. **LOCATION:** 23 Bliss Ave.,
Tenafly (Bergen County). **TELEPHONE:** 201-894-8611. **WEBSITE:** www.
smafathers.org/ind-mus.htm.

Stedman Gallery: A growing collection of art on paper and photography by contemporary American artists highlights this museum,
supplemented by other works in other media and from different
periods and places. There are also changing exhibits from other
museums, private collectors, and artists. Special events include lectures, performances, video programs, and art performances
throughout the year. **HOURS:** Mon.–Wed. and Fri.–Sat., 10–4; Thu.,
10–8. Call for additional evening hours. Closed major holidays and
between exhibitions. **LOCATION:** Fine Arts Center, Rutgers Campus,
Camden (Camden County). **TELEPHONE:** 856-225-6350.

Rutgers Geology Museum: A super-large room ringed by a balcony
comprises this science museum located on the second floor of the
Geology Hall on the Rutgers campus. A reconstructed mastodon
looms in the center, while the walls hold charts of geological periods and cases of small fossils. A newly expanded mineral display
includes Jersey's famous fluorescent rocks. Interesting lectures and
demonstrations for school groups take place here. The small gift
shop offers minerals for sale at reasonable prices. Free. **HOURS:** Mon.,
1–4; Tue.–Fri., 9–12; Sun., 12–4, Sept.–June. Call for summer and holiday hours. **LOCATION:** Hamilton St. & College Ave., New Brunswick.
TELEPHONE: 732-932-7243.

Jersey City Museum: This art and history museum celebrates Hudson
County's culture with eight galleries, a theater, classrooms, cafe, and
a gift shop. All are located in a new 35,000-square-foot facility that

opened in late 2001. The collection includes more than 20,000 regionally significant art and historical objects. There are drawings, paintings, prints, photos, maps, decorative arts, and industrial objects at the museum, including more than three hundred works by local artist August Will. The work of many other established and emerging Hudson County artists are also showcased. Many events are held throughout the year, including a music series, a film series, children's programs, lectures, symposia, and other events. **HOURS:** Wed. & Fri., 11–5; Thu., 11–8; Sat. & Sun., 12–5. **ADMISSION:** $. Discounts: Seniors, students. **LOCATION:** 350 Montgomery St., Jersey City (Hudson County). On-street parking only. Near the Grove St. PATH station. **TELEPHONE:** 201-413-0303. **WEBSITE:** www.jerseycitymuseum.org.

Noyes Museum: This striking, beach-style museum overlooks a lily-pad lake on the edge of a national wildlife refuge. Inside, you'll find many changing exhibits of contemporary paintings, photography, and sculpture by regional and national artists. It also has a growing collection of its own American fine and folk art, including a nice collection of vintage duck decoys. A special gallery for exhibits by students from area schools and community groups adds a nice touch. You'll also find an interesting shop in this museum, which was established by Fred W. Noyes, an academically trained painter and creator of nearby Smithville. **HOURS:** Tue.–Sat., 10–4:30; Sun., 12–5. **ADMISSION:** $. Discounts: Seniors, students. Under 12 free. **LOCATION:** Lily Lake Road, Oceanville (Atlantic County). Off Rt. 9. **TELEPHONE:** 609-652-8848. **WEBSITE:** www.noyesmuseum.org.

Ellarslie, the Trenton City Museum: Housed in a Victorian Italianate villa built in 1848, the museum offers a blend of changing art exhibits and a permanent collection of local historical material. On the second floor, you'll find the permanent collection of fine and decorative arts, cultural history, and industrial artifacts from the area. Included are exhibits of Trenton's renowned ceramic and porcelain companies, such as Boehm, Cybis, and Lenox. On the first floor, there are changing exhibitions of contemporary art in all media. The museum also hosts many special events, musical programs, and art classes. Ellarslie is set in Trenton's Cadwalader Park, designed by Frederick Law Olmstead. Free. **HOURS:** Tue.–Sat., 11–3; Sun., 1–4. Closed major holidays. **LOCATION:** Cadwalader Park, Parkside Ave., Trenton. **TELEPHONE:** 609-989-3632. **WEBSITE:** www.ellarslie.org.

Hunterdon Museum of Art: Housed in an 1836 stone gristmill across a picturesque dam from the Red Mill Museum, the museum has a rustic wood interior that forms a backdrop for changing exhibits of modern and contemporary art by New Jersey and other artists as well as a permanent collection of 500 prints. The museum also offers art classes, workshops, lectures, tours, and a gift shop. **HOURS:** Tue.–Sun., 11–5. Admission by donation. **LOCATION:** 7 Lower Center St., Clinton (Hunterdon County). **TELEPHONE:** 908-735-8415. **WEBSITE:** www.hunterdonartmuseum.org.

Bergen Museum of Art and Science: With most of its collection in storage, a new museum gallery was slated to open in the Bergen Mall. The museum also sponsors special programs in the mall auditorium. **LOCATION:** Lower level of the Bergen Mall, Paramus (Bergen County). **TELEPHONE:** 201-291-8848. **WEBSITE:** www.thebergenmuseum.com.

CHILDREN'S MUSEUMS

New Jersey Children's Museum

This museum is dedicated to the proposition that children learn through play and experience. Set in a reconditioned industrial building in Paramus with 15,000 square feet of space, the museum is 100 percent hands-on. Children from ages 3 to 8 can touch, climb, put on clothes, and play-act to their heart's content. The walls are brightly painted, the floor is carpeted, and the place may remind you of a giant nursery school. But the exhibits are far more expansive than what you would find at your local preschool. There is a real helicopter, for instance. It has been simplified so that a child can climb inside and pretend to fly. There is a genuine backhoe with a hard hat to match, and a fire engine that comes complete with fire hose and bell. Each of the thirty interactive exhibits is designed around a theme, including a fantasy castle, a prehistoric cave where kids can scribble their own "cave paintings" on a blackboard, and a garage where they can repair a jeep. The huge space is divided into sections devoted to dance, music, medicine, and so forth. The "office" has real computers, and the pizzeria keeps the kids busy for hours.

The museum is not meant as a drop-off spot. Parents must supervise their children, and they are welcome to join in the play. There are assistants around to help. No food is allowed, but you can duck outdoors to a nearby fast food place. Birthday parties can be arranged by reservation. Gift shop, of course.

HOURS: Mon.–Fri., 9–5; weekends, 10–6. **ADMISSION:** $$. Under 1 free. **LOCATION:** 599 Valley Health Plaza, Paramus (Bergen County). Call for directions. **TELEPHONE:** 201-262-5151. **WEBSITE:** www.njcm.com.

Garden State Discovery Museum

This interactive children's museum serves the southern part of the state. The two women who run it have filled the 15,000-square-foot center with painted murals on the walls and a number of interesting and innovative exhibits. The theme is New Jersey, so included is a Jersey diner complete with chrome and red vinyl seats, and a kitchen where kids can whip up plastic hamburgers. A "Down the Shore" exhibit lets kids fish off a boat or send rubber ducks down a stream.

Other areas include a rock-climbing wall and the one-hundred-seat theater where the kids can put on costumes and act. A flowered Volkswagen "bug" and a house construction complete with gravel pit and junk musical instruments are also on hand. One section is devoted to the science of sports. The museum directors have wisely included a snack area where you can eat your own sandwiches and augment them with vending-machine items. There is a child-centered gift shop. Geared for childen up to 10 years old—and parents must accompany them. Family membership available, as are overnights and birthday parties.

> **HOURS:** Tue.–Sun., 9:30–5:30; Sat. until 8:30. **ADMISSION:** $$.
> Discount: Seniors. Under 1 free. **LOCATION:** 2040 Springdale Rd.,
> Cherry Hill (Camden County). Not far from N.J. Turnpike, Exit 4.
> Call for directions. **TELEPHONE:** 856-424-1233.
> **WEBSITE:** www.discoverymuseum.com.

Wonder Museum

With a focus on interactive exhibits, this children's museum has more than fifty hands-on educational activities, combining scientific discovery and historical exploration with youthful curiosity. Kids can climb on the Explorer Ship, modeled after Columbus's *Pinta*. Or they can explore a retired 1965 fire truck, an ambulance, a 1948 Gunther biplane or a 1926 Model T. In Dinosaur Valley, they can dig and take home their own fossils or draw their own cave paintings. Or maybe they'd like to crawl inside a real Plains Indian tepee. There's also a frontier cabin, a medieval castle, and the Wonder Grocery & Kids Cafe. They can even relive Neil Armstrong's first step on the moon at the Moon Landing exhibit. The museum hosts art classes for kids, summer camp, games, birthday parties, and group and school trips. There's also a cafe and souvenir shop plus parking on-site. Children must be accompanied by an adult.

> **HOURS:** Mon.–Sat., 10–6; Sun., 10–5. **ADMISSION:** $$. Discount:
> Adults, groups. Under 2 free. Closed Thanksgiving, Christmas,

and New Year's. **LOCATION:** 385 Rt. 130, East Windsor (Middlesex County). One block north of Rt. 571. **TELEPHONE:** 609-371-6150. **WEBSITE:** www.wondermuseum.com.

Monmouth Museum

This is a three-part museum, with one section a museum for adults and two sections devoted to exhibits for children. The Lower Gallery features changing exhibits in art, history, science, and nature. The Becker Children's Wing is geared toward 7- to 12-year-olds and mounts major exhibits on school subjects related to science and cultural history (such as the Western frontier) that run for two years. The third section, the WonderWing, is designed for the six-and-under set. It contains interactive play areas, including a tree house, pirate ship, whale slide, and kelp forest in an under-the-sea setting. A lot of activities are packed into a small setting. Also note that, while the Monmouth Museum is on a public college campus, it is a private institution.

> **HOURS:** Lower Gallery, Tue.–Sat., 10–4:30; Sun., 1–5. Becker Children's Wing, Tue.–Fri., 2–5; Sat., 10–4:30; Sun., 1–5. WonderWings, Fri., Sat., 10–4:30; Sun., 1–5; Tue.–Thu., call for hours. **ADMISSION:** $. Discounts: Seniors, children. **LOCATION:** Brookdale Community College, Lincroft (Monmouth County). Garden State Parkway, Exit 109, then west on Newman Springs Rd. (Rt. 520). **TELEPHONE:** 732-747-2266. **WEBSITE:** www.monmouthmuseum.org.

Other Children's Museums

They're popping up all over the place, and whether you call them Children's Museums, Discovery Museums, Discovery Centers, or what-not, they certainly appeal to double-income working parents who feel they have to do something important with their kids on the weekend. Also popular with grandparents and (probably) divorced fathers. Birthday parties and other group functions are usually available and often take place in a separate room.

Imagine That!! A discovery center with thirty-five hands-on activities. Ballet room, computers, art, music, drama, shadow play, play pirate ship, VW bug, real Piper plane. Lots of crafts here also. Food is available at the in-house cafe. There are two of these franchises in New Jersey. One is at 200 Rt. 10 in East Hanover, Morris County (**TELEPHONE:** 973-952-0022) and the other is located at Rt. 35 north and Harmony Road, Middletown, Monmouth County (**TELEPHONE:** 732-706-9000). **ADMISSION:** $$ for kids (under 1 free), $ for adults. Open daily except for major holidays. **WEBSITE:** www.imaginethatmuseum.com.

Discovery House: More than 100 activities include a live-action TV news show, huge kaleidoscopes, large spin-art table, lots of crafts, magic castle, a Volkswagen "Beetle" (nonmoving of course) in an 8,000-square-foot space. Allow two hours at least. Closed Mondays and major holidays. Located at 152 Tices Lane, East Brunswick (Middlesex County). ADMISSION: $$ for kids and adults: Under 18 months free. TELEPHONE: 732-254-3770.

Jersey Explorer Children's Museum: Inside the East Orange Library, this noncommercial museum is dedicated to bringing the Afro-American heritage alive for children, including older kids. Open to groups only, by reservation: Tue.–Fri. Open to the public: Sat., 10–3. Includes Time-Traveler Theater, arts and crafts, interactive story-telling, and some exhibits. Located at 192 Dodd St., East Orange (Essex County). ADMISSION: $ for adults and kids. Under 2 free. TELE-PHONE: 973-673-6900.

SPECIALTY MUSEUMS

Yogi Berra Museum

Yogi Berra was not only a famous catcher for the New York Yankees and a famous coach for the New York Mets, he is just as famous for his funny sayings that rank up there with those of Reverend Spooner and Samuel Goldwyn. So here's an interesting, well-done museum that adjoins the Yogi Berra Stadium right on the campus of Montclair State University. The Berra family lives in Montclair, which is a major reason that this New York baseball player is honored in New Jersey.

The museum and learning center not only has loads of memora-bilia about Yogi, but lots of general baseball lore as well. Exhibits on the evolution of the catcher's glove or the qualities of wood and alu-minum bats are typical. Also cases of trophies, rings, and newspaper clippings about the Yankees and other teams are on view in the well-lighted space. A new permanent exhibit on the history of the Negro Leagues went up in 2002.

In the 125-seat auditorium you can watch a movie about the glory days of the Yankees. The front area allows for unobstructed viewing from wheelchairs.The center is open late on days when a baseball game is on and you can visit the souvenir shop then also. From a special "group" area you can overlook the outdoor stadium where both the Montclair State baseball team and the minor-league New Jersey Jackals play. If you have a kid who memorizes baseball statis-tics or a relative who remembers the 1961 World Series—take them here! Special programs for school and scout groups.

HOURS: Wed.–Sun., 12–5 (until 7 on N.J. Jackals game nights).
ADMISSION: $. Discounts: Students, children. **LOCATION:** 8 Quarry Road,
Little Falls (Passaic County). North end of Montclair State campus.
TELEPHONE: 973-655-2377. **WEBSITE:** www.yogiberramuseum.org.

The Golf House Museum

Set among the posh country estates of Far Hills, the Golf House,
home of the United States Golf Association, includes a stately house-
museum, an administration building, an interesting research lab,
and a gift shop. There are two floors of exhibit space, that include a
history of the game itself, plus rooms devoted to golfing costumes,
golf clubs, and the evolution of the golf ball.

Some of the well-prized mementos are the golf clubs of presi-
dents Wilson, Franklin Roosevelt, and Eisenhower. Also on view is
the Moon Club used by Alan Shepard to play on the lunar surface.
There are also specific exhibits devoted to golfing greats such as Ben
Hogan and Gene Sarazen and a wood-paneled room devoted to
Bobby Jones.

The house contains a magnificent flying staircase, paintings and
sculpture and a library of 13,000 volumes. Be sure to visit the
Research and Training Center, which is in a separate building
behind the main house. Here there are interactive displays such as
one on velocity tests. You can even watch a machine that tests golf
balls (named "Iron Byron") on the greens outside the Center.

HOURS: Mon.–Fri., 9–5; weekends, 10–4. Closed holidays. **ADMISSION:**
Free. **LOCATION:** Rt. 512, east of Rt. 202, Far Hills, Somerset County.
TELEPHONE: 908-234-2300. **WEBSITE:** www.usga.org.

Vietnam Era Educational Center

The New Jersey Vietnam Veterans Memorial is set on a green
hillock only a short way from the PNC Arts Center and features a
circular black wall engraved with the names of the fallen. A short
distance behind it stands the Vietnam Era Educational Center, a
beautifully constructed building that is easily accessible from the
site. The Educational Center is a revelation: it is dedicated to the
whole Vietnam era—not just the war. It was designed by the same
firm that created the Holocaust Museum in Washington, D.C., and
refurbished Ellis Island. The museum is able to capture the tempo
of the 1960s and early 1970s without taking sides in the great
debate. It is an evenhanded presentation of the events behind the
war. The history of Vietnam, the history of communism, the French
colonization of Indochina, and the Japanese occupation in World
War II are all covered.

A double timeline runs along the walls of the circular building. On top, there is a diorama composed of montaged photos of the culture of the era. Scenes from 1950 television shows, pictures of Marilyn Monroe and JFK, Elvis and the Beatles, the 1970s disco era, presidential conventions and moonshots are featured. Below that, there are pictures and text on our growing involvement in the war. The French defeat at Dien Bien Phu, the Red scare in this country—anyone remember the Domino Theory?

For a personal touch, there are the handwritten letters to mothers, wives and sweethearts back home—many from soldiers who never returned. Interactive TV sets allow you to call up a scene from a specific year—the murder of a Vietnamese official, or a college antiwar rally. The tone of the TV narration changes over time, from brisk reports to "up close and personal" views of battle scenes and burning villages. In the central theater a continuous movie shows "testaments" from various viewpoints—dog soldiers, officers, commanders. From the museum you can walk directly to the New Jersey Vietnam Veterans' Memorial through a row of stately trees. The parking lot has plenty of handicapped parking spaces, and everything is accessible to wheelchairs.

HOURS: Tue.–Sat., 10–4. **ADMISSION:** $. Discounts: Seniors, students. Under 10, veterans, and military free. **LOCATION:** Holmdel (Monmouth County). Exit 116 on Garden State Parkway to PNC Arts Center. Follow signs. **TELEPHONE:** 732-335-0033. **WEBSITE:** www.njvvmf.org.

New Jersey State Police Museum

For mystery buffs, the exhibits in this $2 million edifice offer information about the role of the State Police as well as insights into crime detection. In fact, you'll feel like Sherlock Holmes just trying to locate the place—the museum is tucked inside the grounds of the New Jersey State Police Headquarters. At the entrance you will be checked in by a state trooper who will point out the way to the museum.

The museum buildings include a refurbished log cabin that once was the dormitory for state troopers. It now houses a 1930 Buick touring car and other exhibits of early transportation. You learn that the State Police only began in 1921 and that Colonel H. Norman Schwarzkopf was the first superintendent.

The main building is full of interactive exhibits and easy-to-read posters. The 911 exhibit, for instance, lets the viewer decide whether to send an incoming call to the police, fire, or medical emergency unit. Most interesting is the exhibit called "Scene of the Crime." Through a glass window you see a murder scene. A man is lying on the floor of a kitchen in a pool of blood. Flour is spilled on the counter. Is the dead man the owner of the premises, or is he an intruder? He was shot, but where is the murder weapon? An overhead video walks you through the preliminary investigation and the procedures for collecting and preserving evidence.

But the *pièce de résistance* of the museum is its exhibit on the Lindbergh case. The kidnapping of the baby son of Charles and Anne Lindbergh took place in 1932 from an estate just outside of Hopewell. The State Police played a major role in the investigation, and some of the evidence used to convict Bruno Hauptmann of the crime is on display. You can see the baby's sleeping suit that was sent to the Lindberghs, along with a ransom note. Reward posters, pictures, and memorabilia of the "trial of the century," which took place in Flemington in 1935, are here.

HOURS: Mon.–Sat., 10–4. **ADMISSION:** Free. **LOCATION:** Rt. 175 (River Rd.), West Trenton (Mercer County). Near Exit 1 on Rt. 95 south. **TELEPHONE:** 609-882-2000, ext. 6400.

Franklin Mineral Museum

New Jersey is both the zinc mining and fluorescent rock capital of the world. While this may not be on the same level as a financial or entertainment capital, it does provide a mecca for rock hounds: Franklin Borough in Sussex County. Here, you will find both the Franklin Mineral Museum and the Sterling Hill mine (check separate listing).

Children seem to have a fascination with rocks—as any mother can attest—and they can find plenty here. The museum itself is divided into several sections: a fluorescent rock display, a general exhibit on zinc and other minerals, and a replica of an actual mine.

As part of the tour you are ushered into a long, narrow room where you face a row of gray, ordinary rocks behind a glass case. The guide flicks off the lights, and—lo and behold—the rocks turn into an extraordinary array of shining colors. Green, purple, blue luminous rocks with unusual patterns glow behind the glass. Next is a tour of the mine replica, which is a plaster labyrinth, filled with mock-ups of miners and ore carts. You can also check out the annex dedicated to dinosaur footprints and Indian artifacts. At the gift shop you'll find a good selection of rocks, gemstones, and necklaces.

But for many, the highlight of the trip is the chance to go prospecting in the rock dump at the back of the museum, although the possibility of finding a true specimen is very slim. Check with the museum about equipment and age requirements. There is a picnic area out back as well.

HOURS: Apr.–Nov., Mon.–Sat., 10–4; Sun., 11–4:30. **ADMISSION:** $.
Discounts: Children. Same rate applies for mineral dump.
LOCATION: Evans St., Franklin (Sussex County). Rt. 80 to Rt. 15 to
Sparta, then Rt. 517 north to Franklin. One mile north on Rt. 23.
TELEPHONE: 973-827-3481. **WEBSITE:** www.franklinmineralmuseum.com.

American Labor Museum

Also known as the Botto House, this is a combination historic
house/museum with an emphasis, for a change, on the working
class. This family home of an Italian immigrant worker became a ral-
lying place for striking union members during the 1913 Paterson Silk
strike. Since Haledon had a socialist mayor at the time, and Paterson
itself had banned group assemblies, workers gathered here to hear
John Reed and Big Bill Hayward during the bitter strike.

The Botto House is a sturdy, well-built wooden structure smack-
dab in the center of a middle-income neighborhood in a suburb of
Paterson. It has been restored to the era of 1903–1913 and is kept to
reflect the time when Italian immigrants lived here. The kitchen,
living room, and bedrooms reflect the lifestyle of the skilled
worker of the time. The family took in boarders, grew vegetables,
and lived frugally but not poorly. There is even a bocce court in the
yard.

The museum section of the Botto House offers a video and displays about the early American labor movement. These include
photographs of the unsafe and unsanitary working conditions in
turn-of-the-century factories, and the 1913 silk strike. However,
there are also changing exhibits that emphasize more recent immigrant groups, racial problems, and other aspects of working life.
Labor Day parades sometimes start or end here.

HOURS: Wed.–Sat., 1–4. **ADMISSION:** $. Under 12 free.
LOCATION: 83 Norwood St., Haledon (Passaic County). Call for
directions. **TELEPHONE:** 973-595-7953.

New Jersey Aviation Hall of Fame

Located on one edge of Teterboro Airport is a museum filled with
aviation memorabilia with a focus on the Garden State. There are
loads of model airplanes, a section devoted to women pilots, and
photos of all sorts of early air machines. Hanging from the ceiling
are models of satellites and astronaut uniforms. There is also a small
helicopter you can try out, and a balloon basket that children can
climb into. At the sixty-seat theater you watch a film on the history
of aviation in New Jersey. In the tower room you can listen in on
pilot-control tower conversations. There's also an X-1 rocket engine,

the aircraft used by Chuck Yeager to break the sound barrier; an X-15 engine, a rocket plane that was the first aircraft in space; a 48-cylinder reciprocal engine built by Curtis Wright; and a Hindenburg display with a piece of the ill-fated airship's frame.

Outside, you can climb aboard an old-fashioned propeller plane, and see how the folks in the 1940s and 1950s used to ride. (At least the seats were wider!) And behind the building, a Bell helicopter and a M.A.S.H. unit with jeeps and a truck re-create a Korean War scene. There is even a mess tent for lunch. This is a fun place for those who remember when a Sunday outing with the kids was a jaunt to the airport, and for air force veterans.

> **HOURS:** Tue.–Sun., 10–4. Closed major holidays. **ADMISSION:** $.
> Discounts: Seniors, children, military. Under 5 free. **LOCATION:** 400
> Fred Wehran Dr., Teterboro Airport, Teterboro (Bergen County).
> Off Rt. 46. **TELEPHONE:** 201-288-6344. **WEBSITE:** www.njahof.org.

Air Victory Museum

Set within a hangar in the South Jersey Regional Airport, this museum celebrates American air power and the technology and engineering behind it. The large collection of major aircraft on display includes an F-14A Tomcat, F-4A Phantom II, F104G Starfighter, F-86 Sabrejet, A-4 Skyhawk, and A-7B Corsair II. There are also a number of small helicopters in the hangar, such as the Bell helicopter. Small replicas of famous planes (such as the *Spirit of St. Louis*) as well as wooden and plastic models of a large variety of aircraft can be found throughout the museum. There is also a full display of flight suits, bombardier jackets, and other memorabilia.

Kids can try the Flight Trainer 150 and other interactive exhibits and visit a special area devoted to astronauts and space flight. The museum also contains a cafe and a good-sized gift shop. Outside, you can inspect a full-sized helicopter, capable of carrying fifty-five soldiers.

> **HOURS:** Wed.–Sun., 10–4. Check winter hours. **ADMISSION:** $.
> Discounts: Seniors, children. Under 4 free. **LOCATION:** South Jersey
> Regional Airport, 68 Stacy Haines Rd., Marlton (Burlington County).
> Rt. 38, south on Ark Rd., then left on Stacy Haines Rd.
> **TELEPHONE:** 609-267-4488. **WEBSITE:** www.airvictorymuseum.org.

Other New Jersey Specialty Museums

New Jersey Museum of Agriculture: Part of Rutgers University's Cook College, this huge museum features early farming equipment, a seventeenth-century trading post, tractors, milk carts, plows, buggies, kitchen utensils, and displays of land-clearing in its surrounding research farm. Here you'll find everything from egg sorters to apple pickers, plus the history of New Jersey chicken and produce farms. Weekend family specials once a month may include live farm animals. Lots of elementary school programs are offered during the week. **HOURS:** Tue.–Sat., 10–5; Sun., 12–5. **ADMISSION:** $. **LOCATION:** Off Rt. 1 and College Farm Rd., Cook College, New Brunswick. **TELEPHONE:** 732-249-2077.

Afro-American Historical and Cultural Museum: The museum concentrates on the African-American experience in America. Exhibits include posters and mementos of the civil rights movement, pictures of athletes, quilts, a typical kitchen, and African artifacts. The collection of black dolls goes back to 1860 and numbers in the hundreds. The 4,000-square-foot exhibit space on the second floor of Greenville Library will be expanded. Free. **HOURS:** Mon.–Sat., 10–5. Closed Sat. in summer. **LOCATION:** 1841 Kennedy Blvd., Jersey City. **TELEPHONE:** 201-547-5262.

The Delaware Bay Museum: Exhibits at this museum interpret shipbuilding, oystering, commercial fishing, and recreational uses of the bay. Activities include a wetlands walk, maritime industry tour, and a visit to the *A. J. Meerwald* (q.v.) for groups. **HOURS:** Thu.–Sun., 12–3:30, Apr.–Oct. and by appointment. **LOCATION:** 1727 Main St., Port Norris. **TELEPHONE:** 800-485-3072. **WEBSITE:** www.ajmeerwald.org.

U.S. Bicycling Hall of Fame: The museum features the bicycles, trophies, jerseys, photos, and other memorabilia of famous cyclists and mementos of the Velodrome in Newark. This was a *big* sport in the old days. More than eighty significant notables have been included to date. Somerville also hosts the Tour of Somerville, the oldest bicycle race in the United States, every Memorial Day. Admission by donation. **LOCATION:** 145 W. Main St., Somerville (Somerset County). **HOURS:** Mon.–Fri., 10–4 or by appointment. **TELEPHONE:** 908-722-3620. **WEBSITE:** www.usbhof.com.

Snowmobile Barn Museum: With a collection of more than 400 sleds and thousands of related collectibles, this private museum covers snowmobiling history from the early 1900s to today. There's more here than just snowmobiles, though, including such unique snow machines as a wooden replica of a 1924 Eliason motorized toboggan and a twelve-passenger vehicle built in 1951 as a school-bus/emergency vehicle for the Canadian countryside. The museum also includes farm animals, including a llama, pygmy goats, and emus. Short nature trail and gift shop. **ADMISSION:** $$. Discounts: Children. **HOURS:** Sat., Sun., 10–4, and by appointment. **LOCATION:**

Dixon Rd., Fredon (Sussex County). Rt. 94 to Fairview Hill Rd., then right onto Fredon-Marksboro Rd. Take the first left on Dixon Rd. **TELEPHONE:** 973-383-1708. **WEBSITE:** www.snowmobilebarn.com.

Toms River Seaport Museum: Devoted to small-craft restoration and maritime artifacts, especially relating to Barnegat Bay, the museum is located in the 1868 Carriage House of the estate of Joseph Francis, developer of the Lifecar. The museum also includes forty indigenous watercraft, boat sheds, and a specialized library. A workshop is used for boat restoration, educational programs, and teaching maritime and boat-building skills. **HOURS:** Tue., Thu., Sat., 10–2. Donation. **LOCATION:** Water St. & Hooper Ave., Toms River. **TELEPHONE:** 732-349-9209. **WEBSITE:** www.tomsriverseaport.com.

American Indian Heritage Museum: The Powhatan Renape Nation's museum provides an inside look at Native American culture. Visitors will learn about history, culture, and traditions from guides who gear group tours to visitors' ages. The American Indian staff interprets displays that contain tools, musical instruments, clothing, weapons, and decorative arts. You'll find large dioramas and a gallery of contemporary artwork by American Indian artists and a Native American gift shop. Outdoors, you can explore a re-creation of a traditional woodland village, walk down nature trails, or see the live buffalo. **HOURS:** Sat., 10–3, and Tue. & Thu. by appointment. Call first. **ADMISSION:** $. Discounts: Seniors, children. **LOCATION:** Rankokus Indian Reservation, Rancocas Rd., Rancocas (Burlington County). I-295, exit 45A to Rancocas Rd. **TELEPHONE:** 609-261-4747. **WEBSITE:** www.powhatan.org.

Seabrook Educational and Cultural Center: This museum explains the history of the Seabrook Company and the Japanese-Americans recruited from internment camps in 1944 during World War II. After the war, many continued on as company employees and formed the basis of the area's Japanese-American community. Exhibits depict the settlement history and community life, including a large-scale model of the village in the 1950s and photos and artifacts of life in the company village. **HOURS:** Mon.–Thu., 9–2. **LOCATION:** Upper Deerfield Twp. Municipal Bldg., Rt. 77, Seabrook (Cumberland County). **TELEPHONE:** 856-451-8393. **WEBSITE:** www.co.cumberland.nj.us/tourism/seabrook_museum.

Hungarian Heritage Center: Used as a meeting place for programs and activities for Hungarian Americans, the center includes 10,000 feet of exhibition space. Folk art and immigrant life plus special exhibitions by Hungarian artists are featured here. **HOURS:** Tue.–Sat.,

II–4, Sun., I–4. **LOCATION**: 300 Somerset St., New Brunswick. **TELE-PHONE**: 732-846-5777.

HISTORICAL MUSEUMS
Museum of Early Trades and Crafts

Housed in a handsome Richardson Revival building that once was the Madison Public Library, this museum serves two purposes. The refurbished building, brought back to its circa 1900 glory, with brilliant stained glass windows, bronze chandeliers, and wrought iron balcony, is an architect's delight. Meanwhile the major collection of tools for the thirty-four trades that existed in New Jersey in 1776 are on revolving display. Some of these concern particular trades such as coopering (barrel making), printing, and so forth, from the colonial period onward.

Downstairs, the development of local businesses from their early origins is traced. For instance, the town funeral home is still owned by a family whose patriarch was a carpenter. He made coffins as a sideline, but when funeral parlors came into vogue, he expanded his business. Docents are on hand, and there is a children's "activity" room here.

HOURS: Tue.–Sat., 10–4; Sun., 12–5. Closed major holidays.
ADMISSION: $. Discounts: Seniors, children. **LOCATION**: Main Street (Rt. 124) and Green Village Rd., Madison (Morris County).
TELEPHONE: 973-377-2982.

Ocean City Historical Museum

Life in the 1890s is graphically depicted in this small historical museum, which takes up one whole section of the Community Cultural Center (which also houses the library and art center.) Mannequins in costumes and sections of nineteenth-century family rooms depict the heyday of the Jersey shore when Victorian families headed for Ocean City, the quiet and sober neighbor of Atlantic City. A stained glass window and a complete exhibit are devoted to the wreck of the *Sindia,* a barque that sank on a sandbar beyond the beach and is forever embedded in the sand. Oriental plates and vases, articles, and photos are on display.

HOURS: Mon.–Fri., 10–4.; Sat., I–4. Call for winter hours. **ADMISSION**: Free. **LOCATION**: 1735 Simpson Ave., Ocean City (Cape May County).
TELEPHONE: 609-399-1801.

New Jersey Historical Society

In 1997 the society moved into its new digs (a building that was formerly the Essex Club), which is only a short walk from the much publicized NJPAC (q.v.). This handsome townhouse now contains three floors of exhibits about the Garden State. An extensive collection of books and manuscripts is in the library. Permanent holdings include furniture, paintings, sculpture, and an incredible number of items covering 300 years of history: music, quilting, ship making, and what-have-you.

Revolving exhibits emphasize different periods or themes based on New Jersey history. The opening exhibit in the new building was called "From Sinatra to Springsteen" and traced the evolution of teenagers in the Garden State from the 1940s to the 1980s. Another exhibit followed the life of Paul Robeson, and a later one on the popular Jersey diner. Various interactive exhibits are geared toward school-age children, to keep them involved, but there's plenty for adults here, too.

HOURS: Tue.–Sat., 10–5. **ADMISSION:** Free. **LOCATION:** 52 Park Place, Newark. **TELEPHONE:** 973-596-8500.

Ocean County Historical Museum

Located in the Pierson-Sculthorp House, the rooms of this museum are set up in comfortable nineteenth-century fashion. A music-library room with an Edison cylinder phonograph, a Victor Talking Machine, and a well-set Victorian dining room set the tone. The Victorian kitchen is of particular interest since it is chock full of useful gadgets that have since been deemed nonessential. A gizmo for softening corks had the curators mystified until a tourist told them what it was. Upstairs, the Jeffrey Child's room features a toy and doll collection. The Charles A. Morris School Room, which includes a one-room schoolhouse replica as well as a magic lantern, impresses the youngsters. Downstairs, in the basement, are museum-type exhibits covering the history of the Lakehurst Naval Air Station during the age of dirigibles as well as a diorama of the nearby Blockhouse Fight during the Revolution. Other exhibits include Civil War memorabilia, fossils, Native American artifacts, and Barnegat Bay duck decoys. The Myrtle A. Moore Room is dedicated to early Ocean County industries like cranberry production, boat building, and charcoal and glass making. There are also changing exhibits during the year. The museum also contains a research library with 8,000 volumes on local history.

HOURS: Tue.–Thu., 1–3; Sat., 10–4. Weekend tours on the hour.
ADMISSION: Donation. **LOCATION:** 26 Hadley Ave., Toms River
(Ocean County). Rt. 9 to Washington St., then four blocks to Hadley.
TELEPHONE: 732-341-1880. **WEBSITE:** www.oceancountyhistory.org.

Hopewell Museum

This combination historic house/museum features rooms done up in particular periods as well as a number of specialty exhibits. The house itself is Victorian, built in 1877, but the rooms display Colonial, Empire, and Victorian furnishings. An 1880 organ and a Joseph Bonaparte sideboard are prized possessions here. In the back of the mansion, an addition houses a large collection of Indian artifacts and many costumed mannequins. The costumes include ball gowns, wedding dresses, and other finery worn in the nineteenth century. Upstairs, you'll find a World War I and II memorabilia room, a Hopewell Fire Department memorabilia room, a country kitchen, a glassware room, two children's rooms, a quilt exhibit, and a Civil War room. Guided tour.

HOURS: Mon., Wed., Sat., 2–5. Groups by appointment only.
ADMISSION: Free (donations accepted). **LOCATION:** 28 E. Broad St. (Rt. 518), Hopewell (Mercer County). **TELEPHONE:** 609-466-0103.

Cape May County Historical Museum

This museum in the 1755 John Holmes House is operated by the Cape May County Historical and Genealogical Society. The museum includes a pre-1820 dining room all set up, a children's room with antique toys, and much glassware and china. There's a military collection from the Revolution to today, including the flag from the Civil War ironclad, the Merrimac. The Doctor's Room shows changes in surgical instruments from the Revolution to 1900. The Native American Room contains an extensive arrowhead collection and other Lenni-Lenape artifacts. Across the yard the well-stocked barn features maritime and whaling exhibits, a stagecoach, peddler's wagon, and a restored doctor's sulky. Here also is the original Fresnel lens from the 1859 Cape May Point Lighthouse. Visits are self-guided, with a brochure for regular admission. A 1½-hour guided tour costs an additional fee. The adjacent Genealogy Room is of interest to many historians because of the number of Mayflower descendants in the Cape May area. There is also a small gift shop in the museum proper.

HOURS: Tue.–Sat., 9–4, mid-Apr.–Oct.; Sat. only, Nov.–mid-Apr.
ADMISSION: Adults, $. Discounts: Seniors, children. Under 6 free.
LOCATION: 504 Rt. 9 North, Cape May Courthouse (Cape May County).
TELEPHONE: 609-465-3535. **WEBSITE:** www.cmcmuseum.org.

Camden County Historical Society

Three buildings at the society's complex on the eastern edge of Camden include a museum, library, and Colonial-style mansion.

The Museum of County History showcases life in the region during the past three centuries. It includes early American glass, fire-fighting equipment, military artifacts, and the tools of early handicrafts set up in "shops" of cobblers, blacksmiths, carpenters, coopers, etc. There's also a one-room schoolhouse as well as a harness and storage area for sleighs and a hand pumper from an early fire company. A museum store offers items that relate to museum displays and let younger visitors take a bit of history home with them.

Pomona Hall is an excellent example of early Georgian architecture, furnished as it would have looked when it was a mansion just after the Revolution. The guided tour will take you through many well-furnished rooms, including the plantation office, dining room, dowager's bedroom, and open-hearth kitchen, where demonstrations of old-time cooking are held.

The library has 20,000 books and pamphlets, manuscripts, and newspapers dedicated to the history and genealogy of South Jersey and the Delaware Valley. In addition to its permanent exhibits, the society also has numerous special events throughout the year, from festivals and special tours to historical talks and art exhibits.

HOURS: Wed.–Fri., 12:30–4:30; Sun., 12–5. First & third Sat. of month, 12–5. Closed Aug. & major holidays. **ADMISSION:** $. Under 16 free. **LOCATION:** 1900 Park Blvd., Camden (Camden County). **TELEPHONE:** 856-964-3333. **WEBSITE:** www.cchsnj.com.

Monmouth County Historical Association

Another combination of museum and society headquarters is housed in a handsome, three-story Georgian Colonial not far from the scene of the Battle of Monmouth. Besides its permanent exhibit on the battle, the museum has an impressive collection of mahogany furniture, old china, glassware, and paintings within the historical rooms of the "mansion" (it was actually built in 1931).

The Discovery Room is devoted to a "hands-on experience." Here children can try on period clothes, play at carding wool, and do other colonial tasks. Temporary exhibits on all aspects of Monmouth County can be found here, from steamboats on the Shrewsbury River to Jersey shore memorabilia. The Historical Association also administers several historic houses in nearby towns, including the Allen House and Marlpit Hall.

HOURS: Tue.–Sat., 10–4; Sun., 1–4. Shorter summer hours. **ADMISSION:** $. **LOCATION:** 70 Court St., Freehold. **TELEPHONE:** 732-462-1466.

Other Historical Museums

Meadowlands Museum: This small museum focuses on area history and fine arts. Permanent exhibits include the Homespun Kitchen and Pre-Electric Kitchen on the first floor. Upstairs you'll find an Antique Toy and Game Room plus a Fluorescent Mineral Room containing fossils and minerals, including fluorescents from the Franklin Mine. Changing exhibits range from quilts to art to history. One-hour guided tours are available for groups. **HOURS:** Mon., Wed., Sat., 1–4; Sun., 2–4. Groups at other times by appointment. **ADMISSION:** $. Discounts: Children. **LOCATION:** 91 Crane Ave., Rutherford (Bergen County). **TELEPHONE:** 201-935-1175. **WEBSITE:** www.meadowlandsmuseum.org.

Fort Hancock Historic District: Until 1974 Fort Hancock on Sandy Hook served as part of the coastal defenses. The district contains eighteen Georgian Revival officer homes and other military buildings. The remains of late 1800s concrete fortifications, used to defend New York Harbor, have fallen into disrepair, but there are a few scattered points where you can see them close up. Tours are held in summer (see the park's program guide at the Visitors Center for dates and times). Fort Hancock is also the site of the Fort Hancock Museum, where you can learn about the history of the fort, including displays of military memorabilia (July–Aug., daily, 1–5; Sept.–June, weekends, 1–5). History House, a restored home of Officer's Row, can also be toured (weekends, 1–5). A brochure and map are available at the visitor center. **LOCATION:** Sandy Hook, Gateway National Recreation Area (Monmouth County). **TELEPHONE:** 732-872-5970. **WEBSITE:** www.nps.gov/gate.

Middlesex County Museum: Set in a handsomely restored 1741 Georgian mansion (known also as the Cornelius Low House), the museum offers changing exhibits. A one-theme exhibit (about some aspect of the Raritan Valley, its history, or population) takes up the entire house and usually lasts a few months. Entrance is most easily attained through the Busch Campus of Rutgers University. The interpretive path from the back parking lot here offers a history of the local area. However there is a small parking lot right off River Road. Free. **HOURS:** Tue.–Fri. and Sun., 1–4. **LOCATION:** 1225 River Rd., Piscataway. **TELEPHONE:** 732-745-4177.

Edison Memorial Tower and Museum: The tower is shaped like an electric light with a bulb on top and commemorates the site of Edison's Menlo Park laboratory, birthplace of the incandescent lightbulb. However, the actual laboratory was moved to Greenfield

Village, Michigan, by Henry Ford for his Americana Museum. For a long time the tower itself has not been open to tourists. However, there is a small museum adjacent to it, which is filled with light-bulbs, phonographs, and other mementos of Edison's achievements. Free. **HOURS:** Wed.–Sat., 10–4; Sun., 12:30–4:30. **LOCATION:** 37 Christie St., Menlo Park (Middlesex County). Off Rt. 27 in Edison State Park. **TELEPHONE:** 732-549-3299. **WEBSITE:** www.menloparkmuseum.com.

Heritage Glass Museum: This museum is dedicated to the local glass-blowing industry, with blowing tools and displays of bottles, vases, other glassware, and lots of local memorabilia. Free. **HOURS:** Sat., 11–2 and fourth Sun. of the month, 1–4. Groups by appointment. **LOCATION:** High and Center Sts., Glassboro (Gloucester County). **TELEPHONE:** 856-881-7468. **WEBSITE:** www.glassboroonline.com/glassboro_nj_arts1.htm.

PLANETARIUMS

Aside from the planetariums in major museums, there are a number of places star-seeking New Jerseyans can visit for sky programs. Children under six are sometimes not admitted to programs for good reason—once those doors shut in darkness, there is no escape. Luckily, many planetariums feature special "Stars for Tots" shows. Admission fees run about $5 for adults at college sites. County college planetariums may close down when the college is not in session. Here's what is available.

Ocean County College: The Robert J. Novins Planetarium is located outside the main hurly-burly of Toms River on a large campus. The planetarium not only schedules public shows all year round but also has a special astronomy curriculum for school grades 1–6 during the public school year. Weekend shows (Friday nights and several Saturday and Sunday viewings) are well attended. They do shut down every once in a while to prepare a new show, so call first. The planetarium holds 117 people and is quite modern. **ADMISSION:** Adults, $$. Discounts: Seniors, children. **LOCATION:** College Drive, Toms River. **TELEPHONE:** 732-255-0342.

Raritan Valley College: The newest planetarium in New Jersey seats one hundred people and hosts many school shows plus two public showings on Saturdays. Special pre-school shows are featured. The staff uses both the "canned" slide shows, and their own give-and-take lecture-style sky show. Nighttime laser shows are popular. There is a nice little astronomy museum before you go in. Reservations are required. It is at the top of a long set of stairs, but you can use the elevator in the adjoining building. **ADMISSION:** $. **LOCA-TION:** Lamington Rd. & Rt. 28, North Branch (Somerset County). **TELE-PHONE:** 908-231-8805. **WEBSITE:** www.raritanval.edu.

Morris County College: This automated eighty-seat planetarium offers not only several programs to the local citizenry but also courses for those who really want to delve into the subject. Shows for school and other groups are scheduled during the week and early Saturday. Public showings take place one Saturday per month usually while the college is in session. Since they fill up, best to reserve beforehand. **ADMISSION:** $$. **LOCATION:** Rt. 10 & Center Grove Rd., Randolph. **TELEPHONE:** 973-328-5076. **WEBSITE:** www.ccm.edu.

Trailside Planetarium: At the Watchung Reservation's Trailside Nature and Science Center, Coles Ave. and New Providence Rd., Mountainside (Union County). **TELEPHONE:** 908-789-3670. The planetarium is currently closed during major construction.

NEW YORK MUSEUMS

Metropolitan Museum of Art

This huge Beaux Arts building that covers several blocks of New York's Fifth Avenue is still the grande dame of museums this side of the Atlantic. It is the repository of a European culture wafted to our shores by millionaires whose art collections were donated for reasons of either generosity or tax exemptions. At one time the museum was so old-Europe-centered that it admitted neither American nor "modern" art. However, all that has changed. With the American Wing, you get a museum and a half. The wing encompasses American furniture and decorative arts, re-created seventeenth- and eighteenth-century rooms, paintings, and sculpture. To view it chronologically you must take an elevator and start at the top, descend through the restored rooms, pass the paintings of George Washington and the Frederic Remington sculptures, and end up on the first floor with large canvasses by James Whistler and John Singer Sargent. To get back to the main museum, you cross the beautiful Garden Court with its purple-willowed Tiffany screens and wonderful 1900s ambience.

But to begin at the beginning. When you first enter the Metropolitan's huge marble lobby you may feel as if you've entered Grand Central Station by mistake. Milling crowds, a central information booth, ticket booths, coat-check areas, signs for the restaurant and restrooms, a bookshop and a jewelry counter doing booming business—this is a museum? Well, one traditional feature of the museum is that from the front lobby it's Greeks to the left, Egyptians to the right, and Europeans upstairs.

If you are with children you might go for the mummies and the Egyptian section. The medieval armor on the first floor is another child's favorite. The second floor houses the European paintings, which start with the medieval period. From there you wander through Italian and northern Renaissance, Dutch masters, English portraits, and French landscapes. Other sections of the museum include Asian Arts, fashion design, New Guinea primitives, and modern art.

For the exhausted, there's always lunch where you can wait on line for cafeteria food, or opt for the center restaurant. (Reserve for the restaurant at the Information Booth when you arrive or call ahead at 212-540-3964.) Another stopping place is the roof garden (complete with sculptures), which is open in summer.

HOURS: Tue.–Thu., Sun., 9:30–5:30; Fri., Sat., 9:30–9.
ADMISSION: Suggested donation: $$$. Discounts: Seniors, students. Under 12 free. **LOCATION:** 1000 Fifth Ave. at 82nd St., New York City. **TELEPHONE:** 212-535-7710. **WEBSITE:** www.metmuseum.org.

American Museum of Natural History

The Rose Center for Earth and Space, a seven-floor, 333,500-foot wonder, opened in the spring of 2000 and has given this nineteenth-century museum a new look. The center, which replaced the old Hayden Planetarium, has as its centerpiece an 87-foot sphere that appears to hover within a cube of glass, like the Earth hovering in space. This sphere houses both the planetarium upstairs and a space theater below where visual and audio effects simulate how the universe began.

There are lots of whiz-bang special effects inside, but even the look from the outside is breathtaking. Within, the Hall of the Universe looks like a futuristic airline terminal and the Cosmic Pathway that leads down from the planetarium is a spiral walkway with inserts that cover 13 billion years of cosmic evolution. Within the Rose Center is the Black Hole Theater, the Galaxies Zone, and the Star Zone, and, finally, the Planet Zone, with its 15-ton Willamette Meteorite. Visitors walk through to the Hall of Planet Earth, which has all sorts of rocks, astrophysics exhibits, videos of earthquakes, and the usual interactive computers.

The Rose Center also offers some much-needed amenities such as a parking, garage more public space, a huge cafeteria, and several museum shops. It's best to get reserved timed tickets to the planetarium show, which you can order by phone or the Internet.

As for the main part of the museum—save energy for a visit. You might want to go to the fourth floor to see the dinosaur collection first. The skeleton bones are arranged in poses that today's scientists believe these ancient reptiles would assume. The dinosaurs seem to be poised for flight as if they were birds! On the first floor there are the gems and minerals—a beautiful collection of quartz, sapphires, and jade. A Discovery Room for children offers scientific hands-on exhibits. The museum also hosts an IMAX theater that shows those eight-story-high movies, and a butterfly conservatory in season.

HOURS: Sun.–Thu., 10–5:45; Fri.–Sat., 10–8:45. **ADMISSION:** Combination space show & museum: $$$$. Discounts: Seniors, children, members. **LOCATION:** Central Park West at 79th St., New York City. **TELEPHONE:** 212-796-5100. **WEBSITE:** www.amnh.org.

The Cloisters

High on a tree-covered bluff just minutes from the bustling streets of Washington Heights, there stands a world apart. The Cloisters, a museum built in the style of a fourteenth-century monastery, displays the art and architecture of the Middle Ages in a setting completely devoted to that single age. Unlike its mother museum (the Metropolitan Museum of Art), which tries to cover the span of art from antiquity to the present, this monastic replica covers only the twelfth to fifteenth centuries in Europe. The Cloisters includes both religious and secular art and geographical variety. The red tile roof of the building reflects the style of southern Europe. But inside there are the stones of a Romanesque chapel, and a Gothic hall complete with arched ceiling and flying buttresses. The Cloisters gets its name from the covered walkway around an enclosed garden that was typical of the medieval monastery. Of particular interest to gardeners is the herb garden, where two hundred species of plants sprout among the espalier trees and arcades of a Cistercian cloister.

A star attraction here is the Unicorn Tapestries. Remarkable in their color, preservation, and realism, these panels tell a story which you read by moving from one to the other. The story of the hunt, killing, and resurrection of the Unicorn shows the life of the medieval aristocracy as well as the symbolism of the age. Other top exhibits include illuminated manuscripts and the Chalice of Antioch.

Since the Cloisters is built on a bluff overlooking the Hudson, be sure to drink in the view of Fort Tryon Park and the wild Palisades across the river in New Jersey. John D. Rockefeller Jr. paid for it all—the Cloisters, the park, and the view—when he donated the whole shebang in 1938.

HOURS: Tue.–Sun., 9:30–5:15; Nov.–Feb., 9:30–4:45.
ADMISSION: Suggested donation: $$$. Discounts: Seniors, students.
Includes admission to the Metropolitan Museum of Art. Under 12 free.
LOCATION: George Washington Bridge to Henry Hudson Parkway
north. Take first exit to Fort Tryon Park. Follow signs.
TELEPHONE: 212-923-3700. **WEBSITE:** www.metmuseum.org.

Frick Collection

This little jewel of a museum, housed in the former mansion of the
coke and steel magnate, is a must for art lovers. The European paint-
ings and furniture display a heavy emphasis on both the Renaissance
and eighteenth century. The Fragonard Room with panels painted
for Madame Du Barry and the Boucher Room with panels com-
missioned by Madame de Pompadour have the appropriate French
furniture and ambience to take you back to the reigns of the vari-
ous Louises. Medieval paintings, enamels, Rembrandts, and lots of
eighteenth-century British portraits and landscapes abound.

Since this was once a home, the paintings are hung much as they
would have been in the days of opulence. Gainsborough ladies and
Turner landscapes decorate the comfortable halls, and a lovely
inner courtyard provides an atrium for rest and contemplation.
There is also a lecture hall for free talks.

Only the first floor is open, but this is a formidable collection, so
allow at least an hour to browse through. Children under 10 are not
admitted and those under 16 must be accompanied by adults—they
are serious about art in this place. No lunchroom available. Admis-
sion includes artphone guide.

HOURS: Tue.–Sat., 10–6; Sun., 1–6; Fri. to 9. **ADMISSION:** Adults: $$$.
Discounts: Seniors, students. **LOCATION:** One East 70th St.
(at Fifth Ave.), New York City. **TELEPHONE:** 212-288-0700.
WEBSITE: www.frick.org.

Forbes Galleries

Since Malcolm Forbes was one of New Jersey's most colorful residents, many locals enjoy a peek at the toys of this fabulous millionaire and his family. And toys they are—literally. For in one section of
this museum you will find 12,000 toy soldiers set up in dioramas or
vignettes that include Indians circling cowboys, jousting knights,
marching bands, military formations, and so on.

In another section, called "Ships Ahoy," five hundred toy boats
are on display. These are intricately wrought boats done in all sorts
of materials. You will also see the gold-leafed glass panels from the
grand salon of the old ocean liner, the *Normandie,* along with other
art deco designs.

Other galleries include Presidential Papers (with documents emphasizing the personal side of the presidents) and a Trophy Room. One room is reserved for rotating exhibits, often of "objects de luxe." And of course, since the Forbes collection is famous for them, you do get to see twelve of the jeweled Easter eggs and other ornaments created by the imperial jeweler, Fabergé, for the Russian czars.

The galleries are housed inside the Forbes Magazine building in Greenwich Village. Thursdays are reserved for groups. Children under 16 must be accompanied by an adult.

HOURS: Tue., Wed., Fri., Sat., 10–4. **ADMISSION:** Free.
LOCATION: 62 Fifth Ave. at 12th St., New York City.
TELEPHONE: 212-206-5548. Groups: 212-206-5549.

PENNSYLVANIA MUSEUMS

Philadelphia Museum of Art

It is a Greek temple that surveys the town and the river from an imposing height, with a magnificent flight of steps leading up to its classical columns. The steps, in fact, are as famous as the museum ever since Sylvester Stallone ran up on them in the movie *Rocky*.

But inside the pillared entrance (you can avoid most of the steps by parking in the back parking lot), one of the best collections of art in North America awaits. Galleries of European art include the Johnson Collection on the first floor, which is heavy in Renaissance paintings. Twentieth-century art comes next and includes Marcel Duchamp's famous *Nude Descending a Staircase*. The variety of the museum is evidenced by the fact that there is a medieval cloister, an Indian temple, a Chinese palace hall, and a Japanese teahouse all within these portals.

The kids will find the collection of armor, which includes swords, lances, maces, chain mail, and breastplates, to be fascinating. And one whole wing, devoted to Americana, includes paintings and period rooms filled with Philadelphia-style bonnet-and-scroll bureaus, secretaries, and chests. There is also plenty of early silverware, urns, and other examples of decorative arts.

Tours are offered by volunteer guides at no extra cost. They leave at specific times and originate in the West Entrance hall. Downstairs, there is a pleasant restaurant, cafeteria, and gift shop. Admission price also allows entry to the nearby Rodin Museum, which houses the largest collection of this master sculptor's works outside of France.

The Philadelphia Museum also administers the guided tours of the historic homes in Fairmount Park. Although these classic colonial summer homes are best known for their Christmas decorations, they can be viewed at other times as well. A trolley tram and a Philly Phlash bus can take you from one attraction to another from the back steps of the museum. There is an extra fee for the Fairmount Park house tour.

HOURS: Tue.–Sun., 10–5; Wed. & Fri. to 8:45. **ADMISSION:** $$$. Discounts: Seniors, children. Under 5 free. Sunday: Pay what you want. **LOCATION:** Benjamin Franklin Parkway, & 26th St., Philadelphia. **TELEPHONE:** 215-763-8100. **WEBSITE:** www.philamuseum.org.

The Barnes Foundation

The best collection of Impressionist and post-Impressionist paintings in America can be found in this museum, set in suburban Philadelphia. Visiting hours at this Renaissance-style mansion are somewhat limited. There's also the unusual way the pictures are hung. Paintings cover some walls and even hang over a door transom. African statues and medieval ironwork are interspersed with nineteenth- and twentieth-century art. No biographical data or dates are shown. For visitors conditioned to gallery arrangement based on geography and showing dates of the works, Dr. Barnes's ideas about presentation can require some mental adjustment. He certainly had his own ideas about art appreciation, with color and form paramount. Luckily, the names of painters and titles of paintings are available.

This said, the museum contains two floors filled with a formidable collection: more Matisses than you would expect, including a huge piece entitled *The Piano Lesson;* more Renoirs than you can count; huge Navajo patterned baskets, Cezannes, El Grecos, African masks, and wood sculptures. Downstairs, you can rent audio guides or visit the gift shop. And you can visit the 13-acre arboretum that surrounds the museum. Keep in mind that the number of visitors allowed is limited, and reservations are required.

HOURS: Sept.–June, Fri.–Sun., 9:30–5; July–Aug., Wed.–Fri., 9:30–5. **ADMISSION:** $. Audio tour: $$. Reserved parking: $$. **LOCATION:** 300 North Latch's Lane, off City Ave. (Rt. 1), Merion, PA. **TELEPHONE:** 610-667-0290. **WEBSITE:** www.barnesfoundation.org.

Franklin Institute

The venerable Franklin Institute has always been a pioneer in hands-on exhibits. Exhibits range from the old hands-on favorites to new Disney World–style contraptions. The museum has four main sections: the Science Center, the Mandell Futures Center, the Fels Planetarium, and the Tuttleman IMAX Theater. In addition, there are computer terminals in the halls that can answer your questions about what is where. You will find the following venues:

The Science Center: This is the original museum, which still has many of its popular exhibits. There's a 36-times-life-size heart you can walk through, a steam locomotive in the basement that chugs along for 10 feet every hour, and a giant lever you can swing on. Space Command features an astronaut's suit and interactive tools of the astronauts plus a space academy. And there's a T-33 air force jet trainer you can "fly," plus lots of exhibits on physics, printing, and such.

The Fels Planetarium: The recently renovated 340-seat planetarium is outfitted with a state-of-the-art Digistar projection system and seamless 60-foot dome that give viewers a three-dimensional feel to their star-gazing. Special laser shows, too.

Mandell Futures Center: This brave new world is divided into several permanent exhibits with names like FutureSpace, FutureEarth, and FutureComputers. Here you will find such things as a fiberglass model of a human cell a million times its actual size; a computer that lets you "age" yourself; a model of a NASA space station; a 10-foot globe with fiber-optic lights to show population growth shifts; and an artificial forest and displays involving cyberspace.

The Tuttleman IMAX Theater: Large reclining seats are arranged in steeply angled rows. Above and around you is the movie screen, 79 feet across and four stories high in a hemispheric dome. Lots of loudspeakers project the sound. This is the place for nature films that roar and soar.

3-D Theater: The Stearns Auditorium presents a changing schedule of 15-minute education films. 3-D glasses included.

The museum has underground parking and two restaurants, a huge atrium for resting (unless you want to pay extra to ride the SkyBike 28 feet above the atrium floor), and an outdoor science park (in summer). Expect to spend at least four hours here.

HOURS: Daily, Science Center, 9:30–5; Futures Center, Sun.–Thu., 9:30–5; Fri.–Sat., 9:30–9. Closed major holidays. ADMISSION: Science and Future Centers: $$$; Discount: Seniors, children. Under 4 free. Extra for IMAX. LOCATION: 20th St. and Benjamin Franklin Parkway, Philadelphia. TELEPHONE: 215-448-1200. WEBSITE: www.fi.edu.

Please Touch Museum

When visiting Philadelphia with younger children, this place is sure to be a hit. One of the first hands-on, interactive museums to cater specifically to children under 8, it is also one of the most copied. Starting out in 1976, the museum has changed addresses several times, but it is now ensconced in a multifloored space right in the center of the city's museum district. In fact, it is directly across from the Franklin Institute, which caters to the school-age child (and grownups).

Since this is an urban museum, one display is set up to re-create the city's bus system—there's even the front of a bus on the floor. But there's also an outdoors "set" for boats that go down a river, a TV studio, and the standard kitchen and fruit market areas where kids can re-create grownup activities. A unique stop is the Russian nursery school for an introduction to other cultures. Another exhibit is based on Maurice Sendak's most popular books and includes a giant bed, giant mixing bowl, lots of pots and pans for creating a rumpus, as well as other scenes from the book. *Alice in Wonderland* is another book that is translated into interactive play elements.

During summer months, one can visit Science Park, a joint venture with the Franklin Institute. It is a family-centered, outdoor park with such interactive "elements" as a sky bike, Jumping Fountain, Bubbling Volcano, and so forth. Admission to the park (which is right behind the Franklin Institute) is free with admission to either museum.

HOURS: July 1–Labor Day, daily, 9–6; rest of year, 9–4:30.
ADMISSION: \$\$. Discounts: Seniors. Under 1 free. **LOCATION:** 210 North 21st St. (across from Franklin Institute), Philadelphia.
TELEPHONE: 215-963-0667. **WEBSITE:** www.pleasetouchmuseum.org.

Rosenbach Museum and Library

Located two blocks from Rittenhouse Square in a lovely section of Philadelphia, this 1860s townhouse was the home of rare-book collectors. The books and furnishings of the Rosenbach brothers are at once a paean to the good life and a paradise for collectors. Since one brother searched for antiques while the other concentrated on books, the home is a treasure trove of decorative arts. It is also an important research library.

Stored here are 130,000 manuscripts and 30,000 rare books, which range from medieval illuminated manuscripts to letters written by George Washington and Abraham Lincoln. Lewis Carroll's own edition of *Alice in Wonderland* and the manuscript of James Joyce's *Ulysses* together with hundreds of first editions are shelved in what is essentially still a home with beautiful and delicate furniture.

The dining room where the brothers entertained wealthy guests features an Empire-style table, Venetian Grand Canal scenes, and

Chippendale chairs. A painting by Thomas Sully and a scrolled fireplace adorn the cozy parlor. Upstairs, you can find the re-created Greenwich Village living room of poet Marianne Moore. Now that the museum has acquired the house next door, it has more room to display its large collection, which includes illustrations by children's book author Maurice Sendak and ancient Judaica. The annex will also be used for temporary exhibits and for tour introductory lectures.

Although the Rosenbach brothers lived in their townhouse only from 1950 to 1952, when both were old, the house seems to come out of some turn-of-the century novel by Henry James. It seems incredible that this cultured, even dandified atmosphere existed in the post–World War II period. Yet it's all here—oriental carpets and Herman Melville's bookcase (stacked with first editions of *The White Whale*), seventeenth-century gold chests, and delicate French parlors. The museum is a must for collectors, librarians, art historians, and anyone who wants pointers on how to live with class.

HOURS: Tue.–Fri., 10–4 (Wed. until 8); Sat.–Sun., 10–5. Closed Aug. to mid-Sept. **ADMISSION:** $$. Discounts: Seniors, children. **LOCATION:** 2010 Delancey Place, Philadelphia. **TELEPHONE:** 215-732-1600. **WEBSITE:** www.rosenbach.org.

Brandywine River Museum

From the front, it's a century-old gristmill; from the back it's a strikingly modern glass tower overlooking the Brandywine River, and altogether it is a most pleasant museum where the setting and structure are almost as interesting as the paintings within.

Inside the stone and glass structure, the atmosphere belongs to the Brandywine River artists (a group that formed around Howard Pyle and N. C. Wyeth) and to Wyeth's talented progeny, particularly Andrew and his son Jamie. Both Pyle and N. C. Wyeth were famous illustrators and many an older edition of *Treasure Island* or *King Arthur* contains their realistic action pictures. Although storybook illustrators have never reached the heights of adulation that "purer" artists enjoy, they are still among the most respected painters in America. Howard Pyle began a summer teaching center in the Brandywine Valley in 1898. The artists from this center include Maxfield Parrish, Peter Hurd, and, of course, N. C. Wyeth. But it is Andrew Wyeth, whose painting *Christina's World* is world famous, who holds the most interest for viewers. The strong emotional impact of his canvasses dominates the collection here. You'll find a small number of Jamie's paintings in the permanent collection, plus special exhibits that emphasize other Brandywine artists, American landscapes, and still-lifes. After viewing the exhibits, you can lunch at the cafeteria and view the meandering river and wildflower garden below. This lovely preserve is part of the Brandywine Conservancy, which keeps 5,000 acres in a state of nature—a most poetic place that seems to attract strollers, readers, and young romantics. It is also possible to take trips from the museum by shuttle bus to the N. C. Wyeth house and studio from April to November on specific days and times. Best to reserve for this.

HOURS: Daily except Christmas, 9:30–4:30. **ADMISSION:** $$. Under 6 free. **LOCATION:** Rt. 1 (at Rt. 100), Chadds Ford, PA. **TELEPHONE:** 610-388-2700. **WEBSITE:** www.brandywinerivermuseum.org.

Note: Also see museums that are part of a larger entity. These are mentioned under the title of the larger attraction—e.g., the Museum of American Glass (Wheaton Village), West Point Museum (West Point).

The Classics

Take the ferry from Jersey City to Ellis Island, where millions of immigrants landed. Now a national historic park. *(Photo by Barbara Hudgins)*

Statue of Liberty

Things have changed since 9/11, but now, more than ever, you may want to take the ferry trip across to this icon of freedom. As of December 2002, visitors are no longer allowed inside the statue itself. However, it may surprise you to learn that Bartholdi, the French sculptor who created Lady Liberty, never envisioned the statue as being open to the public. He assumed it would be filled with sand and admired from the exterior only. The elevator to the pedastal and those twenty-two flights of stairs were an American addition.

New Jersey residents can embark from Liberty State Park for the short ride over. Backpacks may be searched and you'd best take as little as possible along. Once aboard the ferry (which stops first at Ellis Island), you get a view from all angles of the glistening lady as the boat turns to make port. As you disembark, the first building you see is the gift and souvenir shop. Here you can stock up on mugs, pennants, and postcards.

There is now more time to explore Liberty Island, which is larger than you might expect. On its 12½ acres are administration buildings, a snack shop, a pleasant tree-shaded picnic area, and walking esplanades that rim the island. Here you can savor the view of Manhattan's towers plus the wide expanse of the harbor and its bustling boats. And there will be plenty of time to get a close-up picture of the "Lady with the Lamp." Both as a visit to a national shrine and a pleasant day's outing between two great ports, a trip to the Statue of Liberty is a must. Best to go in the spring and fall before the out-of-towners arrive. Check the website for updates on access to the statue, which may be affected by security closures.

HOURS: Daily, 9–5. Ferry: Liberty State Park, daily, 9:15–3:45; schedule expands in summer, shortens in winter. Battery Park, NY, daily, every half hour. **ADMISSION:** Ferry fee, adults, $$. **LOCATION:** Liberty State Park (take the N.J. Turnpike to Exit 14B). Parking fee if taking the ferry. **TELEPHONE:** Ferry, 201-435-9499; Liberty State Park, 201-915-3400; Liberty Island, 212-363-3200. **WEBSITE:** www.nps.gov/stli.

Ellis Island

If a visit to the Statue of Liberty is inspiring, a visit to its neighbor, Ellis Island, is absolutely fascinating. Since you get both islands for the same ferry price, it is best to allow enough time to explore both—up to five hours, if you stop at all the exhibits.

Ellis Island is the basic museum commemorating the peopling of America, not only those who set foot on this particular island (for that is only one section), but the story from the beginning, with emphasis on the late nineteenth and early twentieth centuries. A movie, shown in two theaters, recounts the experience of those who left troubled homelands to take the sea voyage to the new land. First, it was in wooden ships that took six weeks to make the voyage and left everyone sick. Later, it was the steamship lines who filled up their steerage section with poor immigrants. If the immigrants were turned back because of sickness or other reasons, the steamship company had to pay for the return passage.

Earlier immigration sites, greed, corruption, and the one-day processing of thousands of people are all covered in the movie as well as the displays. But there is also an amassing of hundreds of trunks, shawls, tickets, flyers, and other mementos of the immigrant experience. A play about typical immigrants is also offered.

Newspaper cartoons depict the rising tide of intolerance against the newcomers, which finally culminated in a restrictive law in 1924 ending the mass migration. Ellis Island was closed in 1954. In its refurbished state it is a wonderful learning experience, and an emotional one as well for anyone who descended from all the Germans, Greeks, Italians, Jews, Irish, Turks, Jamaicans, and others who were among the first to come to these shores.

HOURS: See Statue of Liberty entry. **TELEPHONE:** Circle Line, 201-435-9499; Ellis Island, 212-363-3204. **WEBSITE:** www.nps.gov/elis.

United Nations Headquarters

The first thing you notice as you approach the United Nations complex is the line of colorful flags half-circling the entrance. All member nation flags are flown at the same height—only the U.N. flag is unfurled higher. The next thing you notice is that this place is clean: no old newspapers, candy wrappers, or soda cans litter the area. In the spring, the gardens in back of the buildings sport daffodils and cherry trees, while the rose garden blossoms in June. Outside sculpture includes a gigantic abstract next to the circular fountain and the Japanese Peace Bell.

Tours of the U.N. are still popular, although now you must enter the building through an airport-type security system. The tours (which are done in a number of languages) combine a short history of the United Nations with a description of the building's art and architecture. The number of chambers you enter during the tour depends on whether the various councils are meeting or not. The General Assembly, which is usually open, is a huge hall with high-domed ceiling and more than 2,000 seats. The slatted back walls are interspersed with banks of windowed booths where translators, photographers, and TV people sit. This is the hall most often seen on television when important meetings take place.

Besides the meeting rooms, various member donations are pointed out, such as a crimson Peruvian ceremonial cloak, an intricate Chinese ivory carving, and a wall mosaic based on Norman Rockwell's *The Golden Rule.* The famous Chagall stained glass mural is in the huge public lobby.

The tour ends in the Public Concourse, where you can proceed to the bookstore, gift shops, or postal counter (a mecca for stamp collectors). Handicraft items from around the world, flags, and dolls of all nations are available. The bargain is the fact that there is no sales tax anywhere in the U.N. complex! For hamburgers and french fries

Whatever the world condition, visitors still flock to the United Nations for its tours and interesting grounds. *(Photo by Patrick Sarver)*

there's a good coffee shop here. Visitors who want to sample the lavish international lunch buffet at the Delegates Dining Room (available Monday through Friday only) must reserve ahead. Telephone 212-963-7626 and bring a photo ID—the food and the view of the East River are worth the hassle.

HOURS: Daily, 9:30–4:45. No weekends Jan. & Feb. **ADMISSION:** Free. For tours: $$. Children under 5 not admitted on tours.
LOCATION: 1st Ave. between 45th & 46th Sts., New York City.
TELEPHONE: 212-963-8687. **WEBSITE:** www.un.org.

Empire State Building

After the World Trade Center was destroyed, thousands of people converged upon Ground Zero to pay their respects. The memorial that takes its place will also attract millions over the years. But for those who want to view New York City from a skyscraper, the place to go now is this 1931 Art Deco building. When it was first built, the Empire State was the tallest building in the world. It is now, once again, the tallest in New York City. At night, the observation tower radiates red, white, and blue lights as well as special holiday colors.

For those who make the visit, there is only one entrance now, and you must go through an airport-type security check. You may purchase tickets beforehand (by phone or Website) and skip the ticket line, but everyone must go through the security check. You then are sent by way of two different elevator rides to the 86th floor (the lines can be long).

The 86th floor observatory, at 1,050 feet above the street, has both an enclosed area and an open promenade. High-powered binoculars are available for a fee. Here you will also find a snack bar and souvenir shops. On a clear day, you can see up to 80 miles in all directions. The view to the west offers New Jersey and the Hudson; to the north you get Midtown, Central Park, and beyond; to the east there are the U.N. and Chrysler buildings and Queens; and to the south is Lower Manhattan.

A virtual-reality movie called *New York Skyride* that features a helicopter ride over the city can be seen on the second floor of the building (daily, 10–10; www.skyride.com.), and there is a combination ticket for those who want to add it to the day's outing. For the hungry, there are restaurants, ethnic fast food, and coffee shops in and around the lobby. Throughout the year, concerts and art exhibits take place in the lobby, as well as holiday decorations and shows, plus special annual events like Valentine's Day Weddings and the ESB Run-up. The location is walkable from the PATH station at 33rd St. and 6th Avenue or from Penn Station.

HOURS: Daily, 9:30 A.M.–midnight. **ADMISSION:** $$. Discounts: Seniors, children. Combo ticket with Skyride: $$$$. Under 6 free.
LOCATION: 34th St. and 5th Ave., New York. **TELEPHONE:** 212-736-3100.
WEBSITE: www.esbnyc.com.

South Street Seaport

Boston has its Quincy Market, Baltimore has its Inner Harbor, and New York has its own quaint seaport area. The South Street Seaport has a holiday atmosphere about it that makes it one of the city's most popular tourist spots. The "museum" (as it is called) is actually the entire restoration of eleven square blocks that were the nucleus of New York's earliest seaport. Schermerhorn Row, Water Street, Fulton Street, and South Street boast some of the few remaining federal-style townhouses to be found in the big city. These gracious rowhouses have been beautifully restored and now house shops and restaurants. At the water's edge several ships are available for touring. Tours of the lightship *Ambrose* and the four-masted barque *The Peking* can be fascinating with the right docent. The talks really give you a feeling for the hard work, danger, and close quarters of the old ships.

A more fanciful view of the sea may be obtained from a ride on the Seaport Liberty Cruise Line, a Circle Line that offers a one-hour, bay area version of its standard cruise, or the narrated harbor cruise run by N.Y. Waterways. In warm weather you can also book a two-hour sail on the schooner *Pioneer,* where you have the chance to help raise the rigging. Other cruises may also be available.

Ship tours and rides cost extra, of course, as does entrance to the formal exhibit galleries (the museum part of the Seaport), the Children's Center, and the guided tour of the historic area. Tickets may be purchased at the Pier 16 ticket booth or the Museum Visitor Center at 12 Fulton St.

But the main attraction at the Seaport is the food, shops, and street entertainment. Unfortunately, many of the early quaint shops have been replaced by high-class chains one can find elsewhere. Pier 17, a large building that juts out into the water, is just like a New Jersey mall inside. Luckily, it has balconies that allow you to observe either the street scene or the passing boats. As for the Fulton Market, it has gone through many changes as a food emporium, and still has not found an identity.

The large plaza at Pier 16 attracts performers and musicians, both for impromptu sessions and formal entertainments—one reason that tourists love the spot. Some well-known seafood restaurants are around, but the open-air cafes with their wide plazas also seem popular. There are wide-open walking spaces, and on a sunny day, with the wind off the river, it is New York as we would like it to be. And it makes a photogenic venue for tall ships, fireworks, and other special occasions.

HOURS: Daily for shops and restaurants. **ADMISSION:** Museum, adults, $$. Excursion boats extra. **LOCATION:** Fulton & South Sts., just off FDR Drive, New York City. **TELEPHONE:** Museum, 212-748-8600. **WEBSITE:** www.southstseaport.org.

New York Insider Tours

Since New York is a center for art and theater and New Yorkers are traditionally preoccupied with being "in," it is only natural that some of the most popular tours here are of the behind-the-scenes variety. **Lincoln Center,** for instance, runs escorted tours throughout the whole complex. That means you get a peek at the Vivian Beaumont Theater, the opera, and the State Theater all on one ticket. You may buy tickets at the Tour Desk in the downstairs concourse— the museum runs four tours daily. Call 212-875-5350 for information and reservations. For the one and one-half hour backstage tour of the **Metropolitan Opera** (which runs at 3:45 P.M. on weekdays and 10 A.M. on Saturday) you don't have to be a phantom, but you do have to make reservations. It is highly supervised, but you get to see everything from scenery and costume rooms to a view of the Met stage from the wings and the orchestra seats. Call 212-769-7000 for advance registration.

NBC Television tours are extremely popular, although you are unlikely to see any stars. However, you get to see a few studios and hear a lot of history and inside information on how television actually works. The new jazzed-up tour offers a viewing of HDTV on a 130-degree screen and a chance to "interact" with Jay Leno on a blue screen. There is also a Sweet Shop for chocolates, souvenirs, and whatnot. The tours run every 15 minutes from 9:30 to 4:30 and leave from the main floor of 30 Rockefeller Plaza. Children under 6 are not permitted. It is best to get your tickets as early as possible, since the tours do fill up, or better yet, reserve beforehand. (You're still going to have to stand on line.) Price is way up (adults: $$$$). **TELEPHONE:** 212-664-3700 or go to www.nbcshop.com for information and advance tickets.

Sports lovers and kids will enjoy the All-Access behind-the-scenes tours of **Madison Square Garden,** which are run frequently at the 7th Avenue and 33rd Street site. The arenas, team locker rooms, and suites are covered in this one-hour tour, and you also get a look behind the scenes of the theater section. Tickets are available at the box office, and also online. **TELEPHONE:** 212-465-5800.

For those interested in the backstage machinations of the capitalist world, the **New York Stock Exchange** at 20 Broad Street in the Wall Street area has been allowing visitors for years. You get a quick glimpse of the Exchange floor from a high window. Otherwise, there's plenty of information and hands-on computer stuff to play with in the main education room. It's free, but access is limited, and it's first come, first served. No cameras, no large packages. TELE-PHONE: 212-656-5168. WEBSITE: www.nyse.com.

West Point

West Point has a beautiful view of the Hudson River, gray collegiate Gothic buildings that rise from rocky inclines, parades of cadets on Saturday mornings, and football games in the fall. Nowadays, one must begin the tour at the Visitor Center, which is several blocks outside of the actual gates of the Point. At present, access to the campus is restricted to the official bus tour and to individuals who are attending a specific event such as a graduation, wedding, or football game and reserve ahead. (This may change over time.) Take a photo ID along at any rate.

The Visitor Center, however, has plenty of interesting displays including a mock-up of a cadet's room, a movie about army life, and a busy gift shop. This is the point of departure for bus tours, which leave regularly during the warm weather for a 50-minute tour of the campus. The narrated tour stops at the magnificent Gothic chapel where all those spiffy weddings take place, the old chapel, the Battle Monument, and Trophy Point with its great scenic views.

Before (or after) you take the tour, check out Olmstead Hall right behind the Visitor Center. Here is the fascinating West Point Museum, and it boasts three floors of exhibits, models, mock-ups, and memorabilia. The decisive battles of the world are re-created here. The Dark Ages began because the Roman infantry could not hold out against the Gothic cavalry. The Modern Age began when guns replaced swords, and technology replaced prowess. The point of view here is military history, rather than social or political events. Lots of armor and costumes are around, with everything from a Roman foot soldier with a bearskin headress to a modern astronaut in full outfit.

Another section of the museum is devoted to West Point history and trivia. There was that incident when Benedict Arnold tried to allow the British fleet to sail up the Hudson, but did you know that James Whistler dropped out because he couldn't pass the chemistry course? His watercolors are great, though, and those of Ulysses S. Grant aren't bad, either.

When visiting the Point, you can also take a cruise out on the Hudson on a reconditioned World War I boat. This one leaves from the South Dock at 12:15 on weekdays. Telephone 845-534-7245 for prices, particulars and restrictions.

HOURS: Visitor Center, daily, 9–4:45; museum, 10:30–4:15. ADMISSION: Fee for bus tour. Otherwise, free. LOCATION: Palisades Parkway to Rt. 9W north to Highland Falls, NY. TELEPHONE: 845-938-2638; museum, 845-938-2203. WEBSITE: www.usma.edu. www.westpointtours.com

Independence National Historic Park

This national park in Philadelphia covers several square blocks and includes twenty-four different sites. You can drive right off I-95 into the historic area (via Rt. 676) in a wink. First stop should be the Visitor Center, which has moved to 6th Street and has been considerably enlarged. Here you can watch a thirty-minute film that will give you the necessary background for your tour. Special exhibits are also on view, and sometimes costumed characters are on hand. Of course, there are plenty of maps and brochures to pick up. From the center, proceed to the host of buildings you will want to visit. The new National Constitution Center, now part of Independence Mall, is the first museum devoted exclusively to that most important national document, and you will certainly want to stop by there. Check the Website www.constitutioncenter.org for details.

The two most important sights are the Liberty Bell and Independence Hall. At press time, the bell was being installed into a larger glass pavilion, where there is more space to read the information panels and to take a picture. The bell is huge, of course, and looks just like you would expect it to. A Park Service person may give a talk on the strange history of this particular icon (and how it got its crack) at specified times.

Independence Hall is shown only by a Department of the Interior guide, so there may be a wait, but there is a separate room where you can sit down and hear a preliminary talk. The hall is most impressive, although not very large by today's standards. You can see the inkstand used by the signers of the Declaration of Independence, benches, and so forth. The guide gives a very full explanation of the events surrounding the adoption of the Declaration. Since there is such a crush to see the hall during the heavy tourist season, it is better to make reservations ahead for a specific time by telephone (800-967-2283) or reserve through the Internet at http://reservations.nps.gov. Off-season you can simply get tickets at the visitor center.

Other buildings in the historical park include Carpenters Hall, the Army-Navy Museum, Old City Hall, and several other sites of importance. All have informative displays and are worth visiting. Check in to see Franklin Court (at Market and 4th Streets). This complex includes a steel outline of the original Franklin house (which was torn down) plus an interesting underground museum. As you descend a winding ramp, you pass many displays of Benjamin Franklin's inventions and furniture, until you come to a center with interactive exhibits the kids will like and a film about Franklin. The square outside features a replica of a colonial printing shop and an authentic old-time post office.

> **HOURS:** Some buildings may be closed in winter. Otherwise daily, 9–5. **ADMISSION:** Free. Small charge for advance reservations. **TELEPHONE:** Visitor Center, 215-597-8974 or 800-967-2283. **WEBSITE:** www.nps.gov/inde.

Betsy Ross House: Although her place in history is apocryphal, there is no doubt that the house at 239 Arch Street is a top attraction in Philadelphia. This small red brick building with its narrow staircase is always so crowded that you have little time to glimpse the mannequins who represent Betsy and other colonial ladies busy at their needlework. In fact, the small house is almost overpowered by the adjacent gift shop. Here you can stock up on Liberty Bells, facsimiles of the Declaration of Independence, and, of course, the thirteen-star flag that Betsy is reputed to have sewn. Open daily except Monday. **TELEPHONE:** 215-627-5343.

U.S. Mint: Within the downtown historic district (it's located at Arch and 5th Streets, now officially called 151 National Independence Mall East) is this sturdy building where pennies, nickels, dimes, and quarters are merrily minted along. The upper corridors have loads of exhibits on the history and art of engraved coins, and the downstairs is devoted to sales of coin sets. Unfortunately, the mint is considered a prime target for attack, so there is very heavy security—concrete slabs have been put in front of the building, and you can no longer simply drop in. School classes can still come in by preregistering, but individuals must go through a lot of red tape—a letter from your congressman, for example. **TELEPHONE:** 215-408-0112. However, you can now buy coin sets and get the latest information on visitors' access by going on the Internet. Try www.USmint.gov.

Penn's Landing

When William Penn first landed at this curve of the Delaware River he envisioned a "greene, country towne." What Philadelphia developers envisioned with Penn's Landing was a recreational/educational/entertainment complex that would bring a fading waterfront district back to bloom. It's taken years, but now with the twin development of Penn's Landing and the Camden Waterfront on the other side of the river, and an aerial tramway between the two, the tourists should be tromping in by the thousands, making the town green again.

Penn's Landing is a ten-block-long "district" that includes a museum, a visitor center, an amphiteater for small shows or fireworks watching, two historic naval vessels, a pier for excursion boats, a fancy restaurant, and space for a few more museums and restaurants in the future. Within walking distance is the South Street area of Philadelphia, which is a sort of Greenwich Village with interesting shops and lots of street traffic. The aerial tramway will not only be an attraction in itself, but it will swiftly transport tourists over to Camden's Tweeter Center (q.v.) (for rock concerts), the New Jersey Aquarium (q.v.), and the Battleship *New Jersey* (q.v.).

Of the vessels on the Philly side, you have a choice of different warships. The largest is the *Olympia,* which was Admiral Dewey's flagship during the Battle of Manila Bay (Spanish-American War) and is the oldest steel-sided warship in existence. The other is a World War II submarine named the *Becuna.* Both are available for self-guided tours through the Independence Seaport Museum, a handsome building at the Landing. Inside the museum are exhibits on the *Olympia,* on the Delaware River waterfront history, in addition to lots of boats and interactive exhibits. A single ticket (adults: $$) includes admission to the museum and the ships outside. **TELE-PHONE:** 215-925-5439.

At the moment, Penn's Landing also includes the pier for the *Spirit of Philadelphia,* an excursion boat that does lunch and dinner cruises; the dock for the *Riverlink,* a ferry that crosses to the Camden waterfront; and a new hotel. The Festival Pier, part of Penn's Landing, but several blocks north, boasts an ice-skating rink and an amphitheater for shows and fireworks. More development is expected. In the meantime, between the new amphibious "Ducks" (which take tourists around town and then plunge into the river for a waterside view), the planned water commutes, and the return of the restaurant-ship the *Mosholu,* the Delaware River should be swimming with activity.

Over at the Camden side, the waterfront is dotted with attractions from the Ben Franklin Bridge to the south. First, there is the towering Campbell Fields baseball stadium, then the dome-shaped aquarium with its adjoining colorful children's garden. The treed public waterfront park in front of the aquarium allows visitors some free space to sit and view the Philadelphia skyline. Next, there is the Tweeter Center, a large concert venue, and the majestic U.S.S. *New Jersey,* a battleship that dwarfs the historic vessels at Penn's Landing in size. See separate entries for these attractions.

HOURS: Daily, 9–5 for museum. Vary for other attractions. **LOCATION:** Columbus Blvd. and Walnut St. (parking lot). **TELEPHONE:** Museum, 215-925-5439; Philadelphia Convention Bureau, 215-636-3300.

Theme Parks, Water Parks, and Amusement Parks

Boardwalk amusements are a long-standing tradition at the Jersey Shore. *(Photo by Barbara Hudgins)*

Six Flags Great Adventure

There seems to be an unwritten law for theme parks that each year there is a new and scarier thrill ride, and each year the price goes up. So what do we have at Six Flags, the original multi-acre Great Adventure that shares a theme park with a drive-through safari? (See Animal Kingdom chapter for the safari.) There seem to be two trends: more children's rides, on the one hand, and bigger and faster roller-coasters to attract the teenagers and young adults, on the other.

Great Adventure never had much of a theme from its inception. Now, there are sections of the park that have loosely associated attractions. Because the park is owned by Warner Brothers, one whole area is called Movietown. First came the Batman Ride (an upside down roller-coaster with decor from the second film). Then there was the Chiller, a double-track inverted coaster based on the *Batman and Robin* movie. A Hollywood "commissary" nearby dispenses the usual fast food. Another section is called "Midway," featuring an all-American amusement park theme. Here are the games of chance, some small rides, and the new "Superman, The Ride" (a gravity-defying pretzel-shaped monster of a coaster). At the other end of the park, "Frontier Adventures" has a vague Western theme. The section encompasses the Super Teepee for gifts, the Runaway Mining Train, and a barbeque palace next to the splashing log flume. The Northern Star Arena here hosts large concerts with rock and pop acts.

For those who hate thrill rides (there are, after all, grandparents around) there are variety shows, festivals, and the central Fort Independence arena where the dolphin show reigns. The original carousel, the large Ferris wheel, and a few other tame entertainments are still around. And acrobat and circus acts are usually on hand at the indoor Showcase Theater. The Grandstand at the Lake hosts fireworks (when the park is open until 10 p.m.) and various water-ski shows. For young kids there is the Looney Tunes Seaport, with expanded kiddie rides and some interactive play areas. At Bugs Bunnyland, costumed characters (Bugs Bunny, Daffy Duck, etc.) put on a show at the small theater that youngsters seem to enjoy. More miniature engines, trains, and such are here also.

Patrons who want active rides have a better chance of finding short lines if they choose from the smaller, midway-style ones. And the classic wooden Rolling Thunder and the Great American Scream Machine are quicker to board than the newer Medusa, a "floorless" model with seven loops and sharp curves, and Nitro, a favorite of roller-coaster critics.

As for food, don't expect gourmet fare (although the prices are up there). Veteran visitors bring picnics in their coolers and just tailgate it in the parking lot. (You are not allowed to bring food inside the park except to the designated picnic area near the Safari section.) Bring along towels—there are still flume rides that drench you! Lockers are available. And of course there are plenty of shops, drink vendors, and concession stands along the paths. And, by the way, Six Flags has elongated the season with a Halloween Fright Fest that takes place in October. Rides, ghoul shows, and an atmosphere that is strictly for teenagers are offered.

> **HOURS:** Early Apr.–mid-June, call for hours. Late June–Labor Day, daily, 10–10. Safari, 9–4. Open weekends, Sept., Oct. **ADMISSION:** $$$$$ (safari included). Discounts: Seniors, children 48 inches & under. Under 3 free. Parking extra. Season tickets available. **LOCATION:** Jackson Twp. (Ocean County). N.J. Turnpike, Exit 7A, then Rt. 195 to Exit 16. **TELEPHONE:** 732-928-2000/1821. **WEBSITE:** www.sixflags.com.

Hurricane Harbor

After years of pussyfooting around while water parks opened up all over the place, Six Flags Great Adventure finally took the plunge in the year 2000 to do the same. The largest theme park in the area opened up Hurricane Harbor, a separate water park with its own hours and prices. The entrance is on the left-hand side of the Six Flags parking lot.

This place is large, so you may not be able to handle both parks in a single day, but there is the option of an add-on ticket to the Great Adventure theme park after 4 P.M. Or you can buy a combination ticket to both parks that can be used over a two-day period.

Hurricane Harbor consists of 45 acres of wave pools, high-flying water slides, and roving rivers. Six Flags has spent a lot of money on the "look" of a Caribbean/Polynesian Aztec island. One section has a theme of a shipwrecked inventor on a tropical island. For families there is Discovery Bay, a large wading pool that features a giant bucket that pours 1,000 gallons of water onto the waiting crowd below. As for the thrill seekers—since its debut, the park has added even more multicolored, sky-high water slides each year. These include slides for passenger rafts and bodysurfers plus chutes for the popular enclosed rides. And of course the big wave pool lets everybody get into the act—it has some tranquil moments before the wave machine starts.

Adventure River is a long, meandering tube ride that has a bit more swirls and eddies than the usual ones. It also acts as a transportation river between one part of the park and another, so it is a

Taking the lazy river ride around Six Flags Hurricane Harbor, a water park right next to Great Adventure. *(Photo courtesy Six Flags/ Hurricane Harbor)*

way to get around without getting your feet sore. For younger kids, there are all sorts of climbing nets and water gadgets. Also 1,400 lounge chairs are located within the park for parents who are ready to flop. No outside food or drink is allowed, but remember to bring suntan lotion, hats, towels, and swim sneakers if you have them. Changing rooms and showers are provided; lockers are extra.

HOURS: Mid-June–Labor Day, daily, 10–8. Full season. **ADMISSION:** Adults, $$$$$: Discounts: Seniors, children 48 inches & under. **LOCATION:** Check Six Flags entry for location and telephone.

Mountain Creek

In the old days, Action Park was a thrill-seeking park that appealed to teenagers and young adults. It was transformed into Mountain Creek in the 1990s, with a family orientation. Now it's back to action again with two different areas: a water park and a skate park (as well as a nearby ski area for winter sports).

At Mountain Creek Waterpark, there are more than two dozen rides, slides, and pools. Adventurous rides are emphasized, although there are moderate rides as well. The Wild River Canyons area includes the Colorado River Ride, a 1,600-foot whitewater adventure. Thunder Run and the Gauley are major whitewater tube rides. Adventure Ridge features the Vertex and Vertigo tube speed coasters in the dark. And then there's the H2-Oh-No!, a speed slide that drops you down 99 feet in mere seconds.

Moderate rides include an area called Kids World, featuring the Spraygrounds, an interactive water play fort, the relaxing Lost Island River and, of course, a wading pool. Elsewhere, there are rubber tube rides that twist and turn, straight slides that jackknife you into the water, closed chute rides, and the Tarzan Swings water hole, where you just jump in from a swinging rope. The High Tide wave pool is comparatively tame except when it gets overcrowded, and there's a beach club above it for sunset drinks.

Mountain Creek Skate Park is a separate 20,000 square-foot area for skateboarders, with lots of mini-ramps, launch ramps, fun boxes, and rails, making this a popular place for those who like wheels under their feet. The biggest challenge is the 8-foot vert ramp. There are also two half-pipes and four quarter-pipes. The skating surface is concrete. Snack bar and rentals. **ADMISSION:** $$$. This one stays open longer than the water park: May to October.

> **HOURS:** Varies for water park and skate park. Call. **ADMISSION:** Water World, people 48 inches & taller, $$$$. Discounts: Seniors, children 36–48 inches. Under 36 inches free with an adult ticket. **LOCATION:** Rt. 94, Vernon (Sussex County). Rt. 80 to Rt. 23 north to Rt. 94; go north for 4 miles. **TELEPHONE:** 973-827-2000. **WEBSITES:** Water park, www.mountaincreekwaterpark.com; skate park, www.mountaincreek.com.

Clementon Park

Set on 40 acres about 12 miles southeast of Camden, this venerable amusement park established in 1907 has rides that range from an old-fashioned carousel to a large log flume for families. Newer rides include the Thunderbolt, Sea Dragon, Chaos, Chance Inverter, Samba Tower, and Turtle Whirl. There is an interactive playport for kids, plus traditional kiddie rides. More relaxing rides include the Clementon Belle showboat, the C. P. Huntington Train, and the ten-story Giant Ferris Wheel. Clementon is also home of the Big Cat Encounter, featuring lions and tigers.

Splash World, a 13-acre water park alongside the amusement park, has a separate entry, so you can enter it alone or buy combination tickets. Splashworld includes a Pirate Ship, set in a 10,000-square-foot kiddie pool for the little ones. Caribbean Cove is a 5,000-square-foot activity area for kids, including new pint-sized slides. For the more adventurous, there are the 700-foot enclosed chutes of the Black Viper or the Sky River Rapids, with their three sets of water slides and three splash pools. Besides the other curling and straight slides, one can always find the level 1,200-foot Endless River, a tube ride that eddies through scenic waterfalls and rock formations. Changing rooms, showers, and lockers available.

HOURS: Mid-May–Memorial Day, weekends, 12–9; June, Thu.–Sun., 12–10 (Splashworld, 12–8); July–Labor Day, daily except Mon., 12–10 (Splashworld, 12–8). Times vary in May, June, and late Aug. Closed occasionally for private parties. Check seasonal schedule on the Website. **ADMISSION:** Combination pass, $$$$. Discounts: Seniors. Children under 36 inches tall free. Individual parks, $$$$; after 5, $$$. Free parking. **LOCATION:** 144 Berlin Rd. (Rt. 534) off Rts. 30 or 42, Clementon (Camden County). **TELEPHONE:** 856-783-0263. **WEBSITE:** www.clementonpark.com.

Land of Make Believe

For years this was a simple, down-home amusement park, set in rural Warren County, next to Jenny Jump State Park. It catered to children under 12 at a time when most parks were geared toward teenagers. There were a few mechanical rides and a miniature train ride, as well as such simple attractions as a talking scarecrow, a haunted house with a few scary exhibits, and an old-fashioned hayride.

The park is now more than a half-century old and the space encompasses 30 acres. Every year, Chris Maier, who took over from his father, adds bigger and new attractions. He has also expanded the range of activities. There are two sections: the water park side and the amusement ride side, but the place is small enough that you can easily do both sides within one day. And many of the dry rides are definitely for the younger kids.

The Pirate's Cove water park includes a lazy river ride and several mid-sized water slides. There is a giant wading pool for youngsters, with a life-sized pirate ship in the middle. This one squirts water and has a simple slide. Parents can sit on lounge chairs around the pool and watch. The river tube ride can be used by children and parents alike and is fairly mild. A covered water slide called the Black Hole is geared to older kids (you must be at least 8 years old to use it), while other new water slides seem geared to the faster crowd. Lockers and changing rooms are available, but bathrooms can get crowded.

On the amusement park side there is a carousel, Frog-Hopper, Tilt-A-Whirl, miniature train ride, and a number of small kiddie rides. There is a trend to newer, faster coasters, although not the gigantic types you find in the large parks. Still, in all, many young children prefer putting on costumes and becoming part of the show at the Middle Earth Theater, or going to simple attractions like the petting zoo and the maze. The park still offers free parking and a picnic area (we hope that lasts) plus the usual hamburger, ice cream, and concession stands.

HOURS: Mid-June–Labor Day, 10–5; Sun., 10–6. Call for May, Sept. hours. **ADMISSION:** Children, $$$$; adults, $$$. **LOCATION:** Rt. 80, Exit 12. Two miles south to Hope (Warren County). Follow signs. **TELEPHONE:** 908-459-5100. **WEBSITE:** www.lomb.com.

Wild West City

This northern New Jersey version of a Western "Dodge City" comes complete with marshal, cowboys, the Sundance Kid, shootouts, and a posse of kids. Run by the Stabile family for many years, it is still going strong. On a dusty street flanked by stores and a blacksmith shop, you can lean on the hitching post and watch cowboys twirl ropes and go through a series of lasso tricks. But the big deal of the day is when the bad guys rob the bank or the stagecoach on its way down Main Street. The sheriff "deputizes" all the kids to help round up the villains. Once the bad guys are caught, will they be strung up from the nearest tree? Not if these actors are expected to show up for the next go-round of cowboy activities!

For the last few years, the management has added more educational shows, such as a frontier cooking demonstration, Native American dances, mountain men get-togethers, and other non-violent, politically correct events. However, the main theme here is the Wild West as it was imagined in dime novels and by Hollywood.

The Golden Nugget saloon offers food, but it also hs some simple shows inside at scheduled times. There are two other eateries, and the stores along the street sell real Western goods and plenty of tin guns. You can take an authentic stagecoach ride down the main street or the miniature train ride that circles the town (extra fee for these). And don't be surprised if there's a hold-up on the way. You can also "pan" for gold or visit the petting zoo. Picnicking allowed in a shady grove off the main street, but pizza and other snacks are also available at the shops. Miniature golf and pony rides are extra.

HOURS: Mid-June–Labor Day, daily, 11–6. Open weekends, spring and fall. **ADMISSION:** Adults, $$; kids, $$. **LOCATION:** I-80 to Rt. 206 north (exit 25), Netcong (Sussex County). **TELEPHONE:** 973-347-8900. **WEBSITE:** www.wildwestcity.com.

Tomahawk Lake

This old-fashioned family picnic lake, with tables, ice-cream stand, hamburgers and catering facilities for groups is combined with a new-fashioned kiddie water park, making for an interesting combination. Set in the cool Sussex County hills, the setting is a genuine

18-acre freshwater lake with sandy beach. The low admission fee includes parking, lake use, and a tot-sized water world. Several larger water slides, the bumper boats, and miniature golf are available for an extra fee. There is also an area for those who simply want to swim. Bring your own picnic lunch or buy sandwiches, snacks, ice cream, or beer at the concession stands. Popular for group picnics and for families buying a seasonal ticket, but drop-ins are welcome too. Also open for the Halloween Experience in October.

> **HOURS:** Memorial Day–mid-June, weekends only; mid-June–Labor Day, daily. **ADMISSION:** Adults, $$. **LOCATION:** 153 Tomahawk Trail (off Rt. 15) Sparta (Sussex County). **TELEPHONE:** 973-478-7490. **WEBSITE:** www.tomahawklake.com.

Other Amusement Parks

Fairy Tale Forest: Opened originally in 1957, Fairy Tale Forest still has the look of an old-fashioned kiddie park. It is set in a wooded area of North Jersey, reminiscent of the Black Forest. Molded storybook characters, such as Goldilocks and the Three Bears, inhabit twenty little decorated cottages that you can peek into. Kids can see Hansel and Gretel, Pinocchio, the Three Bears, Snow White and the Seven Dwarfs, and other fairy-tale characters. Magic shows and other acts are held on summer weekends. Singalongs and storytelling are held throughout the day. Kiddie carousel and fire engine rides are available (extra fee). Hot Diggity's Grill offers food. The special Christmas Wonderland (Fri. after Thanksgiving to Dec. 23, 5–9) is a popular outing with tiny lights decorating the houses and lots of action in the gift shop. **ADMISSION:** $$. Under 2 free. **HOURS:** Memorial Day–June, weekends, 11–5; July–Labor Day, Tue.–Sun., 11–5. Closed July 4. Call for fall hours. **LOCATION:** 140 Oak Ridge Rd., Oak Ridge (Passaic County), three-fourths of a mile off Rt. 23. **TELEPHONE:** 973-697-5656. **WEBSITE:** www.fairytaleforest.com.

Blackbeard's Cave: This recreation park south of Toms River includes a wide variety of activities, from a miniature golf course and bumper boats that travel through caves to batting cages and a driving range. For small kids, there's the Adventure Station, a park with numerous kiddie rides and activities. Older kids have an archery range, Water Wars (water balloons), and a quarter-mile Formula 1 Go-Kart track. An unusual form of jousting and Splatter Zone (a paintball arena) are also on hand, as well as an arcade and restaurant. **LOCATION:** Rt. 9, Bayville (Ocean County). **HOURS:** May–Oct., daily, 10 A.M.–midnight; hours vary rest of year. **TELEPHONE:** 732-286-4414. **WEBSITE:** www.blackbeardscave.com.

Bowcraft Amusement Park: Set down on asphalt amid the hurly-burly of Route 22 in urban Union County, this small park has been modernizing over the years. It includes a swing carousel, a miniature train ride, and several other kiddie rides such as a mini-coaster and a frog-hopper. A video arcade and game room keep older kids busy, and the 18-hole miniature golf engages the whole family. Fast food available. Free parking and admission—you pay per ride. Convenient for area people who don't have to battle beach traffic to get here. Open during warm weather. Call for hours. **LOCATION:** Rt. 22, Scotch Plains (Union County). **TELEPHONE:** 908-233-0675. **WEBSITE:** www.bowcraft.com.

Storybookland: This well-known children's park has small structures in the shape of the Gingerbread House, the Old Woman's Shoe, Noah's Ark, etc. The petting zoo, miniature train ride, antique car ride, and other attractions are included in the admission price. It was built for the summer crowd, but now special events also include a Hallowe'en event, and a large, popular Christmas light display from late November to December. Picnic area, snack bar. Ten miles west of Atlantic City. **HOURS:** Mid-May–early Sept., 11–5:30; shorter hours, spring and fall. Special Christmas hours. **ADMISSION:** Children & adults, $$$. Under 1 free. **LOCATION:** Rts. 40 & 322, Black Horse Pike, Egg Harbor Twp. (Atlantic County). **TELEPHONE:** 609-641-7847. **WEBSITE:** www.storybookland.com.

Boardwalk Amusements

There are small arcades, video game rooms, and miniature golf places at any number of Jersey shore resorts. The major amusement centers are concentrated at the boardwalks in a few towns. Although they could use more bathrooms, and sometimes you'll find bubblegum stuck on the boards, these are fun places to visit. The larger amusement piers have become more sophisticated over the years. Rides seem to be larger each year, and now there are huge roller-coasters, swinging pirate ships, and taller rides than ever.

Many boardwalks now offer water parks that are as big as any you'd find at a theme park. What's more, they have plenty of lifeguards around. You'll find a lazy river ride for kids (and timid adults), slides that are partially enclosed (to give you a scarier feeling), slides with mats, and slides where the only cushion on the water is your backside. The only difference from large theme parks is that the rides have been compressed into a smaller space.

At boardwalk amusements you pay per ride by buying tickets (or a roll of tickets). With the water park you usually buy a bracelet that allows you a certain number of hours of use. Often there are specials on less-crowded weekdays. Amusement rides aren't the only boardwalk experience, of course. There is always cotton candy, pizza slices, soft ice cream that melts before you can finish it, games of chance that you can never win, and lots of T-shirts for sale.

Starting from the north, here is a list of major amusement parks.

Keansburg: This is an older area that has been somewhat resurrected with new rides. The boardwalk runs about four or five blocks and includes plenty of kiddie rides, plus a growing number of adult rides, such as the 100-foot-high Double Shot and the Wildcat coaster. There are the also concessions and arcade. Keansburg doesn't have a real beach, but it does have a fishing pier.

Across from the amusement area is a block-long water park called Runaway Rapids that definitely gives class to the area with its large water chutes and slides. A high-speed slide and double-wide slides for tubes make the 12-year-olds happy. A new corkscrew slide puts a new twist on the downhill motion. The park also advertises a huge hot tub. A lazy river ride and a kiddie pool with giant bucket and lounge chairs for parents offer an alternative to the slides. You buy bracelets for two- or three-hour sessions. Grandmas can buy a "dry" spectator bracelet at half price. **DIRECTIONS:** Garden State Parkway to Exit 117, then Rt. 36. Open seasonally, beginning in late March. **TELEPHONE:** 800-805-4FUN. **WEBSITE:** www.keansburg-amusementpark.com.

Point Pleasant: Jenkinson's Amusements at 300 Ocean Ave. dominates the boardwalk here, featuring four indoor arcades and three miniature golf courses for the family crowd. The amusement ride section includes twenty-seven rides, with thirteen strictly for the kiddies. The adult rides vary but none are of the overwhelming variety. The rides are mostly midsize, for both for kids and adults, and they cover several blocks. A large food pavilion that juts out onto the beach has everything from a fast food buffet to sit-down service plus a very active bar.

On the other side of the boardwalk, Jenkinson's Aquarium (q.v.) is open year-round and offers something for rainy days. Special events, such as fireworks and concerts, take place on the beach, usually Wednesday or Thursday nights. **DIRECTIONS:** Garden State Parkway to Exit 98 south to Rt. 34 south to Rt. 35. **TELEPHONE:** 732-892-0600. **WEBSITE:** www.Jenkinsons.com.

Seaside Heights: New Jersey's version of Coney Island has one of the largest boardwalk amusement centers, with lots of amusements and concessions along the boardwalk and the piers. Casino Pier and the skyride along the beach are familiar to many who have visited or even seen Seaside Heights on television when MTV placed its summer Beach House there. The beaches are free on Wednesday and Thursday, and weekly fireworks go off on Thursday nights.

The Casino Pier (800 Boardwalk) includes many large rides, such as the big Ferris Wheel and the Pirate Ship, plus the usual assortment of Trabants, Red Barons, and kiddie rides. Their indoor section features an authentic 1920s American-made carousel. Along the quay are numerous indoor arcades, such as Coin Castle, that include air hockey games and food stands along with the usual Skeeball and video games. Rides are active all day. Across the street, Water Works (732-793-6488) is a full, condensed water park on a square block opposite Casino Pier. Everything from easy tube rides to the "adult" twisting water slides are here.

About a mile down the boardwalk is Funtown Pier (in Seaside Park), which is under new management (it was getting a little drab). New rides here include a Tower of Fear and a looping coaster that join the old Giant Wheel on the pier. Altogether there are forty rides and attractions, and special all-day prices for Wednesdays. **DIRECTIONS:** Garden State Parkway to Exit 82 to Rt. 37 east through Toms River to bridge; keep left for Seaside Heights. **WEBSITE:** www.seaside-heightstourism.com.

Beach Haven: A small cluster of amusements caters to families on Long Beach Island. On the square block between 8th Street and Bay Avenue you'll find Thundering Surf, which is a combination of curlicued water slides, the Crazy Lazy River, and a small kids, area. Next to it is Settler's Mill, a fancy miniature golf complex complete with waterfall (609-492-0869; www.thunderingsurfwaterpark.com). A block away, at 7th Street there is the Victorian-themed Fantasy Island, which includes a small carousel, kiddie rides, Ferris wheel, arcades, and an old-fashioned ice-cream parlor (609-492-4000; www.fantasyislandpark.com).

Atlantic City: The Steel Pier, directly across from Trump's Taj Mahal (Virginia & Boardwalk), is open during the warm-weather season (609-345-4893; www.steelpier.com). Coasters, flume ride, carousel, and many kiddie rides combine with cotton candy, hot dogs, and sporadic thrill shows (such as high-wire walking) from time to time.

The venerable Central Pier (1400 Boardwalk), which looks a little worn, hosts a large video arcade and go-karts at the moment. And across from the centrally located, newly renovated Boardwalk Hall, you'll find a lushly landscaped miniature golf course that overlooks the ocean (609-347-1661). There's a memorial pavilion and gazebo for concerts here also. Most casino hotels keep at least one video arcade room available for their guests' children and outsiders.

Ocean City: A giant Ferris wheel dominates the skyline at Gillian's Wonderland Pier (Boardwalk & 6th; 609-399-7082). This amusement park has other adult rides, such as a log flume and a small coaster, as well as an indoor area with monorail and kiddie rides for inclement weather. Playland's Castaway Cove (Boardwalk & 10th) offers arcade games and more than thirty rides. And Gillian's Island Waterpark (Boardwalk at Plymouth Place) has a water park with a wide range of water slides and other standard waterplay elements packed into a seemingly small space.

The 2-mile boardwalk here also includes a movie theater, karaoke parlor, several restaurants, and the usual beach stores and ice cream stands. The more sedate Music Pier provides popular concerts and shows for the family crowd. There are a record number of miniature golf courses in this town. **WEBSITE:** www.oceancity-nj.com.

Wildwood: The boardwalk stretches almost 2 miles from North Wildwood through Wildwood itself. It includes games of chance, arcades, food stands, and T-shirt and souvenir shops. A tram ride goes up and down the boardwalk for those who get tired. Start with Morey's Pier (Boardwalk & 25th St., N. Wildwood) at the northern end. It's the most visible because of the really high Condor Ride. This pier offers all sorts of thrill rides and amusements plus a complete water park (Raging Waters) at the end of the pier. It includes a kids' area with a dumping water bucket, a lazy river ride, and plenty of turning, twisting slides. Parents can watch from an overview area.

The Morey organization (609-522-3900; www.moreyspiers.com.) owns two other piers. There's the Wild Wheels Pier (Boardwalk & Spencer) with drive-your-own rides, such as dune buggies and go-karts. Mariner's Landing (Boardwalk & Schellenger) includes another Raging Waters park similar to the one at Morey's Pier, with water slides and plenty of paraphernalia for kids. (All this is in sight of a beach that's free.) The awesome coiling Sea Serpent coaster, other thrill rides, and kiddie rides are all packed onto the pier here, too.

Midway down the Wildwood boardwalk, Castle Dracula used to dominate the scene as part of the inward-facing Nickel's Midway Pier. But ever since the castle burned down in 2002, a water park called Splash Zone has taken up the space. For general information, check out the **WEBSITE:** www.the-wildwoods.com.

OUT OF STATE—PENNSYLVANIA
Sesame Place

When Sesame Place first opened, it was the first activity park devoted directly to the younger set. Children from 3 to 13 were supposed to stretch their minds and muscles in a series of innovative "play concepts," such as swimming in thousands of plastic balls and climbing up cargo netting. While these activities still exist, the park is now more commercially oriented, with enough grown-up rides to interest Dad, Mom, and older siblings. A mild roller-coaster called "Vapor Trail" is now on tap.

As for the water rides—they come in large and small sizes. For those who like it slow, there is Big Bird's Rambling River, a level waterway for rubber tubing. The Rubber Ducky ride is for small-fry who want to take a tube ride with a little roll to it. The larger water rides are exactly like the ones at the Jersey shore—metal structures where you chute down on a cushion of water. Some twist and turn, some are partially enclosed, and some are straight down; you end up in a small pool of water all the same. The lines are long, but they move in an orderly fashion, and the park personnel make sure you don't bump into your neighbor. For those who are scared of water rides, there is a simple fountain in the center of the park where everybody can just jump around and get wet. In another section, a tropical island allows kids to squirt water guns and play steel drums.

Lockers are available for a fee (you better get on line immediately if you want to grab one), as well as changing rooms (which can get pretty messy, so wear your bathing suit when you come).

What if you hate water? Well, there are shows: one features bird or animal acts; another is a song-and-dance revue starring Bert, Ernie, Elmo, and others. Every afternoon a musical parade by costumed characters rocks down Sesame Street and affords plenty of picture-taking opportunities. There are a few eateries—but expect lines. Unfortunately, you can no longer bring picnics into the park (but since this is a fairly concentrated space, you can probably race out to the cooler kept in the car at least once). When is the best time to visit Sesame Place? Because season tickets are bought by nearby families, and daycare buses come in droves on weekdays, this park is often overcrowded. Early morning and late afternoon are suggested. Bring hats, towels, and suntan lotion.

HOURS: June–Aug., daily, 9–8; shorter hours off season. Sept.–Oct., weekends, 10–5. **ADMISSION:** $$$$$. Age 2 and under free. Parking fee. **DIRECTIONS:** Rt. 1 south through Trenton to Oxford Valley Mall, Langhorne, PA. Turn right at New Oxford Valley Rd. just before the mall. **TELEPHONE:** 215-757-1100. **WEBSITE:** www.sesameplace.com.

Dorney Park and Wildwater Kingdom

This is basically a double-personality park. On one side is Dorney Park—once a standard, old-fashioned amusement park (it's been around since 1884). When corporate owners Cedar Faire bought it in 1992 they started souping it up with new rides and attractions. Since Cedar Faire is known for its roller-coasters, a 200-foot-high inverted megacoaster called "Steel Force" and a huge Dominator that sends you down twin shafts were introduced. Every year there have been more thrill rides, such as the new, green, double-looping Laser.

For those who like nostalgia, Thunderhawk is an old-fashioned wooden coaster left over from Dorney's old days. A replica steam engine train takes passengers around the park, and the Center Stage features acts and song-and-dance revues. There's also Camp Snoopy, a section for kids which includes costumed characters, easy rides, and some interactive play elements. Another kiddie ride section is the "Tot Spot."

On the other side of Dorney park is Wildwater Kingdom, a highly popular water park that offers water slides in all sorts of variations. You will find looping, speeding, inner tube, and kiddie water slides here. The taller water rides include the Pepsi Aquablast, which features a raft for four or six people that hurtles down a slide. The newest curving slide is so tall and long that dominates half of the water park.

The giant wave pool (which manufactures artificial waves every 10 minutes) has two sections: one for those who ride plastic surfboards and mattresses, and one for those who stand and jump. Don't expect to be able to swim in all this mass of bodies. But the park does provide plastic sun chairs and lounges so that parents can sit and sun while their offspring surf and slide. Locker rooms and showers are available, as are surfboard rentals.

There is a special section for young children in each park. Wildwater Kingdom has Lollipop Lagoon, a large wading pool interspersed with water umbrellas and a "submarine" with play elements. Dorney Park is just beyond Allentown and is no farther away than other major parks for many New Jerseyans. Food is no longer allowed inside the gates (they do cater picnics for groups). Parking is extra. However, their entry price for seniors and children under 48 inches tall isn't bad.

HOURS: Daily, 10–10, full season. Shorter hours Apr. to mid-June & Sept. **ADMISSION:** Combo ticket, adults, $$$$$. Discounts: Seniors, children age 4 to 48 inches tall. Under age 3 free. Season ticket available. **LOCATION:** 3830 Dorney Park Rd., Allentown, PA. Rt. 78

past Allentown to Exit 16B. **TELEPHONE:** 610-395-3724; 800-551-5656. **WEBSITE:** www.dorneypark.com.

Other Out-of-State Amusement Parks

Camelbeach Waterpark: The Camelback Ski area in the Poconos is transformed each summer into a water park, complete with a wave pool and plenty of water slides. The Titan, which parallels the mountain, is eight stories tall and 819 feet long, a world's record. There are also lazy river tube rides, a swimming pool for grownups, bumper boats, miniature golf, and a "skyride" (the ski lift) for a scenic view. For lunch there is a sit-down place in the lodge and hot dog and ice cream stands outside. **ADMISSION:** Adults, $$$$. Discounts: Seniors, children. **LOCATION:** Tannersville, PA (off Rt. 80). **TELEPHONE:** 570-629-1661. **WEBSITE:** www.camelbeach.com.

The Jersey Shore

Some Jersey beaches have amusements, some don't, some are free, some charge admission—but what they all have in common is sand, the Atlantic Ocean, and lots of umbrellas! *(Photo by Patrick Sarver)*

There are 127 miles of beach along the coast of New Jersey, offering swimming, boating and fishing. But for most people, going to the Shore means visiting one particular portion of that coastline. Here's a quick look at the various types of shore resorts that await the new-comer or old-timer.

First of all, there are the beaches. Some are narrow and some are wide, but few are free except off-season. Sandy Hook (run by the U.S. Park Service) charges a parking fee during season but can become crowded nevertheless. Atlantic City and the beaches of the Wild-woods are free. Island Beach State Park charges a per-car admission. Most other beaches require beach badges (which you buy at the beach or town hall) or admission through a private bathhouse. The price of badges varies depending on whether you buy per day, week, or season. If you stay at a hotel that owns its own beachfront, you don't have to bother with all this. Guest houses and motels usually provide beach tags to clients. There are a few select beaches that are accessible to club members only. No matter where you go in the summer, parking can be hard to find, and none too cheap in many towns.

Cottage and beach-house rentals vary according to size, closeness to beach, and the social status of the town. Guest houses remain the cheapest accommodation, especially if you don't mind walking a few blocks to the beach. Bed & Breakfasts, their rich cousins, charge more than motels. Most motels offer efficiency apartments for those who want to cook in. Motel rates compare well to other beach areas along the Atlantic Coast. Major amusement areas are found at Point Pleasant, Ocean City, Seaside Heights, and Wildwood. Otherwise, arcades and miniature golf are in close proximity to beach-goers, even in towns where boardwalks are noncommercial.

THE UPPER SHORE

Sandy Hook to Island Beach State Park

The closest and most accessible to the crowded urban and suburban areas of northern New Jersey, the upper Shore is naturally very popular for daytime and weekend trips as well as two-week vacations. Sandy Hook is part of the Gateway National Park and is run by the National Park Service. The beach is free, but there are parking fees mid-June to Labor Day. Sandy Hook also offers the oldest lighthouse in the United States, a nature center, Visitor Center, tours of Fort Hancock, and surf fishing.

Below Sandy Hook begins a string of beachfront communities, each with a slightly different personality. Some, like Belmar and Manasquan, cater to a young, singles crowd who share cottages and guest houses. Others, like Deal, are quiet and rich and interested primarily in full-time residents and full-summer rentals. (It does have one admission-free beach, though.) Avon, with its lovely hotels and guest houses, looks like a beach painting, and has a pleasant, nontacky boardwalk. Long Branch has a spa-hotel and a public beach called Seven Presidents Park (small admission fee).

Asbury Park is an older resort that's a faded remnant of its former self. It is best known for its rock clubs, including the Stone Pony, where Bruce Springsteen began his career. The boardwalk is practically deserted, although talk of a renaissance is always just over the horizon. Separated from Asbury by a canal, Ocean Grove is quiet, reserved, and Victorian, with a well-known auditorium. The turn-of-the-century Victorian houses here remain from the early religious camp meeting days and are popular now with yuppies.

To the south is the so-called Irish Riviera, towns from Bradley Beach and Avon to Belmar, Sea Girt, and Manasquan, where many of North Jersey's Irish traditionally spent their summers in years past. You can find Spring Lake here, with its turreted late-Victorian homes and little old lady customers, plus a good smattering of singles. The late-night scene is often more important at some of the singles beach resorts than is the beach.

Farther south is Point Pleasant and Point Pleasant Beach, towns with a large fishing fleet and residential areas, including an increasing number of condos. Summer rentals, popular amusements, and several marinas keep this area bustling. Lots of seafood restaurants are here, also. Point Pleasant has a classical concert on summer Wednesday nights and fireworks on certain nights, too. But for the young single crowd, Jenks nightclub on the boardwalk is the place to be.

From Bay Head south to Ortley Beach, things get pretty residential—almost suburbia-by-the-sea. Things get more down to earth by the time you reach Seaside Heights, Seaside Park, and Dover Township. There are hundreds of guest cottages here, some of them minimal-comfort types with just two rooms and a couple of screened windows. Almost one hundred motels also service the many vacationers who come to this popular area, with its large amusement center. Island Beach State Park at the southern end of this long peninsula has pristine beaches that draw many daytime visitors (the park often closes its gates on summer weekends when the lot gets full).

Long Beach Island

For many middle executive families the place to go is Long Beach Island, only an hour and a half away from North Jersey's affluent suburbs and an hour from Cherry Hill. A long, narrow strip of beach that extends from Barnegat Light to Holgate, the island is actually a series of little towns connected to the mainland by a bridge. Here you will find closely quartered beach houses and a few motels leading up to the dunes. The clean air reminds one of Cape Cod. Since most people rent beach homes or apartments for at least two weeks, there is an air of leisure and permanence about Long Beach Island. Also, there are some very fancy digs near Loveladies and Harvey Cedars.

Courses in art photography, yoga, and such are offered at both the Foundation of Arts and Sciences and at St. Francis Center. The Surflight dinner theater assures visitors there's more to summer life than basking on the beach. An amusement area and boutique shopping center attract both teenagers and families with kids to Bay Avenue between 7th and 9th Streets in Beach Haven. Of course, a trip to Long Beach Island would not be complete without a visit to Barnegat Lighthouse State Park. The park allows picnicking, surf fishing, and a view of the panorama from the red and white nineteenth-century lighthouse—it takes only 217 steps to climb it. The only access to Long Beach Island is the one road, Route 72, from the mainland to the center of the island. For the Atlantic City area you must return to Route 9 or the Garden State Parkway.

THE JERSEY CAPE

Ocean City to Cape May

Like Atlantic City, this last strip of coastline is considered Philadelphia's shore as well as New Jersey's. However, people from all over come to these beaches, especially Canadians. Ocean City, the first down the line, bills itself as America's oldest family resort. It has never allowed liquor to be sold in its environs, the beach is wide and clean, and the long boardwalk is filled with stores, arcades, major amusement centers, a water park, and a movie house.

South of there is Sea Isle City, largely residential. Then comes Avalon, with a growing number of upscale condos and a beautiful beach. On the same island is Stone Harbor, which has rental houses and apartments plus a bustling main boulevard filled with boutiques, bistros, and yuppies. Good restaurants are a major attraction here.

The Wildwoods have the largest number of boardwalk amusements at the shore. Wildwood Crest may have the advantage of getting the biggest family crowd, but the beaches all along this area are very wide and are kept quite clean, and are able to handle the huge crowds that come on weekends. The surf is definitely milder down here and shallow enough for a toddler to wade a little. And the beach is free—no badges required. North Wildwood, Wildwood, and Wildwood Crest are solid motels from top to bottom with guest houses and rental houses a block behind. Wildwood has the boardwalk amusements and the swinging nightclub crowd, while the Crest is more family centered.

At the very tip of New Jersey lies Cape May. This is a beautiful Victorian town with colorful Victorian gingerbread houses and green lawns set against a placid shore. The beaches here are generally narrow, even after periodically receiving new sand (the jetty at the Cape May Canal traps the natural flow of sand in Wildwood). Automobile congestion is a real problem in the town—or trying to get into it—because of the narrow, old-fashioned streets and the town's popularity. Cape May has one of the largest collections of Victorian houses in the country, along with quaint boutiques, gaslight lamps, and brick walkways. The arts and crafts shops lining Washington Mall offer an evening's entertainment in themselves.

West of town, Cape May Point offers a wide beach, a refurbished lighthouse (you can climb all those steps for a fee) at Cape May Point State Park, and those little pieces of clear quartz known as Cape May Diamonds at Sunset Beach. And the sunsets themselves can be quite impressive there, too. A little north on the Delaware Bay side, there's the Cape May–Lewes Ferry, which takes you to Delaware for outlet shopping or the beach at Rehoboth.

SIGHTSEEING AND EXCURSION BOATS

River Belle and **River Queen**: The *River Queen,* a simplified version of a Mississippi River sternwheeler, cruises for lunch, afternoon sightseeing, etc., from Bogan's Basin in Brielle (Monmouth County). Its sister ship, the *River Belle,* leaves from Broadway Basin in Point Pleasant (Ocean County). Both are popular with groups, especially senior citizens. The boats cruise the inland waters of the Manasquan and Metedeconk Rivers and Point Pleasant Canal to Barnegat Bay, so the water is calm, and sightseeing is mostly of the docks of shore homeowners plus an occasional bridge. Luncheon, brunch, dinner, and sightseeing cruises are available. Sightseeing cruises offer narration. Dinner cruises feature a DJ. Late June through Labor Day. **TELEPHONE:** 732-528-6620. **WEBSITE:** www.riverboattour.com.

Cape May Whale Watcher: Summer cruises include morning Cape Island dolphin watch cruises, afternoon ocean whale and dolphin watches, and sunset dolphin watches and dinner cruises. Daily, 10, 1, and 6:30 in summer; May, Sept., & Oct., 10 and 1. Late Mar.–early May and Nov., weekends at 1. Under 6 free with adult. Also, special three- and five-hour Delaware Bay lighthouse cruises. Docked at Miss Chris Marina, 2nd Ave. & Wilson Dr. (across Rt. 109 from Lobster House), Cape May (Cape May County). **TELEPHONE:** 800-786-5445. **WEBSITE:** www.capemaywhalewatcher.com.

Delta Lady: This 1850s riverboat offers narrated tours of the Cape May Canal, inland waterways, marinas, and other sights along the way. Enclosed and open-air seating, with snack bar, and dinner cruises in the summer are available. There's a wildlife and nature cruise, sunset buffet dinner cruise, cruise with "Captain Kidd," and a fireworks banjo cruise on Friday nights. Three trips a day in summer. Discount: Under 12. Under 2 free. Docked at Wildwood Marina, Rio Grande & Susquehanna Aves., Wildwood (Cape May County). **TELEPHONE:** 609-522-1919. **WEBSITE:** www.deltalady.com.

River Lady: This old-time riverboat sails on Barnegat Bay and Toms River. Lunch cruises, extended lunch cruises, historical sightseeing cruises, dinner and dance cruises, and early bird dinner cruises. Cruises May–Sept., Tue., Thu., Sat. and second and fourth Wed. and Fri. Advance purchase required. Docked at 1 Robbins Pky., Toms River (Ocean County). Off E. Water St. **TELEPHONE:** 732-349-8664. **WEBSITE:** www.riverlady.com.

Black Whale Cruises: A fleet of passenger vessels offers trips from Long Beach Island to Tuckerton Seaport, daily Atlantic City casino excursions, and cruises on Tuckerton Bay. One-hour evening bay cruises are available daily on the *Crystal Queen,* a riverboat paddle-wheeler. Operates May–Oct. Docked at the Black Whale Dock, Centre St. & Bayfront, Beach Haven (Ocean County). **TELEPHONE:** 609-492-0333. **WEBSITE:** www.blackwhalecruises.com.

Atlantic City Cruises: *Cruisn 1* is a double-deck boat that carries one hundred passengers, including an enclosed bar and galley, as well as plenty of open-air seating. Cruises range from morning skyline tours and marine mammal cruises to a harbor tour, cocktail cruise, and moonlight dance party. Operates May–Oct. Docked at Gardner's Basin, 800 N. New Hampshire Ave., Atlantic City (Atlantic County). Fares vary by cruise type. **TELEPHONE:** 609-347-7600. **WEBSITE:** www.atlanticcitycruises.com.

Cape May–Lewes Ferry: The ferry now offers a new $27 million, four-deck ship that makes the trip across Delaware Bay to Lewes in 70 minutes. Boats run about every 40 minutes in peak season. As ferries, their main business is transportation. However, the new ships resemble cruise liners in that they have elevators, modern decor, fancy restaurants, and can cater to groups. Older ferries also make regular runs (and sometimes have special events), so call first if you want the "fast" ferry. The terminal is at the Delaware Bay end of the Cape May Canal, where Route 9 ends (Cape May County). **TELEPHONE:** 800-64-FERRY. **WEBSITE:** www.capemaylewesferry.com.

LIGHTHOUSES

Sandy Hook: The pure white column and red top of the oldest working lighthouse in America is familiar from hundreds of postcards and calendars. The lighthouse stands on a small circle of grass inside Fort Hancock, not by the ocean, in the Gateway National Recreation Area. Tours: 12–4:30 on weekends, Apr.–mid-Dec. There's a sign-up sheet for tours at the building adjacent to the lighthouse. A maximum of eight people at a time is led to the top. There's a height minimum of 4 feet, so smaller children won't be able to accompany you. The lighthouse is free, but there's a $10 parking fee for the park in summer, so if you're not headed for the beaches, off-season is more affordable and you'll have a better chance of finding parking near the lighthouse. Take Garden State Parkway, Exit 117, to Rt. 36 east to Sandy Hook exit. TELEPHONE: 732-872-5970.

Twin Lights: An unusual brownstone building that looks more like a castle than a lighthouse, Twin Lights is perched on a bluff in Highlands with a sweeping view of Sandy Hook and the ocean. The "twin" lights (one is square and one octagonal) are towers on either side of the main building. The first Fresnel lights were used here in 1841. The present fortress-like structure was built in 1862 and was the scene of many "firsts." The museum inside includes exhibits on early life-saving equipment and Marconi's demonstration of the wireless from this site. Part of the enjoyment is also the climb up the stairs. The spiral staircase involves only sixty-five steps and leads to an excellent view. Next to the museum is a small gift shop; outside are a picnic area and several historical markers. Donation requested. HOURS: Daily, 9–5 in summer. Closed Mon. & Tue. rest of year. LOCATION: Lighthouse Rd., Highlands (Monmouth County). Rt. 36 east; make right turn just before Highlands Bridge, then right onto Highland Ave. Follow signs. TELEPHONE: 732-872-1814. WEBSITE: www.twin-lights.org.

Sea Girt: This lighthouse stands atop a four-story square brick tower in an L-shaped Victorian brick house in a residential area of Sea Girt. The interior has been restored and furnished according to the 1890s, when it was first commissioned. Free. Tours 1–4 the first Sun. of the month, Apr.–Oct. Beacon Blvd. and Ocean Ave., Sea Girt (Monmouth County). Rt. 71 to Beacon Blvd. Left at end to Ocean Blvd. TELEPHONE: 732-974-0514. WEBSITE: www.lonekeep.com/seagirtlighthouse.

Barnegat: Probably the most famous New Jersey lighthouse, "Old Barney" guards the tip of Long Beach Island. It was built by General

George Meade of Civil War fame (who also constructed Absecon and Cape May lights). Its classic red-and-white design stands against a backdrop of ocean and bay in a state park of the same name. You can climb the 217 steps to the top (small fee in summer; under 12 free) or simply walk around the esplanade and view the tip of Island Beach State Park across the inlet. The park also includes some nature trails among the dunes, a maritime forest,

You can climb to the top of Barnegat Lighthouse on Long Beach Island for a view of the sparkling inlet. *(Photo by Patrick Sarver)*

and a picnic pavilion. A private museum with lots of material on the lighthouse and its Fresnel lens is several blocks away. Daily, 9–4:30 in summer; 9–3:30 rest of year. **DIRECTIONS:** Take Garden State Parkway, Exit 63, to Rt. 72 to Long Beach Island, then 9 miles north to Barnegat Light. **TELEPHONE:** 609-494-2016. **WEBSITE:** www. state.nj.us/dep/forestry/parks/barnlig.htm.

Absecon: Just northwest of the casino strip, this recently restored lighthouse stands on a sandy inland block just off the boardwalk, surrounded by a fence. Now painted its original cream and blue, it features a wrought-iron spiral staircase with 228 steps. Absecon, at 171 feet, is the tallest of the Jersey lights, and the view up top encompasses the beach, inlet, and ocean as well as the town. There's also a reconstructed keeper's house with displays of photos and artifacts about the lighthouse as well as a gift shop. **ADMISSION:** $. Museum free. Open Thu.–Mon., 11–4. **LOCATION:** Pacific and Rhode Island Aves., Atlantic City. **TELEPHONE:** 609-441-9272. **WEBSITE:** www. abseconlighthouse.org.

Hereford Inlet: This is a true lighthouse, in that it is a house with a short tower for the light. Surrounded by lovely gardens and a park, this building in North Wildwood sports a furnished interior and Victorian architecture that make it a landmark worth seeing. Originally built in 1874, it has been restored to its Swiss Gothic style. The gardens are landscaped in the English "cottage" style and include two hundred varieties of flowers. There's a fee for the furnished "house" section. **ADMISSION:** $. Discounts: Children. Combo with Cape May Point lighthouse: $$. **HOURS:** Daily, 9–5, mid-May to mid-Oct.; rest of year, Wed.–Sun., 11–4. **LOCATION:** 1st & Central Aves., North Wildwood (Cape May County). **TELEPHONE:** 609-522-4520. **WEBSITE:** www.herefordlighthouse.org.

Cape May Point: Lovingly restored a few years ago, this lighthouse is the center of a state park well known for bird-watching, a beach, and a nature center. There's a small museum at the base and several historic plaques on the way up the gleaming black spiral staircase. The view from the top includes Delaware Bay, Sunset Beach, Cape May, and the amusement rides at Wildwood. The lighthouse is maintained by the Coast Guard, but the Mid-Atlantic Center for the Arts operates guided tours for a small fee. **HOURS:** Daily, Apr.–Nov., 9–8; limited times rest of the year. The "keepers on duty" allow you to meet the last keepers of the light at the top and ask questions about their life and times in the 1920s. There's also a museum shop in the original oil house. Off Sunset Rd., Cape May

Point. **TELEPHONE:** Park, 609-884-2159; tours, 609-884-5404. **WEBSITE:** www.capemaymac.org.

East Point Lighthouse: This last remaining Delaware Bay lighthouse in the state stands atop a two-story red brick structure built in 1849 at the mouth of the Maurice River. The interior is being restored as a museum of local maritime heritage. Open third Sun. of month, Apr.–Oct., 1–4. Also open for Bay Day, first Sat. in June; Lighthouse Challenge Weekend in mid-Oct.; and annual open house the first Sat. in Aug. Groups by appointment. East Point Rd., Heislerville (Cumberland County). Off Rt. 47. **TELEPHONE:** 856-327-3714.

The Animal Kingdom

Animals have the right of way at Six Flags Wild Safari. *(Photos courtesy Six Flags/Wild Safari)*

ZOOS

Safari at Six Flags

The largest safari outside of Africa takes about an hour to drive through and covers six miles and six "continents." Some animals, such as camels, elk in heat, jealous giraffes, and short-tempered rhinos can get almost too close for comfort. The brochure warns that you should keep car windows closed at all times, so take an air-conditioned vehicle if you're visiting on a 90-degree day. The road through the safari is three lanes wide, and you can travel at your own speed. Each area is separated from the other by wire fences, so you must wait for guards to open the gates between one habitat and another. Surprisingly, the warning signs to keep windows closed are apparent only in the dangerous cat sections. I noticed a number of cars with open windows and people who nuzzled deer and fed popcorn to camels. Camels, in fact, seem like the beggars here; they sidle up to cars looking for handouts. (Of course, there is a sign warning not to feed the animals.) Ostriches, on the other hand, are very surly creatures that would just as soon peck at your finger as your window. In the African Plains section you can watch herds of elephants eat and socialize. And nothing can make you feel smaller than to sit knee-high to a giraffe as he nudges up against your car. The animals have right-of-way here, so if you get in real trouble, honk for a safari guard. The Australian section is unique: kangaroos, wallabies, wallaroos, and the flightless emu strut, waddle, and bound across the hilly terrain.

As you drive slowly from one section to the next, you will see a Bengal tiger in its own Indian pavilion and, later on, brown bears that are usually up a tree or taking a dip in the stream. For those with metal-topped cars, the ride through monkey territory is always of interest. These curious simians will scamper all over your car, check on the occupants, pull on hood ornaments, knock your grillwork, and then pass on to the next car. If you want to avoid these monkeyshines, you can use the by-pass road to the exit. An air-conditioned bus ride through the whole park is an alternative to driving your own car, but there is an extra charge for that.

HOURS: Late June–mid-Sept., daily, 9–4; Apr., May, open weekends. **ADMISSION:** Safari, $$$$. Combo: Free with Six Flags/Great Adventure admission. **LOCATION:** Jackson Twp. (Ocean County). N.J. Turnpike, Exit 7A, then Rt. 195 east to Exit 16. **TELEPHONE:** 732-928-1821. **WEBSITE:** www.sixflags.com.

Cape May County Zoo

Cape May County has poured a lot of money into this park, and the landscape artists have been out in force to make it attractive. Various animal enclosures are arranged along meandering paths with pleasant foliage all about. Some of the enclosures simulate the natural terrain of the animals. Others, particularly those for the big cats, are the traditional cement floor cages. But the zoo is within a park filled with the tall scrub pine and sandy soil of the region, so the general effect is of seeing animals within their natural environment.

Among the many species here you will find zebras, llamas, tigers, jaguars, alligators, bears, spider monkeys, a lion, and even a white-maned tamarin. Quite a variety of birds are on hand also, including cockatoos, toucans, a mynah bird, peacocks, eagles, and barnyard fowl. The reptile house, which had burned down, is now completely restored.

This is one of the best-looking zoos in New Jersey, with colorful plantings and bridges over ponds. It offers a complete African savannah where giraffes and oryx roam and visitors can watch from a shaded gazebo. Outside the zoo there is a lunch concession and farther on, a children's playground and a picnic area. All in all, a very pleasant outing. Still free, but during tourist season, there's a man at the park entrance taking "donations." A few dollars should do it, and it's well worth it. Note: the parking lot gets really crowded on summer weekends!

HOURS: Daily, 10–4:45, weather permitting. **LOCATION:** Rt. 9 & Crest Haven Rd., Cape May Court House. **TELEPHONE:** 609-465-5271 or 465-9210. **WEBSITE:** www.capemaycountyzoo.com.

Space Farms Zoo

This is a private zoo (in itself an endangered species) in a rural area that closely approximates the natural surroundings of many of the animals housed here. The trip takes you well into the hills of northern Sussex County, past farms and horses grazing peacefully among the green hills. The family name here is Space, and, yes, it was a farm before it became a zoo. The granddaughter of the original owner has a degree in animal biology and now administers the place.

The entrance building to the property includes a Museum of Americana (everything from Indian arrowheads to old clocks) and a stuffed rendition of Goliath, the giant grizzly who was once the main attraction here. You can also find a full snack shop with booths and the inevitable gift shop. Buy your entrance tickets here (and perhaps some food munchies for the animals).

Space Farms is set up for family outings, with many picnic tables, swing sets, and other attractions available for youngsters. A hundred hilly acres are devoted to rather simple cages of bears, lions, tigers, hyenas, monkeys, and such. A large pond at the center of the acreage allows ducks and geese to paddle about while pens of yak, llamas, buffalo, and goats dot the surrounding hills—500 animals altogether. There is a separate den for snakes and a special enclosure for otters.

On the hills to the left of the zoo are the museums: several buildings filled with antique cars, sleighs, old buggies, tractors, dolls, farm machinery, toys, and everything else but the kitchen sink. Between the animals, the museums, the swings, and the slides you can make a day of it. Picnic lunches allowed.

HOURS: Daily, 9–5, May–Oct. **ADMISSION:** $$$. Discounts: Children. Under 3 free. **LOCATION:** 218 Rt. 519, Beemerville (Sussex County). 7 miles north of Rt. 206 or 5 miles south of Rt. 23. **TELEPHONE:** 973-875-5800. **WEBSITE:** www.spacefarms.com.

Turtle Back Zoo

There are new walls and walkways at this zoo, but the animal collection still falls short of what it used to be. However, the zoo does have a new sea otter building and a prairie dog area. The Wolf Woods is a naturalistic exhibit where you can watch a family of wolves from behind a see-through shield. Penguins have taken over the old seal pond, and a peacock struts freely around. The Essex Farm petting zoo, which is always popular with kids, returns April to November with goats, pigs, and lambs. There are also pony rides at the farm, and a miniature train travels through the surrounding South Mountain Reservation. You'll also see a few large cats, such as cougars and bobcats, in cages. And, of course, there are always birds, turtles, and deer. Food and gift concessions (except in winter) and a picnic area are available.

HOURS: Mon.–Sat., 10–4:30; Sun., 10:30–5; winter, Thu.–Sun., 11–3. **ADMISSION:** $$. Discounts: Seniors, children. Under 2 free. **LOCATION:** 560 Northfield Ave., West Orange (Essex County). Behind South Mountain Arena. **TELEPHONE:** 973-731-5800. **WEBSITE:** www.angelfire.com/nj4/turtlebackzoo/home.html.

Bergen County Zoological Park

This popular small zoo in Van Saun Park exhibits animals from North and South America, so you won't see any tigers, giraffes, or elephants here. There is a North American Great Plains exhibit, plus Central and South American animals and a North American Wetlands Aviary. Some large cats, including a mountain lion, are on display. The 200 animals here include elk and bison and exotic species like the golden lion tamarin.

A favorite with young children is the miniature train ride, pony ride, and 1890s farmyard with its sheep, goats, and chickens. A gift shop and snack bar are also on hand. The zoo is part of a 140-acre park that features picnic tables, a fishing pond, and biking and hiking trails.

> **HOURS:** Daily, 10–4:30. **ADMISSION:** $. Fri.–Sun. and holidays, May–Oct. Discounts: Seniors, children. Under 12 free. Free, Mon.–Thu. **LOCATION:** Forest Ave., Paramus (Bergen County). Off Rt. 4. **TELEPHONE:** 201-262-3771. **WEBSITE:** www.co.bergen.nj.us/parks/Parks/Zoo.htm.

Lakota Wolf Preserve

This preserve at Camp Taylor near the Delaware Water Gap is home to more than thirty tundra wolves, timber wolves, and arctic wolves as well as some foxes and bobcats. Co-owner and handler Jim Stein presents wolves in their natural surroundings. The preserve is a scenic walk from the campground (rides available on request). The observation area is in the center of four packs of wolves. You'll talk with people who raised the wolves and will learn about the social structure of wolf packs, their eating habits, interaction with humans, and many other aspects of the animals' lives. You'll be able to see the wolves interact with each other, play, and perhaps howl. Guided photo sessions are also available from $125 to $500.

> **HOURS:** Open daily. Admission only at guided tour times, 10 and 4 during daylight savings time; 10 and 3:30 rest of year. Tours also by appointment. **ADMISSION:** $$$. Discounts: Children. **LOCATION:** 89 Mt. Pleasant Rd., Columbia (Warren County). Rt. 80, Exit 4 to Rt. 94 north, 2.5 miles to Mt. Pleasant. **TELEPHONE:** 908-496-9244. **WEBSITE:** www.lakotawolf.com.

Other Zoos

Cohanzick Zoo: New Jersey's first zoo, founded in 1934, is set in an 1,100-acre park that borders the Cohansey River in Bridgeton. The more than two hundred animals include Asiatic bear, leopard, monkeys, white tiger, llama, alligator, reindeer, eagle, falcon, owls, and many others. You can find some unusual species—many in modern, naturalistic settings—as well as a walk-through aviary. The zoo also includes a "zoovenir" shop and concession area. The surrounding park contains plenty of picnic areas, nature trails, and lots more. Free. **HOURS:** Summer, daily, 9–5; fall–spring, daily, 9–4. **LOCATION:**

City Park, Bridgeton (Cumberland County). Rt. 49 to Atlantic St. Follow to Mayor Aitken Dr. **TELEPHONE:** 856-455-3230, ext. 242. **WEBSITE:** www.co.cumberland.nj.us/seedo/attractions/cohanzick_zoo/index.html.

Popcorn Park: This is a 7-acre licensed zoo that caters strictly to injured, abandoned, and unwanted wildlife. One section houses rescued animals, such as lions, tigers, and llamas. Another includes the kennels of abandoned pets waiting for adoption. The facility is run by the Associated Humane Society. **HOURS:** Daily, 11–5. **ADMISSION:** $. **LOCATION:** Humane Way and Lacey Rd., Forked River (Ocean County). **TELEPHONE:** 609-693-1900.

NEARBY OUT-OF-STATE ZOOS

Bronx Zoo

While the smaller zoos of New Jersey are fine for younger children, once the kids have reached third grade it's time to take them to the largest urban zoo in America. Although there are still some old-fashioned ornate zoo houses here, most of the acreage is devoted to open landscapes that allow the animals to roam free while visitors watch them from across moats or behind plastic shields. Since there are more than 5 miles of terrain to cover and 6,000 animals to see, it's a lot easier to take either the skyride or monorail (or both) when they are in season. There is also a tramride that transports visitors (one-way-only fare) from the entrance plaza to Jungle World, an indoor tropical forest, on the other side.

The Bronx Zoo is divided into geographical sections. There is Wild Asia (open only in warm weather), a 40-acre habitat where elephants, rhinos, deer, and antelope roam free. Visitors view them from the glassed-in monorail, the *Bengali Express*. In Africa, lions, gazelles, antelopes, zebras, and gnus roam the grassy slopes. You can view them from surrounding walkways and bridges or from the slow-moving safari ride. South America is a smaller section devoted to anteaters and llamas. North America features a walk-in Wolf Wood, polar bears, and lots of bison, bull elk, and grizzly bears on its plains.

But the Congo Gorilla Forest is the star attraction right now. You can get up close and personal (through glass) with a lowland gorilla family, besides viewing mandrills, colobus monkeys, okapi, and lots of instructional material. Other special houses offer interesting treats. At the World of Darkness, there's a top-notch display of bats, owls, and other nocturnal animals. Special lights allow you to watch the raccoons, porcupines, and bush babies cavort on the forest floor. The World of Birds is housed in an ultramodern concrete cylindrical building. Here you will find three floors of birds in a unique setting. Trees vault up the three stories while a variety of birds perch on the first-, second-, and third-story branches. Other special houses include the Penguin, Aquatic Bird, the extensive Reptile House, and the Zoo Center.

The Children's Zoo offers a host of fun things, especially for kids under 10. Giant rope "spider webs" to climb, snail "shells" to ride in, and prairie dog burrows to explore turn this into an educational amusement park. Extra fee, but well worth it—you could spend almost an hour here alone. If you don't bring a sandwich (and there are plenty of tables if you do), there is a cafeteria that is open all year round. But watch out for those prices for soft drinks in souvenir cups! When it comes to concession stands, it's a jungle out there.

HOURS: Weekdays, 10–5; weekends, 10–5:30; winter hours, 10–4:30. **ADMISSION:** Adults, $$$. Discounts: Seniors, children. Wed.: Donation. Parking fee. **LOCATION:** George Washington Bridge to Cross Bronx Expressway east to Bronx River Parkway north. Take exit marked "Bronx Zoo." **TELEPHONE:** 718-367-1010. **WEBSITE:** www.bronxzoo.org.

Central Park Zoo

If you are in Manhattan with children, a good place to stop is the Central Park Zoo on the east side of the park. This is a small zoo (officially, it's the Wildlife Conservation Park), but it is set up much like its bigger brother, the Bronx Zoo. The largest exhibit is indoors, called Jungle World. It's nice and warm in here; in fact, it is a transported tropical rain forest with chattering monkeys and colorful toucans moving along the three stories of foliage. Even tiny animals like leafcutter ants and other jungle insects are displayed.

The sea lion pool is always popular at feeding time, and farther along the plaza you will find the polar bears. They have limited space but seem to enjoy splashing into their vertical pool. Visitors certainly enjoy photographing them. An adjoining indoor "cave" is devoted to penguins. It is quite dark in here, and you can watch these funny creatures dive-bomb through the water when they aren't waddling about. Beyond the regular zoo, there is a small children's zoo that has been retrofitted with interactive play areas for children with some small animals about. A snack bar, tables, and a gift shop are also available. The zoo is open 365 days a year.

HOURS: Daily, 10–5. **ADMISSION:** $$. Discounts: Seniors, children. **LOCATION:** 830 Fifth Ave. (at 64th St.), New York City. **TELEPHONE:** 212-861-6030.

Philadelphia Zoo

This is America's oldest zoo, but like most others, it is quickly changing old-fashioned zoo houses into modern landscaped habitats. Their outstanding new Peco Primate Reserve features lowland gorillas, orangutans, gibbons, and lemurs in a lush habitat of 2.5 acres. There is also Carnivore Kingdom, a big draw with the rare white lion as one of its stars. African Plains re-creates the African veldt, featuring giraffes, zebra, sable antelope, and secretary birds, while Bear Country specializes in bruins. Elephants and rhinos, giraffes and zebras are always on hand.

Besides the lions, tigers, and hooved animals that one would expect at a major zoo, you can also find Australia's gift to the world, kangaroos and wallabies, plus a Rare Animal Conservation Center filled with some unusual varieties of monkeys and other species.

The zoo is known for its Treehouse, a special exhibit that allows kids to climb into a ficus tree, ride on a caterpillar, and explore a river, a marsh, a meadow, and other environmental features. One can smell the rain forest, hear the birds chirping, feel the skin of various animals, and generally have a good time at this popular hands-on exhibit.

The Children's Zoo's exhibits let kids interact with animals and their keepers. There are also several specialized zoo houses and a baby animal nursery where you can watch the newborns frolic. Other features include a monorail ride around the premises (extra fee), the ZooBalloon (extra fee), and some new swan boats. This 1,600-animal zoo covers 42 acres, which makes it large but not impossible to cover in one day. It offers some nice picnic areas, plus two major eateries. It is located inside the huge Fairmount Park, which also houses several Philadelphia museums, gardens, and historic houses.

HOURS: Open daily, Feb.–Nov., 9:30–5; Dec.–Jan., 9:30–4. **ADMISSION:** $$. Discounts: Seniors, children. Under 2 free. Parking: $$. **LOCATION:** 34th & Girard in Fairmount Park, Philadelphia. Girard Ave. exit off Rt. 76. **TELEPHONE:** 215-243-1100. **WEBSITE:** www.phillyzoo.org.

AQUARIUMS

New Jersey State Aquarium

This modern concrete building was considerably jazzed up a few years ago with the addition of a colorful walkway, a children's garden, and a family of penguins. Since you can really cover the aquarium in less than two hours, having the Camden Children's Garden (q.v.) up front affords plenty of interactive activity for kids and grownups too, while waiting for the seal or diver's "show."

When you enter the building, you find yourself facing a set of Megalodon jaws, featuring 275 fossilized teeth from a prehistoric monster-size shark. Then you encounter the huge 760,000-gallon Open Ocean tank that houses over 2,000 fish, including more than a dozen sharks, stingrays, and sea turtles. From a theater you can watch volunteer scuba divers go into the big tank and answer questions or wave to a turtle.

Altogether there are eighty freshwater and saltwater exhibits here, including a special exhibit on South American fish and birds upstairs. The aquarium also features a mangrove lagoon, a Caribbean beach, and the replica of an ironclad mail ship that sank in 1867. At the touch tanks, children can feel the surface of sharks, sting rays, sea stars, and crabs.

Outside, at the Seal Shores section, a daily "training session" allows visitors to watch as harbor and gray seals take on such audience-pleasing chores as catching Frisbees and leaping to touch a suspended ball. Meanwhile, over at the penguin area called Inguiza Island, a colony of twenty African blackfooted penguins waddle around. This exhibit includes a beach, rocks, and a pool with an underwater viewing area so you can watch the birds swim rather than walk. Daily feedings let visitors enjoy the birds up close and learn about them from trainers.

The aquarium also offers a cafeteria on the first floor. It has an outdoor deck with a nice view of Philadelphia across the river and a large gift shop filled with stuffed animal versions of whales and penguins.

HOURS: Apr. 16–Sept. 15, daily, 9:30–5:30; rest of year, weekdays, 9:30–4:30; weekends, 10–5. **ADMISSION:** Adults: $$$. Discounts: Seniors, students, children. Under 3 free. **LOCATION:** 1 Riverside Dr., Camden (Camden County). Parking garage across street (fee). **TELEPHONE:** 800-616-JAWS. **WEBSITE:** www.njaquarium.org.

Pequest Trout Hatchery

This sparkling modern concrete building complex has three purposes. One is to raise the trout that are later thrown into the state's streams and lakes to become some lucky fisherman's catch. The second is to introduce youngsters to proper fishing techniques and educate them on wildlife conservation. The third is to manage this huge acreage and the wildlife that lives within it (including birds whose chirping is amplified in the main building).

The Visitor Center includes a large room with many hands-on exhibits. There are also charts, displays, and a tankful of adult trout so that even those who do not fish can get a look at these big specimens. In another room a continuous video shows how the fish are bred, fed, and finally transported by truck to be dumped in freshwater streams. Then you can go outside to see the ponds where the young fish are. A look into the glass-sided building will allow you to see hundreds of tiny fingerlings swimming about. About 600,000 brown and rainbow trout are raised here.

This is a popular place for school and scout groups, because during the group tour, kids often get to wield a fishing rod. There are also special Saturday classes on fishing techniques. You can buy fishing and hunting permits here plus the special trout stamps that help to fund this state center. Individuals don't get a tour but can visit the exhibits, hike the trails in the surrounding 1,600 acres, or picnic at the nearby tables.

> **HOURS:** Daily, 10–4. **ADMISSION:** Free. **LOCATION:** 605 Pequest Rd., Oxford (Warren County). Off Rt. 46. **TELEPHONE:** 908-637-4125.

Ocean Life Center

Atlantic City once had an aquarium on the boardwalk. Now it has a new one at Gardner's Basin on the inlet. Only this one is much larger and more environmentally correct than the old dinky tanks at Central Pier. Ocean Life Center is a multimillion dollar aquarium/ marine learning center that is meant to anchor the quaint maritime park of Gardner's Basin, which also sports two restaurants and several excursion boats, and is the scene of several festivals.

The center includes some large tanks of fish, both tropical and local, including giant moray eels, and a diorama showing local species. A larger aquarium tank has recently been added. The maritime section includes a diving suit, the wheel of a boat, and lots of explanations about barrier reefs and life along the sea. Kids will like the many computer stations here. There is a nice open deck on the upper floor where you can walk out and watch the boats. The jitney now stops at Gardener's Basin, so you can visit from the boardwalk area.

> **HOURS:** Daily, 10–5. **ADMISSION:** $$. **LOCATION:** 800 N. New Hampshire Ave., Atlantic City. **TELEPHONE:** 609-348-2880.
> **WEBSITE:** www.oceanlifecenter.org.

Other Aquariums

Jenkinson's Aquarium: A popular spot at Point Pleasant Beach on the boardwalk near Ocean Ave., about a block north of the amusement rides. It is roomier than you would expect inside, and it includes tanks of small sharks and rays, a penguin area, an alligator pit, and some hard-working seals. The centerpiece is the sunken ship, the

Youngsters try out the Touch Tank at the Ocean Life Center in Gardner's Basin. *(Photo courtesy Atlantic City Convention & Visitors Authority)*

Bounty, with freshwater tropicals flitting in and around it. Coral reef fish and colorful parrots are here as well, and you can walk around the center to get a view from all sides. New tropical forest exhibit. **HOURS:** Summer, daily, 10–10; winter, daily, 10–5. **ADMISSION:** $$. **TELEPHONE:** 732-899-1659.

Marine Mammal Stranding Center: Located in the beach town of Brigantine just north of Atlantic City, this center was created mainly as a rescue center, so don't expect to find dolphins or whales here, because the garage-sized pool isn't large enough to hold them. You may find harbor seals or turtles. The Visitor Center contains a really large fish tank where you can peer through a magnifying glass at some exotic species. There are also animal replicas, exhibits on conservation, and a gift shop filled with T-shirts and educational items. **LOCATION:** 3625 Brigantine Blvd. (on the curve of the circle), Brigantine (Atlantic County). **TELEPHONE:** 609-266-0538.

WHALE AND DOLPHIN WATCHES

Another way to visit fish and other sea creatures is to go out to meet them in their own environment. There are a number of boats at the Jersey Shore that run excursions for whale and dolphin watches or skim through the interior canals to view birds and swamp life. Here are a few. Please note that although sailing times are listed for the reader's convenience, dates and schedules may change at any time due to weather or other circumstances. Always check ahead.

Cape May Whale Watch and Research Center: The M/V *Whale Watcher* is a 75-foot catamaran designed for whale and dolphin watching, complete with food service. An on-board naturalist instructs passengers on spotting techniques. Whale watches last three hours, dolphin watches two. Trips at 9:30, 1, and 6 in summer; May, Sept., Oct., 9:30 and 1. Fare: Whale watch, $$$$; dolphin watch, $$$. Discounts: Children. Under 7 free. **LOCATION:** 1286 Wilson Dr., Cape May. Rt. 109 to Wilson Dr. **TELEPHONE:** 609-898-0055. **WEBSITE:** http://capemaywhalewatch.com.

Silver Bullet: This ocean-going 70-foot speedboat offers dolphin watching trips daily at 9:30, 12, & 2:30 and an added trip at 4:30 Tue.–Thu. Fare: $$$$. Discounts: Children. Under 2 free with adult. Docked at Wildwood Marina, Rio Grande & Susquehanna Aves., Wildwood (Cape May County). **TELEPHONE:** 609-522-1919. **WEBSITE:** www.silverbullettours.com.

Wildlife Unlimited Tours: An enclosed pontoon takes you on two-hour back bay and river wildlife trips. These salt-marsh safaris include birdwatching and talks on marsh life. A limited supply of binoculars are also available. N.J. Audubon sponsors some of the marsh birdwatching trips as well as special bald eagle water tours down the Maurice River in spring, leaving from Millville. Sailings: summer, three trips daily; fall, two trips. Fare: $$$. Discounts: Children. Under 6 free. **LOCATION:** Docked at Miss Chris Marina, 2nd Ave. & Wilson Dr. (across Rt. 109 from Lobster House), Cape May. On Wed. and Thu., from late June to Labor Day, sails from Wetlands Institute (q.v.) in Stone Harbor. **TELEPHONE:** 609-884-3100. **WEBSITE:** www.skimmer.com.

NEARBY OUT-OF-STATE AQUARIUM

The New York Aquarium

It's in Brooklyn, not Manhattan, and you can get there easily from the Verrazano Bridge since it is right smack in the middle of Coney Island. Many people prefer visiting in the spring or fall to avoid getting caught up in the hurly-burly of boardwalk amusements. For northern New Jersey residents, this is the only decent-sized aquarium within easy driving distance.

This concrete aquarium is home to whales, sharks, seals, penguins, and a variety of tropical fish. The whales swim around lazily in the big tank—what you mostly see is their underbellies, but when you do get a glimpse of the heads of these smooth white mammals they always seem to be smiling. This is a characteristic of the Beluga whale, a group that is on the small side and quite handsome.

Outside, there is a touch tank and cove where children can handle starfish, as well as a building just for sharks (mostly smaller tiger sharks). But the most dramatic exhibit is at Sea Cliffs where a 300-foot re-creation of a Pacific coastline cliff is home to walruses, penguins, sea otters, and seals. You can watch them on the crags or in the water.

In warm weather, a training show takes place in an outside arena. A dolphin jumps up and learns to take a fish from the trainer. The days of the cutesy dolphin shows are over, and this one is properly educational for all concerned. However, in the summer the sun can get really hot out here, so take a hat along.

In any season there are always the yellow tangs, the electric eel, and other strange and beautiful denizens of the deep in their various tanks. Although not as large as the big aquariums in Mystic or Baltimore, this place does have a good mix of species and of course those crowd pleasers, the seals, whales, and dolphins. There is a souvenir stand, a cafeteria, and a nice view of the Atlantic Ocean.

HOURS: Weekdays, 10–4:45; weekends, 10–6. **ADMISSION:** Adults: $$$. Discounts: Children, students. Under 2 free. Parking fee. **LOCATION:** West 8th St. & Surf Ave., Brooklyn. Take Verrazano Bridge to Belt Parkway (direction of JFK Airport) until 8th St. exit. Look for signs. **TELEPHONE:** 718-265-FISH. **WEBSITE:** www.nyaquarium.com.

WILDLIFE REFUGES AND NATURE CENTERS

Great Swamp National Wildlife Refuge

The remains of a glacial pocket, the swamp serves as both a refuge for animals and as a 7,500-acre barrier to suburban development. It was saved in 1960 from being turned into an airport by local conservationists and donated to the federal government. The area is a combination of marshes, grassland, swamp, woodland, and hardwood ridges.

Wooden boardwalks at the Wildlife Observation Center on Long Hill Road let visitors traverse the wetlands and observe whatever wildlife is around. Mostly it's small—woodchucks, muskrats, frogs, geese, ducks, herons. There are deer, wild turkeys, and fox, too, though they tend to stay in the interior. There are blinds for picture taking. Swamp officials recommend visits in the early morning or late afternoon. There's also a bird-watching overlook on Pleasant Plains Road not far from the headquarters. About half the swamp is a wilderness area, and 8 miles of hiking trails cross this part of the refuge. Old sneakers or waterproof shoes are recommended. Insect repellent is especially advisable. Free. **HOURS:** Dawn until dusk. **LOCATION:** Headquarters, 152 Pleasant Plains Rd., Basking Ridge (Morris & Somerset Counties). **TELEPHONE:** 973-425-1222. **WEBSITE:** http:// greatswamp.fws.gov.

While headquarters facilities in the Great Swamp are limited, there are three nature centers of interest bordering the refuge.

Somerset County Park Environmental Education Center: Located in Lord Stirling Park on the western edge of the Great Swamp, this modern building features classrooms, exhibits about the swamp, a book and gift shop, and photography and art shows. More than 8 miles of trails and wooden walkways pass ponds and cross woods and wetlands in the park's 950 acres. Bird-watching, guided hikes, cross-country skiing, school programs, and trips are offered each year. **HOURS:** Park, daily, dawn–dusk. Center, daily, 9–5. **LOCATION:** 190 Lord Stirling Rd., Basking Ridge (Somerset County). **TELEPHONE:** 908-766-2489. **WEBSITE:** www.park.co.somerset.nj.us/environmentaleducation2.htm.

Great Swamp Outdoor Education Center: Adjacent to the eastern edge of the Great Swamp, this 40-acre Morris County facility contains natural history exhibits on animals, a library, and classrooms. There is also an exhibit of art with a nature theme that changes monthly. Nature trails, guided walks, and wooden boardwalks lead into the swamp. Special programs such as maple sugaring are offered, plus scout and family programs. **HOURS:** Daily, 9–4:30. **LOCATION:** 247 Southern Blvd., Chatham Twp. (Morris County). **TELEPHONE:** 973-635-6629. **WEBSITE:** www.parks.morris.nj.us/parks/ gswampmain.htm.

The Raptor Trust: This is a wildlife rehabilitation center for wounded birds, primarily birds of prey like owls, hawks, and falcons. Those that cannot be released are kept in aviaries for public display, for breeding purposes, and for educational purposes. Run by a nonprofit organization that also offers educational programs for school, scout, and adult groups. **HOURS:** Daily, 8–5 (call first). **ADMISSION:** Donation. **LOCATION:** 1452 White Bridge Rd., Millington. **TELEPHONE:** 908-647-2353. **WEBSITE:** www.theraptortrust.org.

Edwin B. Forsythe National Wildlife Refuge

There are two divisions of this refuge, Brigantine and Barnegat. Both attract bird-watchers, photographers, and naturalists. There are over 43,000 acres of grassy tidal marsh interspersed with tidal bays and channels with some brushy upland areas that support deer, fox, and other small animals. But the main use is to protect waterfowl that use the Atlantic flyway. The snow goose, Canada goose, brant, and black duck are among the many birds that stop here. The refuge offers a seasonal calendar of wildlife events.

The Brigantine Division is only 11 miles from Atlantic City, and you can see the towers of Atlantic City beyond the marshland vistas. But it's a world of immense quiet and peace. An 8-mile self-guided drive circles waterfowl impoundments. Spring and fall are best, but hundreds of birds are here year-round. There are two short trails through the woodlands and salt marsh as well as places where you can stop your car to take pictures. During the warm months the insect population is heavy here, so bring repellent. The Noyes Museum (q.v.) is located just before the entrance. There is a small entrance fee. The refuge headquarters, across Route 9 in Oceanville, also offers changing wildlife displays.

The Barnegat Division offers less access, but visitors can see wildlife from an observation platform on Bay Shore Drive as well as on the mile-long DeCamp Wildlife Trail, located at Mantoloking and Adamston Roads in Brick Township. The Holgate Unit of the Barnegat Division covers 400 acres of beach, dunes, and salt marsh at the southern tip of Long Beach Island. It is open off-season, Sept.–Mar., to pedestrians and 4WD vehicles for wildlife and nature study. Closed in summer for the piping plover nesting season.

HOURS: Headquarters, daily, 8–4; refuge, daylight except during hazardous conditions. **LOCATION:** Brigantine Division, Great Creek Rd., Oceanville (Atlantic County). Off Rt. 9. **TELEPHONE:** 609-652-1665. **WEBSITE:** http://forsythe.fws.gov.

Wetlands Institute

Set in the middle of 6,000 acres of publicly owned salt marsh, not far from the beach at Stone Harbor, this attractive cedar shake education center includes classrooms, an exhibit hall, and six research laboratories. There is a large separate room that houses a touch museum for children and other exhibits. A saltwater aquarium and a large book and gift shop are also on hand. There is also an observation tower that provides a view of the surrounding wetlands (and an osprey nest). The building is surrounded by native plant gardens. Periodic guided tours of the marsh, plus a number of lectures and ecology classes are available. There's also a salt marsh trail available anytime during visiting hours, with guided talks during the summer. A 120-foot pier at the end extends over a tidal creek and offers views of the world's largest colony of laughing gulls. Once a year, the institute hosts the "Wings 'n Water Festival," a popular wildlife art event on the third weekend in September that includes wooden duck carving, seafood dinners, boat rides, and open houses.

> **HOURS:** May 15–Oct. 15, Mon.–Sat., 9:30–4:30; Sun., 10–4. Closed Sun. and Mon. rest of year. **ADMISSION:** $. Discounts: Children. Under 2 free. **LOCATION:** 1075 Stone Harbor Blvd. (Rt. 657), Stone Harbor (Cape May County). Off Garden State Parkway, Exit 10B. **TELEPHONE:** 609-368-1211. **WEBSITE:** www.wetlandsinstitute.org.

Meadowlands Environmental Center

The Hackensack Meadowlands Development Commission's Environmental Center is a modern circular building that sits in the center of an urban salt marsh. Inside, a wide observation room offers panoramas of the surrounding marshland, with the Turnpike and Manhattan skyline visible in the distance. An outside deck allows closer inspection. It is part of the larger Richard W. DeKorte Park, which includes several trails. The Marsh Discovery Trail leads across a pontoon walkway through the reeds and marshlands, where you can spot ducks, egrets, sandpipers, gulls, and ospreys. There's also a shorter trail through the adjacent Lyndhurst Nature Preserve.

The former Trash Museum is now gone, but there are some interesting displays inside. The main lobby showcases a 30-foot diorama of a salt marsh and its inhabitants. The newest addition is the Meadowlands Experience, which opened in late 2002 as an interactive learning center. With kiosks, updated diorama, and other features, the new exhibits add a professional touch to the center. A gift shop offers stuffed animal toys and environmentally related merchandise. The center runs regular public educational programs, guided nature walks, and pontoon boat tours.

> **HOURS:** Weekdays, 9–5; weekends, 10–3. **ADMISSION:** $. Under 12 free. **LOCATION:** 2 DeKorte Park Plaza, Lyndhurst (Bergen County). From Rt. 3, take Rt. 17 south, exit onto Polito Ave., then left on Valley Brook Ave., 2 miles to end. **TELEPHONE:** 201-460-8300. **WEBSITE:** www.hmdc.state.nj.us/ec/index.html

Other Nature Centers

Flat Rock Brook Nature Center: 150 acres of forest with trails and brook surround a visitor center that offers animal and nature exhibits. Various weekend activities, such as tree identification and other classes for schoolchildren. Run by a self-supporting environmental organization. Park: Open daily, dawn to dusk. Building: Tue.–Fri., 9–5; weekends, 1–5. **LOCATION:** 443 Van Nostrand Ave., Englewood (Bergen County). **TELEPHONE:** 201-567-1265. **WEBSITE:** www. flatrockbrook.org.

James A. McFaul Environmental Center: An 81-acre center run by Bergen County, this well-stocked center includes snakes, turtles, and other small animals, a waterfowl pond, nature trail, and garden. The Wildlife Exhibit Hall shows films and slide shows plus museum programs. Exhibit hall **HOURS:** Daily, 8–4:45; weekends, 1–4:45. **LOCATION:** Crescent Ave., Wyckoff (Bergen County). Rt. 208 to Goffle Rd. north to Goodwin Ave., then one quarter mile to Crescent. **TELEPHONE:** 201-891-5571. **WEBSITE:** www.co.bergen.nj.us/parks/Parks/McFaul.htm.

Trailside Nature and Science Center: A part of Watchung Reservation, this modern building includes an auditorium and a natural history museum with a fluorescent mineral room, children's discovery room, and natural history exhibits, as well as weekend programs, nature walks, and numerous children's programs. Thirteen miles of hiking trails surround the center. Planetarium is temporarily closed. **LOCATION:** Coles Ave. & New Providence Rd., Mountainside (Union County). **TELEPHONE:** 908-789-3670. **WEBSITE:** www.unioncountynj.org/park/trailside.htm.

Buttinger Nature Center: This popular center, located in the Stony Brook Reserve, features a Discovery Room with changing nature exhibits and numerous educational programs. There's also a Demonstration Organic Farm, a butterfly preserve, plus 8 miles of trails through the 800 acres surrounding the center. Building **HOURS:** Wed.–Sat., 10–4. **LOCATION:** 31 Titus Mill Rd., Pennington (Mercer County). Off Rt. 31, 2.5 miles north of Pennington Circle. **TELEPHONE:** 609-737-3735. **WEBSITE:** www.thewatershed.org.

Merrill Creek Reservoir Environmental Preserve: Hiking, wildlife observation, and photography are offered in a 290-acre preserve. The Visitor Center has hands-on wildlife exhibits and two aquariums displaying local fishes. Guided field trips and other activities are offered. Numerous trails. Pick up a map at the Visitor Center. **HOURS:** Open daily; preserve, dawn–dusk; Visitor Center, 8:30–4:30. **LOCATION:** 34 Merrill Creek Rd., Washington Twp. (Warren County). Rt. 57 to Montana Rd., left on Richline Rd., then left on Merrill Creek Rd. **TELEPHONE:** 908-454-1213. **WEBSITE:** www.merrillcreek.org.

Poricy Park Nature Center: This 250-acre township park offers trails, a nature center, fossil bed, and a colonial farmhouse. A modern building houses nature and fossil displays, art programs, and an extensive list of school programs. Poricy Brook Fossil Beds are just a short drive away where you can explore for fossils. Guided tours are available for groups. The Joseph Murray Farm, built before 1780, is the site of special historical programs throughout the year and monthly tours. **HOURS:** Trails, dawn to dusk; nature center, Mon.–Fri., 9–4; Sun., 12:30–3:30; farmhouse, 1–2:30 last Sun. of month (exc. Oct., Feb., & May). **LOCATION:** Oak Hill Rd., Middletown (Monmouth County). Just west of Rt. 35. **TELEPHONE:** 732-842-5966. **WEBSITE:** www.monmouth.com/~poricypark.

Sandy Hook Visitors Center: Summer activities include canoe trips and dune walks. The center has slide show, some terrariums, and an exhibit on the U.S. Life-Saving Service (once headquartered in the building). Year-round weekend activities include holly forest walks and school classes. Brochures for lighthouse, Fort Hancock, and beaches are available here. **LOCATION:** Sandy Hook, Gateway National Recreation Area (Monmouth County). **TELEPHONE:** 732-872-5970. **WEBSITE:** www.nps.gov/gate.

Cooper Environmental Center: The center exhibits live reptiles and fish, plus hands-on seasonally oriented displays about the local environment. It offers guided hikes through 500 acres of fresh and saltwater marshes and upland forest as well as bird-watching lessons, slide shows, and a junior naturalist program. **HOURS:** Daily, 8–4:30. **LOCATION:** Cattus Island County Park, 1170 Cattus Island Blvd., Toms River (Ocean County). **TELEPHONE:** 732-270-6960.

Tenafly Nature Center: The Nature Center Building on this 50-acre site next to Lost Brook Preserve offers interpretive displays as well as a variety of nature and wildlife education programs. Free. **HOURS:** Trails, open daily, dawn–dusk; building, Tue.–Sat., 9–5; Sun., 10–5. **LOCATION:** 313 Hudson Ave., Tenafly (Bergen County). Right off Engle, just north of Clinton Ave. **TELEPHONE:** 201-568-6093. **WEBSITE:** www.tenaflynaturecenter.org.

Wells Mills Nature Center: The nature center is set amid a 900-acre county park that includes a scenic lake and cedar swamp. The Exhibit Room features a variety of rotating displays on Pinelands environment, history, and wildlife. Nature programs are offered. Canoe rentals, spring to fall. **HOURS:** Park, daily, dawn to dusk; center, daily except holidays, 10–4. **LOCATION:** Wells Mills Rd., Waretown

(Ocean County). Garden State Parkway northbound, Exit 69, west on Rt. 532 (Wells Mills Rd.); or southbound, Exit 74 to Lacy Rd., east to Rt. 9 to Rt. 532 west. **TELEPHONE:** 609-971-3085.

Woodford Cedar Run Wildlife Refuge: The Education Center on this 184-acre preserve offers workshops, field trips and hands-on exhibits about wildlife. The refuge also has a wildlife rehabilitation hospital that treats 2,000 animals a year and includes an outdoor live-animal compound. Wonderful Wildlife Weekends (Sat., 10–4, and Sun., 1–4) focus on specific species. Outdoor Adventures include Pinelands canoe trips, off-road biking, guided hikes, tracking by compass, and outdoor skills. **HOURS:** Mon.–Sat., 10–4; Sun., 1–4. **LOCATION:** 6 Sawmill Rd., Medford (Burlington County). Rt. 73 to Marlton, east on Rt. 541, right on Hopewell Rd. to W. Centennial, then to Borton Rd. Make a right, then a left onto Sawmill. **TELEPHONE:** 856-983-3329. **WEBSITE:** www.cedarrun.org.

Warren E. Fox Nature Center: Displays depict area history, ecology, and environmental principles. The greenhouse has a live animal collection. Programs include bird-watching, orienteering, night excursions, reptile and amphibian walks, and other themes. Field studies combine lecture and on-site, hands-on instruction. **HOURS:** Weekdays, 8–4:30; weekends, 8–4. **LOCATION:** Estell Manor County Park, Rt. 50, Mays Landing (Atlantic County). **TELEPHONE:** 609-645-5960. **WEBSITE:** www.aclink.org/parks/mainpages/nc.asp.

New Jersey Audubon Society

The society operates a number of centers, wildlife sanctuaries, and bird observatories throughout the state. (908-204-8998; www.njaudubon.org.) Here you might find art shows, gift shops chock full of books and binoculars, libraries, sample backyards with lots of birdhouses, and trail maps for the surrounding fields or forests. The centers include the following.

Scherman-Hoffman Sanctuary: Headquarters for the society, the site is a combination of two former estates. The 276-acre sanctuary runs programs such as nighttime or morning rambles, slide programs, art shows, school programs, canoe trips, birding weekends, and more. Free nature walks Fri. and Sat., 8–9 A.M. Lots of upland and streamside trails. There is also a nice nature center inside and a well-stocked gift shop. **HOURS:** Tue.–Sat., 9–5; Sun., 12–5. **LOCATION:** 11 Hardscrabble Rd., Bernardsville (Somerset County). Exit 30B from Rt. 287. Cross 202 to Childs Rd., then right on Hardscrabble. **TELEPHONE:** 908-766-5787.

Lorrimer Sanctuary: This center, in a late 1700s house, has an exhibit and lecture room, interpretive and hands-on displays, gift shop, and nature trails on 14 surrounding acres. Activities include nature programs and workshops and numerous programs for school kids. Lots of bird-watching. **HOURS:** Wed.–Fri., 9–5; Sat., 10–5; Sun., 1–5. **LOCATION:** 790 Ewing Ave., Franklin Lakes (Bergen County). One mile off Rt. 208. **TELEPHONE:** 201-891-2185.

Sandy Hook Bird Observatory: This new site, replacing Owl Haven Center in Tennent, has a Visitor Center, observation deck overlooking New York Harbor, and hiking trails. The observatory offers field trips, morning bird and butterfly walks, bird migration watch mid-Mar. to mid-May, workshops, and many school group programs. **LOCATION:** 20 Hartshorne Dr., Fort Hancock, Gateway National Recreation Area (Monmouth County). **TELEPHONE:** 732-872-2500.

Weis Ecology Center: Nestled on a 160-acre preserve adjacent to Norvin Green State Forest, this center offers numerous on-site programs covering wildlife, outdoor skills, and interpretive hikes. Campsites and cabins are available, as is a dormitory for school and scout groups. Special residential programs include meals. **HOURS:** Wed.–Sun., 8:30–4:30. **LOCATION:** 150 Snake Den Rd., Ringwood (Passaic County). Take Rt. 287 to Exit 55 to Rt. 511 north for 4 miles. Left on Westbrook Rd. Left again at fork, then second left onto Snake Den. Take left fork on Snake Den. **TELEPHONE:** 973-835-2160.

Plainsboro Preserve: A 631-acre preserve features an environmental education center with interactive displays, a nature bookstore, an observation deck overlooking McCormack Lake, and more than 5 miles of trails. There are natural history programs, interpretive hikes, and slide programs for groups. **HOURS:** Tue.–Sun., 9–5. **LOCATION:** 80 Scotts Corner Rd., Plainsboro (Middlesex County). Rt. 1 to Scudders Mill Rd., then left on Dey Rd to Scotts Corner. **TELEPHONE:** 609-897-9400.

Rancocas Nature Center: This is a favorite for bird-watchers. It covers about 120 acres on the edge of Rancocas State Park and has nature displays, a book and gift shop, and a classroom inside and nature trails beyond. **HOURS:** Tue.–Sat., 9–5; Sun., 12–5. **LOCATION:** 794 Rancocas Rd., Mt. Holly (Burlington County). **TELEPHONE:** 609-261-2495.

Nature Center of Cape May: The nature center on the harbor has exhibit aquariums, classrooms, a gift shop, and display gardens. A full schedule of natural history programs runs throughout the year. Extensive program for schools and other groups. **HOURS:** Varies by season, opens around 10 A.M. **LOCATION:** 1600 Delaware Ave., Cape May (Cape May County). **TELEPHONE:** 609-898-8848.

Cape May Bird Observatory: The Northwood Center is the prime bird-watching area in the state. It is famous for its Cape May Weekend in early May, when millions of birds can be tracked, but there is birding activity year-round. There's also an information center and book and gift shop. **HOURS:** Daily, 9–4:30. **LOCATION:** 701 East Lake Dr., Cape May Point (Cape May County). **TELEPHONE:** 609-884-2736.

The Center for Research and Education: This is an 8,600-square-foot building surrounded by 26 acres of marsh and upland that offers lecture rooms, a large gift shop, observation deck, wildlife art gallery, a model backyard habitat and displays, and much educational activity. **HOURS:** Daily, 9–4:30. **LOCATION:** 600 Rt. 47, Goshen (Cape May County). **TELEPHONE:** 609-861-0700.

The Great Outdoors

Canoeists wind up a fun day on the Delaware River at the Delaware Water Gap National Recreation Area. *(Photo by Patrick Sarver)*

SKI AREAS

Due to some warm winters over the last few years, many ski areas have closed and others have limited operations. Not all trails or facilities may be available. Unless otherwise noted, snowmaking is available at all areas. The number of trails (and trails available) change all the time. The number of lifts may be upgraded from one season to the next. Typical price for adult day ticket is $45. Please call first.

New Jersey Ski Areas

Mountain Creek: By far the largest ski area in New Jersey, covering 175 skiable acres. Ski and snowboard instruction is available at all levels. Night skiing and half-day tickets are available. Eleven lifts, including a gondola. Three peaks, 45 trails, ski and snowboard rentals. Cafeteria and bar at base lodges. Vertical drop of 1,040 feet. For snowboarding, there's a Zaugg superpipe and five terrain parks, with more than twenty rails, including a 60-foot roller-coaster rail, S-rail, double kink rail, and many EZ-slide rails for learners. A total of sixty "hits" in all. There are also seven snowtubing runs. Construction is also underway on a new resort village. A new lodge and stores will be ready for the 2005–6 season, with the rest of the village being built over a ten-year period. **HOURS:** Weekdays, 9 A.M.–10 P.M.; Sat., 8 A.M.–10 P.M.; Sun., 8 A.M.–5 P.M. **LOCATION:** Rt. 23 to Rt. 94 north, between McAfee and Vernon (Sussex County). **TELEPHONE:** 973-827-2000 for general information, 973-827-3900 for ski reports. **WEBSITE:** www.mountaincreek.com.

Hidden Valley: Once partially private, now a public ski area with day, twilight, and night skiing. Twelve trails, four lifts, a variety of trails, 620-foot vertical. Ski lessons, rentals, and separate racing program. Snowboarding terrain park. Cafeteria, bar, lodge entertainment. **HOURS:** 9 A.M.–10 P.M. **LOCATION:** 44 Breakneck Road, Vernon (Sussex County). Rt. 23 north to Rt. 515, 8 miles, then right on Breakneck. **TELEPHONE:** 973-764-4200. **WEBSITE:** www.hiddenvalleynj.com.

Campgaw Mountain (Bergen County): For beginners and intermediates. 100% snowmaking equipment. Five beginner and intermediate trails, two double chairlifts, one tow, one conveyor lift, vertical drop of 300 feet. Lighted for night skiing; cafeteria in lodge. Lessons daily and seasonal ski and snowboarding rentals. Six runs for snowtubing with two surface lifts, half-pipe, and freestyle terrain park for snowboarding. **HOURS:** Weekdays, 1–9; Sat., Sun., & holidays, 9–9. **LOCATION:** Campgaw Rd., Mahwah (Bergen County). Off Rt. 202. **TELEPHONE:** 201-327-7800. **WEBSITE:** www.skicampgaw.com.

Note: Cross-country skiing is available at most state parks and in many county parks in New Jersey.

Poconos Ski Areas

Shawnee Mountain: Just beyond the Delaware Water Gap, Shawnee offers nine lifts, twenty-three trails, snowmaking, ski school, accessory rental, cafeteria, bar, and nursery, and a 700 foot vertical. Day, night, and twilight skiing. Snowboarding, snowtubing with two tows. Family packages. **LOCATION:** Rt. 80, Exit 309, then north on Rt. 209 for 6 miles. **TELEPHONE:** 570-421-7231; snow report, 800-233-4218. **WEBSITE:** www.shawneemt.com.

Jack Frost/Big Boulder: You buy a combination ticket for these two popular mountains. Jack Frost has nine lifts, one ski carpet, and many trails that run the gamut from "Powderpuff" to "Thunderbolt." Rentals, ski school, cafeteria, nursery. There are fourteen slopes at Big Boulder, thirty at Jack Frost. Twenty-four snowtubing chutes with nine lifts combined. Terrain park and half-pipe at both. **LOCATION:** Lake Harmony and White Haven, PA. Rt. 80, Exit 284. **TELEPHONE:** 800-468-2442. **WEBSITE:** www.jfbb.com.

Camelback: Located 15 miles west of the Delaware Water Gap and part of Big Pocono State Park, Camelback offers a variety of trails and attracts a pleasant crowd. There are thirty-three trails, thirteen lifts. This 2,100-foot mountain is the largest in the area. Three base lodges. Snowboarding, snowtubing. **LOCATION:** Tannersville, PA. Rt. 80, Exit 299. **TELEPHONE:** 570-629-1661; snow report, 800-233-8100. **WEBSITE:** www.skicamelback.com.

New York State Ski Areas

Hunter Mountain: For groups and more advanced skiers, Hunter is very popular. A bit of a drive, but there's a 1,600 foot vertical and a large variety of trails on three peaks for all levels. Ten chairlifts, one tow, fifty-three trails; all services available. Snowboarding terrain park and half pipe. Variety of eateries. Snowshoeing with high-tech shoes on the mountain summit. Snowtubing park with three tows (daily except Tue.). **HOURS:** Daily, 8:30–4. **LOCATION:** Garden State Parkway to N.Y. Thruway, Exit 20, to Rt. 32 to Rt. 32A to Rt. 23A, west 10 miles. **TELEPHONE:** 888-HUNTERMT. **WEBSITE:** www.huntermtn.com.

Ski Windham: Seven miles west of Hunter. Two peaks with a 1,600 foot vertical with thirty-nine trails and seven lifts. Includes a base lodge, restaurant, night club, cafeteria, ski school, nursery. Snowboard terrain park and half pipe. **HOURS:** Sat. & hol., 8 A.M.–10 P.M.;

Thu., Fri., 9 A.M.–10 P.M.; Sun.–Wed., 8–4. Snowtubing park with three lifts open Friday evening, weekends, and holiday Mondays. **LOCATION:** Windham, NY. Take N.Y. Thruway, Exit 21, to Rt. 23 for 25 miles. **TELEPHONE:** 518-734-4300; snow report, 800-729-4766. **WEBSITE:** www.skiwindham.com.

Ski Sterling Forest: Less than 10 miles over the N.Y. border in Tuxedo Park. This ski area focuses on families and is pleasant for beginners and intermediates. Four double chairlifts, seven trails, 400-foot vertical. Base lodge, cafeteria, warming hut, lessons, rentals. Snowboarding terrrain park. **HOURS:** Open daily plus weekend eves.; every day and eve. in Jan. & Feb. **LOCATION:** Rt. 17 north to Exit 17A west; just north of Tuxedo, NY. **TELEPHONE:** 800-843-4414. **WEBSITE:** www.skisterlingforest.com.

HIKING

An overwhelming majority of federal, state, and county parks offer hiking of some kind or other. In fact, according to the state, there are almost 1,200 miles of hiking trails on public land in New Jersey.

The Appalachian Trail traverses 75 miles of the northern tip of the state on its way from Maine to Georgia. It crosses into the state at the Delaware Water Gap and follows the Kittatinny Mountain ridge through Worthington State Forest, the Delaware Water Gap National Recreation Area, Stokes State Forest, and High Point State Park. It then turns east along the New York border to Wawayanda State Park and Abram Hewitt State Forest before heading north and out of the state at Greenwood Lake. All of these parklands offer miles of other prime hiking trails for all levels of hiker.

The Pine Barrens in southern New Jersey offer a completely different experience. The terrain is flat but the flora and fauna of the region are unusual. Trails and old sand roads wind through the pines and swamps. At 50 miles, the Batona Trail is the longest, extending from Carpenter Spring in Brendan Byrne (formerly Lebanon) State Forest to Batsto in Wharton Forest, then east to Bass River State Forest. Another, shorter trail in the Pine Barrens is the Absegami. Since trails in the Pine Barrens can be confusing and people have gotten lost, it is best to start your hike at Batsto, where you can talk with the rangers at the Visitor Center and obtain hiking guides. Check Bass River and Wharton State Forest in the state parks and forests listings.

Among the most popular county parks for hiking are the following. *North:* Watchung Reservation in Union County; South Mountain Reservation and Lenape Trail in Essex County; Mahlon Dickerson

Reservation, Pyramid Mountain Natural Area and Patriot's Path in Morris County. *Central:* Lord Stirling Park and Sourland Mountain Preserve in Somerset County, Musconetcong Gorge in Hunterdon County, Hartshorne Woods in Monmouth County. *South:* Wells Mills County Park and Cattus Island in Ocean County, and Estell Manor Park in Atlantic County.

In addition, there are hundreds of miles of trails in almost all the state parks and forests. There's a list of these parks later in this chapter.

A good place to contact for hiking advice is the Sierra Club's local chapter in Princeton. Their hikes are led by responsible guides who are very knowledgeable about New Jersey and nearby trails. **TELE-PHONE:** 609-924-3141. Numerous hiking and other outings are described on the N.J. chapter's Website at http://njsierra.enviroweb. org/njs_outings.htm.

Another hiking group is the Appalachian Mountain Club, whose local New York/New Jersey chapter can be reached at 212-986-1430, or the Delaware Valley chapter at 215-628-4344. See chapter Websites at www.amc_ny.org, or www.amcdv.org for a list of upcoming hikes.

FISHING

Saltwater Fishing

Many people think of saltwater fishing in New Jersey as offshore fishing, but there are also many opportunities for surf fishing as well as shore and small boat angling on the numerous bays along the Jersey shore. Whether you're on the water or along the shoreline, saltwater fishing requires no license in the state.

Fishing boats are available for walk-ons at almost every coastal harbor in the state, from Raritan Bay to Cape May as well as along the Delaware Bay shore. Party boats go out seven days a week during the summer as well as quite often at other times of the year. Usually half- or full-day excursions are offered. Some boats offer overnight fishing for tuna, including trips to the offshore canyons; they come complete with tackle, bait, food and drink, although you pay for the extras, of course. These boats can often handle over a hundred people and are designed to go well out into the ocean in their quest for bluefish, weakfish, tuna, fluke, and striped bass. Charter boats are usually smaller and can be hired by groups for the day. In the busy season they must be reserved weeks in advance. Check the sports section of most newspapers (Friday editions, especially) for the names of party and charter boats. Or write or call the N.J. Division of Fish, Game and Wildlife, CN 400, Trenton, NJ 08625 (609-292-2965), for the Party and Charter Boat Directory. Or download it from www.state.nj.us/dep/fgw/prtyboat.htm#directory.

Freshwater Fishing

Fishermen have several traditional favorites in New Jersey, many of them in state parks. Anyone over 14 years of age must have a license for freshwater fishing, which you can get at any sporting goods or bait-and-tackle store. For those who like lake fishing, Round Valley Reservoir (Hunterdon County) is deemed by some to have the best fishing, with twenty-two species of fish, including rainbow and lake trout and large- and smallmouth bass. Nearby Spruce Run is another favorite for trout, bass, and muskellunge. Big and Little Swartswood Lakes in Swartswood State Park (Sussex County) are both known for their fishing quality. Greenwood Lake (Passaic County and New York State) is a huge lake, popular with anglers with boats.

Trout fishing seems to attract a lot of interest, especially in spring, when cooler waters throughout the state support an active trout-stocking program. Among the notable trout streams in the northwestern part of the state are the Pequest River, Flat Brook, and the Paulinskill and Black Rivers, not to mention the South Branch of the Raritan in the Ken Lockwood Gorge Wildlife Area.

Trout fishing is popular from spring to fall in the many streams and rivers in the state's many parks and forests. *(Photo by Patrick Sarver)*

The Delaware River from Trenton north to High Point on the state's western border is also a popular fishing area, especially during the spring shad run (Lambertville even has an annual shad festival). But there are also large and smallmouth bass, muskellunge, and many other species. The best fishing in the Delaware is by boat, since the deeper part of this broad river is often inaccessible from shore. But there are many areas of public access along the river.

With so many bays in southern New Jersey, saltwater fishing tends to be more popular here. However, the Pine Barrens still offer some good freshwater fishing, especially for pickerel, bass and catfish. Try the Batsto and Wading Rivers and the many lakes in parks throughout the southern part of the state, such as Parvin and Bass River State Forests.

Boating ramps are available at most state parks, but you must bring your own boat. Canoes and rowboats can also be rented in selected areas.

CAMPING

New Jersey has many state parks that offer beautiful, clean, and well-equipped campgrounds. All you have to do to enjoy them is bring your own camping equipment, a minimal entrance fee, and tote your own garbage out (state policy; they provide the bags). Call the campgrounds for details. (A listing of state parks can be found at the end of this chapter.)

Bass River and Swartswood state parks are excellent for family outings. Campsites are adequately sized. Facilities include flush toilets and showers, and they are kept fairly clean. Swimming, boating, and picnic areas are close to the sites. At Bass River, the shallow lake allows for canoeing and paddle boating. Swartswood Lake is good for sailing as well. Canoes, rowboats, and paddle boats can be rented.

For good-weather weekend camping, reservations are recommended. At most state parks, half of the available sites can be reserved ahead so long as you stay a minimum of two days. The rest are given out on a first-come, first-served basis. Group sites can always be reserved in advance. Your chances are always better in midweek, especially if you just show up looking for a camping spot.

Wawayanda and Worthington parks are definitely primitive. Wawayanda is especially suitable for group camping and day trips to the beach or for fishing. Group campsites are served by outhouses. However, toilets, changing rooms, and food concessions are found at the beach area. No flush toilets are to be found at Worthington on the Delaware. Located a few hundred feet from the Delaware, this large open site will appeal to those who choose to fish, raft, or canoe on the river. For the truly hardy, scenic Round Valley Reservoir offers real wilderness camping. Campers must hike or boat to the sites. The key interest here is sailing, boating, and fishing. Spruce Run, with facilities for boating, fishing, and swimming, takes camping out of the woods and puts it in the sunshine, where, in the heat of summer, it doesn't belong. Sites are on a hill and there is no shade. Again, there is a beach for swimming with the usual facilities.

Swimming, boating, and fishing in state parks are also usually available daily in season for noncampers.

There are also hundreds of sites in many private campgrounds around the state. The Pine Barrens and the southern portion of New Jersey abound with these camps, which usually offer more sophisticated facilities than the state-run sites (higher rates, too). A limited number of county parks offer camping also (check park listings later in chapter). For a brochure from the N.J. Campground Owners Association listing private camping and RV sites in the state, call 800-2-CAMP-NJ. **WEBSITE:** www.newjerseycampgrounds.com.

ADVENTUROUS OUTINGS

For those who like to add the element of adventure to their summer activities, a number of options are available. You don't have to live in California to windsurf, skydive, parachute, or raft down a river. Here are a few of the places where you can jump into action.

Gliding and Diving

Skydiving/Parachuting: If you want to learn how to skydive and parachute, you can learn both in one day. You get jump training on the ground, then you're taken up and out. One outfit specializing in freefall and tandem jumping is Skydive Sussex, affiliated with the U.S. Parachute Association. They are located at the Sussex Airport, scene of a popular summer air show, on Rt. 639, Sussex. Open Apr.–Nov. **TELEPHONE:** 973-702-7000. **WEBSITE:** www.skydivesussex. com.

Two skydiving schools with lessons tailored for new and experienced skydivers are offered at Freefall Adventures/Skydive Cross Keys. Freefall Adventures introduces beginners and novices to the sport, while Skydive Cross Keys is geared for experienced and licensed skydivers. **LOCATION:** Cross Keys Airport, Rt. 555, Williamstown (Gloucester County). Rt. 322, 5 miles east of Glassboro to left on Rt. 555. **TELEPHONE:** 856-629-7553. **WEBSITE:** www.freefall-adventures.com.

Plane Gliding: You soar in a glider (which is towed aloft by an airplane) over the Delaware Water Gap, the Kittatinny Ridge, and other scenic areas. Good picture-taking possibilities. Contact Yards Creek Soaring, 36 Lambert Rd., Blairstown Airport, Blairstown (Warren County). TELEPHONE: 908-362-1239.

Hot Air Ballooning

Hot air ballooning offers fancy flights (often with champagne included) at prices to match. Flights are almost always at sunrise and about two hours before sunset, because that's when wind conditions are calmest. If winds are up or if the weather's bad, then the flights are canceled. A few places fly year-round, but most operate spring to fall. The hotbed for ballooning in the state is Hunterdon and Somerset Counties, largely along the Rt. 78 corridor, with three major balloon ports along Rt. 173 near Clinton. There are some scattered balloon flights elsewhere in the state, as well. Some of the larger companies are the following:

In Flight Balloon Adventures leaves from the Coach 'n Paddock restaurant in Clinton (Hunterdon County). TELEPHONE: 908-479-4674. Website: www.balloonnj.com.

Balloons Aloft flies out of the Sky Manor Airport in Pittstown (Hunterdon County). TELEPHONE: 800-608-6359. WEBSITE: www.njballoon.com.

Avian AdVentures flies from the Clinton area (Hunterdon County). TELEPHONE: 908-208-1869. WEBSITE: www.njhotair.com.

Balloonautics is located in Phillipsburg (Warren County) and flies from the Rt. 78 corridor. TELEPHONE: 877-438-6359. WEBSITE: www.aeronuts.com.

Odyssey Hot Air Balloons, located in Moorestown, flies out of the South Jersey Regional Airport in Lumberton (Burlington County). TELEPHONE: 856-234-5165. WEBSITE: www.njballoons.com.

Have Balloon Will Travel is also out of Phillipsburg (Warren County), around Rt. 78. Or they will travel to other locations. TELEPHONE: 800-608-6359. WEBSITE: www.haveballoonwill-travel.com.

Dancing on Air flies in the Flemington area (Hunterdon County). TELEPHONE: 877-HOTAIR4. WEBSITE: www.hot-air-ride.com.

Blue Sky Adventures is located in East Brunswick (Middlesex County). TELEPHONE: 732-940-6558.

Balloons ascend over the Hunterdon County countryside in a mini-festival of color. *(Photo by Thomas Baldwin/Courtesy www.balloonnj.com)*

Tewksbury Balloon Adventures launches near White House (Somerset County). **TELEPHONE:** 908-439-3320.

If you just like to watch hot air balloons, then head to the New Jersey Festival of Ballooning, held at the Solberg Airport in Readington (Somerset County) in late July. There are usually around 125 balloons, many with special shapes, along with concerts by pop music stars. **TELEPHONE:** 800-HOTAIR9. **WEBSITE:** www.balloonfestival.com/NJ.html.

ADVENTUROUS WATER SPORTS

Windsurfing

Popular areas are at lakes in such state parks as Round Valley and Spruce Run. The bay side of the Jersey shore also offers windsurfing territory for experienced practitioners. Sandy Hook is popular, and you can find windsurfing rentals on Long Beach Island and other Shore resorts.

Canoeing, Kayaking, and Tubing

Kittatinny Canoes in Dingman's Ferry, PA, is one of the biggest canoe renters along the Delaware River, and also offers rafting, kayaking, and tubing trips. A number of trips are available, from north of Port Jervis, NY, to the Bushkill area. From 2.5-mile tubing trips to overnight canoe camping. **TELEPHONE:** 800-FLOAT-KC. **WEBSITE:** www.floatkc.com.

Further south is Bucks County River Country, which offers canoeing, leisure rafting, kayaking, and river tubing upriver to Point Pleasant, PA (Bucks County). A variety of trip lengths are offered, from two hours to overnight. Picnic facilities are available at the base. **TELEPHONE:** 215-297-TUBE. **WEBSITE:** www.rivercountry.net.

The other prime area for canoeing in New Jersey is the Pine Barrens, with canoe and kayak outfitters scattered throughout the southern part of the state. Among the popular waterways are the Wading, Mullica, Oswego, and Batsto Rivers, which run through Wharton State Forest and other state forests of the region. The New Jersey Pinelands Commission maintains a list of outfitters in this area on its **WEBSITE:** www.state.nj.us/pinelands/canoe.htm.

Mohican Outdoor Center: This southernmost Appalachian Mountain Club facility stands near Catfish Pond and the Appalachian Trail in the Delaware Water Gap National Recreation Area. An extensive program of outdoor-skills workshops is offered here from April to November. Courses include rock climbing, backpacking, yoga and hiking, mountain biking, orienteering, wilderness first aid, birdwatching, Native American lore, photography, and astronomy. There are cabins and campsites, along with a dining hall with meals available in summer. **LOCATION:** 50 Camp Rd., Blairstown (Warren County). Rt. 94 west of Blairstown to Mohican Rd. Left on Gaisler Rd., then right on Camp Rd. **TELEPHONE:** 908-362-5670. **WEBSITE:** www.mohicanoutdoorcenter.com.

STATE PARKS AND FORESTS

Following is a listing of the state parks and forests in New Jersey. Park areas with swimming charge a parking fee on summer weekends; some charge every day in summer. Other parks are free. The state offers special yearly park passes, which can be a bargain if you visit a lot of parks in summer. For more information on state parklands, visit www.state.nj.us/dep/forestry/parks.

State Parks

Allaire State Park, Rt. 524, Allaire (Monmouth County): its 2,260 acres includes restored Allaire Village, a narrow-gauge railroad, picnicking, hiking and horse trails, camping, fishing, golf course, nature center, lively calendar of events. TELEPHONE: 732-938-2371.

Allamuchy Mountain State Park, Allamuchy (Warren County): Mostly undeveloped forested hills with some fishing and trails. Also the site of Waterloo Village (q.v.). TELEPHONE: 908-852-3790.

Barnegat Lighthouse State Park, Barnegat Light (Ocean County): This is a 172-foot lighthouse with a 217-step spiral staircase. Picnicking, fishing from restored jetties, no swimming. Nearby museum. TELEPHONE: 609-494-2016.

Cape May Point State Park (Cape May County): Picnicking, tours of restored lighthouse, wetlands boardwalk trails, bird-watching, swimming, nature center, surf fishing. TELEPHONE: 609-884-2159.

Cheesequake State Park, off Garden State Parkway, Exit 20, Matawan (Middlesex County): A 1,274-acre park consisting of wetlands and upland forest. Several miles of hiking trails lead through a variety of terrain, including a boardwalk through a cedar swamp. There's also camping, a swimming beach, fishing, picnicking, and a nature center. TELEPHONE: 732-566-2161.

Corson's Inlet State Park, Rt. 619 south of Ocean City (Cape May County): Beach, small boat launch, fishing. (Call Belleplain State Forest.)

Delware & Raritan Canal State Park (Somerset County): There are two separate sections to this park: Bull's Island Recreation Area on the Delaware near Stockton (Hunterdon County), and a long, narrow strip of land between the old canal and the Millstone River. Canoeing, fishing, bicycling, hiking. TELEPHONE: 732-873-3050.

Double Trouble State Park, Double Trouble Road (Rt. 530), Berkeley Twp. (Ocean County): Includes a small historic village, hiking trails beside cranberry bogs, and canoe trips on Cedar Creek. **TELEPHONE:** 732-341-6662.

Farny State Park, off Rt. 513, Marcella (Morris County): A wilderness-type area, it offers hiking trails through the Farny Natural Area and overlooking the adjacent Splitrock Reservoir. (Call Ringwood State Park.)

Fort Mott State Park, Fort Mott Rd., Salem (Salem County): A 104-acre park surrounding the remains of an 1890s fort (q.v.). Picnicking, playgrounds, and fishing. Next to Finn's Point National Cemetery. Ferry to Pea Patch Island and Fort Delaware, a Civil War prison. **TELEPHONE:** 856-935-3218.

Hacklebarney State Park, 119 Hacklebarney Rd., Long Valley (Morris County): Off Rt. 124 west of Chester. The Black River cascades through a scenic, boulder-lined gorge. Trout fishing in the river and in Trout Brook, streamside and upland hiking, picnic area, and a playground. **TELEPHONE:** 908-879-5677.

High Point State Park, Rt. 23, Sussex (Sussex County): The highest point in the state is marked by the 220-foot High Point Monument. Swimming beach at Lake Marcia. The Appalachian Trail passes through this park, part of more than 50 miles of trails at High Point. Kuser Natural Area includes a cedar swamp. Three lakes and a pond offer fishing and boating. Camping, nature tours, bicycling, and a cross-country ski center. **TELEPHONE:** 973-875-4800.

Hopatcong State Park, Landing (Morris County): Small public beach at the southern end of Lake Hopatcong, New Jersey's largest lake. Picnicking, swimming, boating, fishing. **TELEPHONE:** 973-398-7010.

Island Beach State Park, Central Ave. south of Seaside Park (Ocean County): Popular 9.5-mile-long beach with ocean swimming, bathhouses, surfing area, fishing, picnicking, bicycling, and two natural areas with nature trails. Year-round parking fee. **TELEPHONE:** 732-793-0506.

Kittatinny Valley State Park, Andover (Sussex/Warren County): Hike the 27-mile Paulinskill Valley Trail along the scenic Paulinskill River and 20 miles of the Sussex Branch Trail, both on former railroad rights-of-way. The Sussex Trail is still being developed. 973-786-6445. For monthly hike information, call the Paulinskill Valley Trail Committee at **TELEPHONE:** 908-852-0597.

Liberty State Park, Jersey City (Hudson County), Exit 14B of N.J. Turnpike: This Hudson River–front park is known as the home of the Liberty Science Center (q.v.) and for the ferry to the Statue of Liberty and Ellis Island. There is also a 1.3-mile Liberty Walk along the Hudson, which offers great views of Lower Manhattan, Ellis Island, and the Statue of Liberty. Other points include the restored Central Railroad of New Jersey terminal, a salt marsh natural area and interpretive center, a butterfly and sensory garden at Millennium Park, a marina, boat ramps, playground, picnicking, New York ferry, and special events throughout the year. **TELEPHONE:** 201-915-3400. **WEBSITE:** www.libertystatepark.com.

Long Pond Ironworks State Park, Rt. 511, Hewitt (Passaic County): Historic village, museum, and early American ironworks (q.v.) at Hewitt. Hiking trails lead to a small waterfall and go along Wanaque River beyond the ironworks. Fishing, boating at Monksville Reservoir. (Call Ringwood State Park.)

Monmouth Battlefield State Park, Bus. Rt. 33, Manalapan (Monmouth County): Visitor Center, historic sites, and yearly reenactment commemorate the Battle of Monmouth of the Revolutionary War (q.v.). Picnicking and 25 miles of hiking trails. **TELEPHONE:** 732-462-9616.

Parvin State Park, Rt. 540, Pittsgrove (Salem County), 5 miles west of Vineland: This 1,100-acre wooded park surrounds Thundergust and Parvin Lakes. It offers campsites and cabins, a swimming beach, boating, fishing, picnicking, a canoe rental, 15 miles of hiking trails, and a scenic natural area and cedar swamp. **TELEPHONE:** 856-358-8616.

Princeton Battlefield State Park, 500 Mercer St., Princeton (Mercer County): Small park with historic Clark House and Revolutionary War monument on the grounds. Open fields for walking, hiking, and picnicking. **TELEPHONE:** 609-921-0074.

Rancocas State Park, Mt. Holly (Burlington County): Nature center, hiking, and fishing highlight the activities in the heavily wooded preserve. (Call Brendan Byrne State Forest.) Or call the Audubon Center at the park at 609-261-2495.

Ringwood State Park, Ringwood (Passaic County): Three areas of the park include Ringwood Manor, Skylands, and Shepherd Lake. Ringwood Manor includes the mansion of millionaire Abram Hewitt; Skylands includes a Tudor manor and the state botanical gardens (q.v.); and Shepherd Lake is a recreation area offering a swimming beach, boat rentals, and fishing. Several hiking trails cross the park, and there are nice picnicking grounds in many areas. **TELEPHONE:** 973-962-7031.

Round Valley Recreation Area, Rt. 629, Lebanon Twp. (Hunterdon County): Wilderness camping, boating, fishing, hiking, swimming beach, and picnicking at the second largest lake in the state. TELEPHONE: 908-236-6355.

Spruce Run Recreation Area, Clinton (Hunterdon County): A large, scenic lake that offers fishing, boat rentals, sailing, a swimming beach. and picnicking. TELEPHONE: 908-638-8572.

Stephens State Park, now combined with Allamuchy Mountain State Park, Hackettstown (Warren County): Camping, fishing, picnicking, and a playground in woods lining the Musconetcong River. TELEPHONE: 732-852-3790.

Swartswood State Park, Rt. 619, Swartswood (Sussex County): Excellent fishing, boating, hiking, boat rentals, picnicking, camping, and a swimming beach on two scenic lakes. TELEPHONE: 973-383-5230.

Voorhees State Park, Rt. 513, High Bridge (Hunterdon County): Hiking, picnicking, camping, nature study, and an astronomical observatory in a wooded hillside preserve. TELEPHONE: 908-638-6969.

Washington Crossing State Park, Rt. 29, Titusville (Mercer County): Rolling hills along the Delaware River offer a nature center, outdoor theater, picnicking, playing fields, hiking, camping, and historical museums (q.v.). TELEPHONE: 609-737-0623.

Washington Rock State Park, 16 Rock Rd., Green Brook (Somerset County): Picnicking and views from atop a bluff (q.v.) overlooking the Plainfields and beyond. (Call Liberty State Park.)

Wawayanda State Park, 885 Warwick Tpk., Hewitt (Passaic/Sussex Counties): There are two main areas of the park. One, near Highland Lakes, offers camping, fishing, boat rentals, a swimming beach, hiking, and horseback riding in the forest surrounding Wawayanda Lake. The second, off Bearfort Rd., offers fishing and wilderness-style hiking. TELEPHONE: 973-853-4462.

State Forests

Abram S. Hewitt State Forest, West Milford (Passaic County): Some hiking and cross-country skiing, but still largely undeveloped. (Call Wawayanda State Park.)

Bass River State Forest, New Gretna (Burlington/Ocean Counties): Garden State Parkway, Exit 52, follow signs. This sandy Pinelands park surrounds scenic Lake Absegami. Swimming beach, picnicking, hiking, nature study, fishing, boat rentals, canoeing. Lakeside cabins and campsites. TELEPHONE: 609-296-1114.

Belleplain State Forest, Rt. 550, Woodbine (Cape May/Cumberland Counties): Lake Nummy, surrounded by a pine, oak, and cedar forest, offers beach swimming, picnicking, hiking, nature trail, interpretive center, boat rentals, camping, and fishing. The forest also includes East Creek Pond on Route 347. TELEPHONE: 609-861-2404.

Jenny Jump State Forest. Hope (Warren County): Mountaintop trails lead to rocky overlooks of the Delaware Water Gap and Great Meadows. A separate section about 2 miles south near Mountain Lake includes hilly woodland hiking trails. There's picnicking, camping, hiking, nature study, and an astronomical observatory. TELEPHONE: 908-459-4366.

Brendan Byrne State Forest, Rt. 72, New Lisbon (Burlington County): Pakim Pond offers swimming, picnicking, hiking, and camping amid Pinelands forests and cedar swamps. Whitesbog Village (q.v.) offers a look at historic cranberry bogs and town. TELEPHONE: 609-726-1191.

Norvin Green State Forest, Ringwood (Passaic County): Hiking trails begin from a nearby Audubon nature center and lead to a panoramic view atop Wyanokie High Point that includes Manhattan in the distance. (Call Ringwood State Park.)

Penn State Forest, off Rt. 563, Jenkins (Burlington County): Lake Oswego offers swimming, picnicking, hiking, fishing, camping. A few paved roads beyond the lake have wide potholes but most are just sand. (Call Bass River State Forest.)

Ramapo Mountain State Forest, Skyline Dr., Oakland (Bergen/Passaic Counties): A streamside trail climbs from lower parking area off I-287 to scenic Ramapo Lake, which is circled by a level path. A semipaved, private road from an upper parking area is much more level and great for biking. A lot of people also seem to bring their dogs here. A side trail leads to Castle Point and the ruins of a 1910 stone mansion. A nice place for hiking, bicycling, fishing, and picnicking. (Call Ringwood State Park.)

Stokes State Forest, Rt. 206, north of Branchville (Sussex County): The forest includes Tillman Ravine, a 10,000-year-old hemlock-lined gorge, great views from atop Sunrise Mountain, a swimming beach at Stony Lake, beaver meadows along Big Flat Brook, and more than 17 miles of marked trails. Plenty of swimming, picnicking, hiking, camping, and fishing throughout the forest. TELEPHONE: 973-948-3820.

Wharton State Forest, Rt. 542, Hammonton (Burlington, Atlantic, and Camden Counties): At 110,000 acres, this largest parkland in the state lies deep in the heart of the Pinelands. At Batsto (q.v.), there is a historic village and a scenic lake and stream. Atsion Recreation Area on Route 206 offers a swimming beach, bathhouse, and nearby camping and cabins. There's a boat ramp on the Mullica River at Crowley's Landing east of Batsto on Route 542. There are canoe launch areas off Route 542 near Batsto, at Atsion, and on the Wading River south of Jenkins and at Speedwell on Route 563. Plenty of camping, canoeing, hiking, and picnicking throughout the forest, including the Batona Trail. TELEPHONE: 609-561-0024.

Worthington State Forest, Rt. 80, Exit 1 (Warren County): Because of its location, a lot of people think it's part of the Delaware Water Gap National Recreation Area, but it's actually state land. Among the attractions are the Dunnfield Creek hiking area, where the Appalachian Trail leads to Sunfish Pond atop the Kittatinny Ridge · and other trails lead to the top of Mount Tammany, overlooking the Water Gap from 1,500 feet. Along the Delaware north of the Water Gap you'll find the historic Copper Mine Inn and campgrounds. Alternate trails lead from this area to Sunfish Pond. Plenty of fishing, hiking, picnicking, backpacking, and camping in this area. TELE-PHONE: 908-841-9575.

COUNTY PARKS

The extent of county parks varies considerably throughout the state, with some counties, like Morris, having a well-developed system of nature-oriented parks while other counties have fewer or focus more on urban amenities. However, you'll find some nicely developed county parks throughout the state. Unlike state parks, they rarely charge entrance or parking fees. There may be a fee for programs, however. Here is a selection of the more notable ones. Call for directions, since many large parks have several entrances. Also check the "Garden Variety" chapter for gardens run by county parks. Nature centers and zoos in county parks are described in more detail in the "Animals" chapter.

Atlantic County Park, in Estell Manor: This park consists of 1,742 acres and includes a nature center, biking, cross-country ski and hiking trails, fishing, and picnic areas. Historic sites. Rt. 50 south of Mays Landing. TELEPHONE: 609-625-1897, 645-5960.

Berlin Park, Park Drive, Berlin (Camden County): Almost 150 acres, with fishing, hiking, picnic area, and playground. Site of Camden County Environmental Studies Center. TELEPHONE: 856-795-7275.

Campgaw Mountain Reservation, Mahwah (Bergen County): Winter ski area, plus hiking trails, and camping. **TELEPHONE:** 201-327-7800.

Cattus Island County Park, 1170 Cattus Is. Blvd., Toms River (Ocean County): Nature center and hiking trails on a peninsula in Barnegat Bay. **TELEPHONE:** 732-270-6960.

Colonial Park, Mettlers Rd., Franklin Twp. (Somerset County): Rose garden and fragrance gardens, arboretum, tennis courts, boating, fishing, hiking, and picnic areas. **TELEPHONE:** 908-722-1200.

Cooper River Park, Haddonfield (Camden County): The paved Cooper River Trail follows the stream for 9 miles through the Camden County suburbs.

Davidsons Mill Pond Park, off Rt. 130, Deans (Middlesex County): Fishing and picnicking at old mill pond. **TELEPHONE:** 732-745-3995.

Duke Island Park, Old York Road, Bridgewater (Somerset County): Fishing, picnicking, concerts, hiking along Raritan River. **TELEPHONE:** 908-722-1200.

Eagle Rock Reservation, Eagle Rock Ave., West Orange (Essex County): Overlook atop Watchung Mountain offers great views of New York skyline, a 9/11 memorial, and hiking in the woods. Private restaurant in park (Highlawn Pavilion).

Garret Mountain Reservation, Valley Road, Paterson (Passaic County): Hilltop park includes Lambert Castle (q.v.), scenic overlook of Paterson and Manhattan skyline, hiking, fishing, stables, and riding trails. **TELEPHONE:** 973-881-4832.

Hartshorne Woods Park, Middletown (Monmouth County): The Rocky Point section offers woodland trails with overlooks of the Navesink River. **TELEPHONE:** 732-842-4000.

Holmdel Park, Longstreet Rd., Holmdel (Monmouth County): Reconstructed farm, large arboretum, picnic pavilion, fishing lake, and hiking. **TELEPHONE:** 732-946-2669.

Hunterdon County Arboretum, 1020 Rt. 31, Lebanon Twp.: This 73-acre park includes a 20,000-square-foot display garden, picnicking, wetlands study area, and hiking trails. **TELEPHONE:** 908-782-1158.

Johnson Park, River Rd., Piscataway (Middlesex County): Large picnic areas, small horse track, small animal zoo, ball fields, hiking trails, and restored village on the banks of the Raritan River. **TELEPHONE:** 732-745-3900.

Lewis Morris Park, Rt. 124, Morris Twp. (Morris County): Woods and grassy fields adjoin Jockey Hollow. Lake offers swimming beach and fishing. Hiking, picnic areas, and ice skating. TELEPHONE: 973-326-7600.

Lord Stirling Park, Basking Ridge (Somerset County): Home of the Environmental Center adjacent to the Great Swamp (q.v.), this 900-acre park has 8.5 miles of trails and boardwalks that cross forests and wetlands, as well as a public riding stable. TELEPHONE: 908-722-1200.

Mahlon Dickerson Reservation: Weldon Rd., Jefferson Twp. (Morris County): Large park offers hiking, mountain biking, equestrian trails, fishing, canoe rentals, and group picnic area. Small camping area for trailers and some tents. TELEPHONE: 973-326-7600.

Manasquan Reservoir: Windler Rd., Howell Twp. (Monmouth County): More than 1,200 acres and a lake for rowboats, fishing, and hiking. TELEPHONE: 732-842-4000.

Mercer County Park, Rt. 535, West Windsor Twp. (Mercer County): Includes a large lake with a marina, fishing, ice skating, picnic facilities, and hiking trials. TELEPHONE: 609-989-6530.

Musconetcong Gorge Park, off Rt. 519, Holland Twp. (Hunterdon County): Scenic hikes in undeveloped woodland hills above the Musconetcong River. TELEPHONE: 908-782-1158.

Ocean County Park, Rt. 88, Lakewood (Ocean County): Once a vacation site for John D. Rockefeller, today it includes a swimming lake, fishing lake, playgrounds, and mature trees. Cross-country skiing in winter. TELEPHONE: 732-506-9090.

Pyramid Mountain Natural Historical Area, Boonton Ave. (Rt. 511), Montville Twp. (Morris County): Its 1,000 acres of rocky hills offer hiking and overlooks. Main feature is Tripod Rock, a huge boulder balanced on three smaller rocks since the last ice age. TELEPHONE: 973-326-7600.

Roosevelt Park, Oakwood Ave., Edison (Middlesex County): A compact park known for its summer theater series in an outdoor amphitheater. Lake fishing, trails. TELEPHONE: 732-745-3900.

Schooleys Mountain Park, Camp Washington Rd., Long Valley (Morris County): Swimming beach and lake, boating, hiking, bridle trails, summer environmental center. TELEPHONE: 973-326-7600.

Scotland Run Park, Clayton-Williamson Rd., Clayton (Gloucester County): Nature center, boating, swimming, fishing, picnicking, and hiking on almost 1,000 acres. TELEPHONE: 856-881-0845.

South Mountain Reservation, Northfield Rd., West Orange (Essex County): Includes ice skating rink, Turtle Back Zoo, fishing, hiking, scenic views, cross-country skiing, and picnicking.

Thompson Park, Newman Springs Rd. (Rt. 520), Lincroft (Monmouth County): Beautiful mansion holds art shows. Grounds include a display rose garden, fitness trails, picnic area. Many activities with summer theater in barn. TELEPHONE: 732-842-4000.

Turkey Swamp Park, Georgia Rd., Freehold (Monmouth County): One of the few county facilities to include camping (with a restroom and showers). There are sixty-four campsites plus a lake for boating. Trails, playgrounds, ball fields. TELEPHONE: 908-462-7286.

Van Saun Park, Forest Ave. off Rt. 4, Paramus (Bergen County): Includes Bergen County Zoo (q.v.), lake, fishing, ice skating, large picnic area, playground, and walking paths. TELEPHONE: 201-262-2627.

Warinanco Park, St. Georges Ave., Roselle (Union County): Lake for rowing, fishing, ice skating in winter. Picnic area. TELEPHONE: 908-298-7850.

Watchung Reservation, Mountainside (Union County): Part of the Watchung Mountains, includes trails, picnic areas, planetarium, nature center, horseback riding stables, and fishing. TELEPHONE: 908-789-3670.

Wells Mills County Park and Nature Center, 905 Wells Mills Rd., Waretown (Ocean County), 5 miles west on Rt. 532: Inside the Pinelands, this 810-acre park includes a nature center, hiking trails, cedar swamp, lake fishing, and canoe rentals in season. TELEPHONE: 609-971-3085.

FEDERAL AND INTERSTATE AREAS

Sandy Hook

This division of the Gateway National Recreation Area encompasses the Visitor Center with nature displays, pamphlets, and maps; several guarded beaches with bathhouses, changing rooms, and concession stands. Picnicking allowed. Although most people come for the beach, there is also Fort Hancock (q.v.), which has a small museum, restored officers' quarters, and remnants of 1890s concrete gun emplacements; the Sandy Hook lighthouse (q.v.); and hiking and bird-watching in the natural areas. Fishing is allowed at several points. Windsurfing and snorkeling on the bay side.

LOCATION: Across bridge from Highlands (Monmouth County). Rt. 36 east from Garden State Parkway, Exit 117. **TELEPHONE:** 732-872-5970. **WEBSITE:** www.nps.gov/gate.

Delaware Water Gap National Recreation Area

This scenic parkland encompasses forests, Appalachian ridges, historic villages, and 40 miles of the Delaware River along the northwestern edge of the state. The **Appalachian Trail** cuts 25 miles through the New Jersey side of this park on its way from Maine to Georgia. There are lots of other hiking trails as well as picnicking, canoeing, swimming, fishing, bicycling, and historic sites. You'll find some real back roads here, where you can travel miles without seeing a house. You might, however, see a bear or two if you're lucky.

The Kittatinny Point Visitor Center off Route 80, sits above the banks of the river, where the 1,500-foot-high Kittatinny Ridge is dramatically cut by the Delaware River, giving the area its name. The center offers books, park and trail maps, and nature displays. Outside is a picnic area as well as a boat and canoe launch area. Across the highway is the Dunnfield Creek hiking area.

The Mohican Outdoor Center (q.v.), accessible from Blairstown on the eastern side of the park, is set in a scenic nature area on Catfish Pond. It is also an overnight stop along the Appalachian Trail that is run by the Appalachian Mountain Club.

A number of scenic spots lie north of Kittatinny Point along the scenic Old Mine Rd. Nine miles north of the Visitor Center is the Depew Recreation Site, a popular summer beach and picnic ground along the river. Just beyond that lies Van Campens Glen, where a trail leads alongside a stream in a scenic gorge to upper and lower Van Campens falls. A mile or so north on the road (or by trail) is the Watergate Recreation Site, a popular picnicking and fishing spot with ponds set amid a large, open, grassy area (parking fee). Millbrook Village (q.v.) is a restored town from the 1800s farther along the park road. Blue Mountain and Crater Lakes, on a turnoff north of Millbrook, offer swimming, picnicking, fishing, canoeing, and hiking amid deep forests. The gravel road leading to Crater Lake also offers turnouts with sweeping views of the Paulinskill Valley from atop Kittatinny Ridge.

Continuing north, you'll find the Walpack Valley Environmental Education Center in Walpack Center, a small town along the Flat Brook, known for its trout fishing. Turn right into the town and continue across the brook. Just past the cemetery, turn right, then travel a mile or so on a pot-holed gravel road to Buttermilk Falls, where a stream tumbles 75 feet down a steep, forested hillside. A wooden stairway climbs to two overlooks beside the falls, which is more dramatic in spring when water flows are greater.

If you turn left off the main park road a couple of miles before reaching Walpack and travel down a long gravel road, you'll pass the restored Van Campen Inn. This historic 1740s stone structure was an important stop on the Old Mine Road in colonial times. Tours are held one Sunday a month. Call the park for dates and times. Nearby is the Military Trail, where a French and Indian War encampment is held in mid-October.

The Peters Valley Craft Center, north of Walpack, offers crafts displays and demonstrations on weekends, 2–5, from mid-May to mid-Sept. Watch students and teachers create pottery and weave, as well as practice woodworking, blacksmithing, silkscreening, and jewelry-making skills. A store and gallery in the village are open year-round (daily exc. Thu., 11–5). You can also enroll in crafts workshops designed for beginners to advanced skill levels that run for two to ten days. Peters Valley also sponsors a crafts fair, held at the Sussex County Fair Grounds in Augusta on the last weekend in September.

There are also more sites of interest across the Delaware in the Pennsylvania side of the park, including Smithfield Beach, the Pocono Environmental Education Center, and Dingmans Falls. The Dingmans area, where a boardwalk trail leads to two high waterfalls, lies across the Delaware on an old private toll bridge (a tolltaker on foot asks for tolls) not far from Peters Valley.

LOCATION: Rt. 80, Exit 1. Also accessible on Millbrook Rd. from Blairstown and via Rts. 206 and 560 near Layton. **TELEPHONE:** Kittatinny Point Visitor Center, 908-496-4458; park headquarters, 570-588-2435; Peters Valley, 973-948-5200. **WEBSITES:** Park, www.nps.gov/dewa; Peters Valley, www.pvcrafts.org.

Palisades Interstate Park

This Scenic park stretches along the Hudson River from Fort Lee to the New York border and beyond. Hiking trails run atop the cliffs and down to the river below. Fishing is allowed in the Hudson. The undercliff park road is often closed to traffic, which adds to its popularity as a bicycling area. There are also riverside picnic areas and boat basins in Alpine, Englewood, and Fort Lee. You'll also find an historic area at Fort Lee (q.v.) plus scenic clifftop overlooks of the river at Fort Lee, State Line Lookout, and elsewhere.

ADMISSION: Parking fees are charged at riverfront areas in the summer. **TELEPHONE:** 201-768-1360. **WEBSITE:** www.njpalisades.org.

Bushkill Falls

For those who wish to avoid the crowds of amusement parks, this scenic attraction offers a day in the country with the simpler amusements of an earlier time set in a primeval forest in the foothills of the Poconos. The area is cool in the summer and colorful in the fall. Though the main waterfall is nowhere near Niagara, it does present photographers and hikers with a pleasant outing.

You enter through a "nature" museum to a pathway through the forest. Although you can get a good view of the cascading water from above, it is more impressive to see it from below by way of a "natural" log and stone stairway. The Main Falls drop over the edge of a 100-foot cliff to a deep pool below. From that point the water drops another 70 feet through a large gorge strewn with gigantic boulders. The falls are fairly narrow, but the drop is spectacular.

There are three routes to follow to the falls. The short route, with a green trail marker, takes only 15 minutes to walk. It is the "chicken" trail to a lookout where you can take a picture, then sit down. The second or "popular" route takes 45 minutes and is for those who want their money's worth. This takes you down and around the bottom of the main falls and back on a rustic wooden boardwalk through a scenic gorge. The third route takes 1½ hours. Here you travel down below the falls, then cross the stream on a long loop trail. Along the way, you pass a series of mist-laden falls and climb to a lookout where you can enjoy a panoramic view of the Delaware Valley before circling back to the gorge.

It is absolutely necessary to wear good walking shoes. Check the map in the brochure you receive with your ticket. It clearly marks the trails to follow. Food service, concessions, gift shop, paddle boats, and beer are available for those who need rest and relaxation after their exertions. Picnic tables are present as well.

HOURS: Apr.–Oct., Mon.–Fri., 9–6; weekends, 9–7; Nov., daily, 9–5, weather permitting. **ADMISSION:** Adults: $$. Discounts: Seniors, children. Under 4 free. **LOCATION:** Bushkill, PA. Rt. 80 to Exit 309, then take Rt. 209 north 11 miles to Bushkill Falls Rd. Follow signs. **TELEPHONE:** 570-588-6682. **WEBSITE:** www.visitbushkillfalls.com.

The Garden Variety

The charming Leaming's Run Garden is a colorful oasis along Route 9 in Cape May County. *(Photo by Victor Di Sylvester/Courtesy Cape May County Dept. of Tourism)*

Duke Gardens

Open from October to May and one of New Jersey's foremost attractions, the Duke Gardens feature a series of interconnecting hothouses with an amazing variety of plants. They are part of the Duke Estate in Somerville. Indeed, from the moment you board the little van in the parking lot that takes you through a winding road you are aware that this is millionaire's territory. The administration building where you get your tickets and wait for the tour is a Tudor-style cottage replete with rich woods and carpets. From here the guide takes you across to the hothouses, where you enter a different world.

Each hothouse contains a shortened version of an international garden. The layout of the flowers and the walkways are all planned to reflect the atmosphere of that particular garden. The first one you enter is the Italian Romantic garden. Here you find statuary amid overgrown plants, birds-of-paradise, and the type of Mediterranean setting that threw nineteenth-century poets into ecstasy. Each garden is controlled for climate and humidity. Enter the Edwardian Conservatory and it's warm. Here, in a hothouse with tropical plants such as sego palms and elephant ears, the English gentleman would propose to his lady love (or at least he did in all those old movies on late night television). He would probably clip an orchid and hand it to her. For there are enough big, fat orchids in here to send an entire graduating class to the senior prom.

The long English garden, on the other hand, is temperate. A brick walkway takes you through sedate rows of hollyhocks, primroses, and manicured boxwoods. A small herb garden is here as well.

The French garden is formal, with flowers set out in greenery shaped in a fleur-de-lis pattern. Latticework covers all, and a statue of a noblewoman reminds you that this is a small version of what you might find at Versailles.

The Chinese garden, with its overhanging willows, stone walkway, and arched bridge over a goldfish pond is for serene meditation. The scent of the fragrant tea olive permeates the air. Among the other gardens you will find an Arizona desert with succulents and tall cacti; a Japanese rustic-style meditation garden; and a geometric Persian garden with decorated tiles and fountains.

Many gardeners attend the plantings, so the display flowers change seasonally, but the overall scheme remains intact. This is a favorite destination of garden clubs, but individuals enjoy the gardens as well. Advance reservations are requested, however. High heels are not permitted (you'll understand why when you walk on those arched stone bridges). You can bring a still camera as long as you don't hold up the group. Although the hothouse gardens are closed in the summer, reserved bus tours of the richly landscaped Duke estate are now a possibility.

HOURS: Oct.–May, daily, 12–4, by reservation. **ADMISSION:** $$. Discounts: Seniors, children. Under 6 free. **LOCATION:** Rt. 206, south of Somerville (Somerset County). Turn at Duke Parkway. **TELEPHONE:** 908-243-3600.

Leaming's Run Gardens

Leaming's Run Gardens was created as a bulwark of quiet woods and colorful plantings against the encroachment of motels and gasoline exhaust fumes near the southern shore. It can transport you back to your childhood. Everyone has probably explored a forest at least once, felt the crackling of pine needles underfoot and heard the whippoorwill above. That's the kind of woods that covers 30 acres of sandy soil here, all interspersed with colorful gardens.

You come across the gardens at each bend of the road. There are over twenty of them, and many are assemblages of color. The yellow garden mixes gourds, gladiola, banana peppers, and taller plants. Another garden is a medley of oranges. The English garden and reflecting pool are typical of a cottage landscape in Britain. Each garden is planted to provide color and texture during the entire season from late spring to early fall. The most recent is a sweetheart garden in the shape of a heart that attracts romantic picture takers.

Three acres are set aside for a replica colonial farm. Here you will find a traditional early-American log cabin with a fenced-in kitchen and herb garden The interior of the cabin is quite authentic and outside you'll find goats and chickens. Beyond the farm are nooks and crannies in the road—with snapdragons, pinks, and a cinnamon walk. There are benches where you can enjoy the view. (If you visit during August you'll see plenty of hummingbirds around also.)

At the end of the one-mile walk, you come to The Cooperage, a shop where you can buy a variety of dried flower arrangements and other gifts. There are a few rules for the gardens, by the way: no smoking, no pets, no drinks, and no radios.

HOURS: Mid-May to mid-Oct., 9:30–5. **ADMISSION:** \$\$. Discounts: Seniors, children. Under 6 free. **LOCATION:** 1845 Rt. 9, Swainton (Cape May County). Garden State Parkway to Exit 17, to Rt. 9, then south. **TELEPHONE:** 609-465-5871.

Branch Brook Park

When it's cherry blossom time in Newark's Branch Brook, hundreds of visitors descend upon New Jersey's oldest county park. Not only do the cherry trees outnumber the ones in Washington, D.C., but Branch Brook itself is an outstanding example of the informal urban parks that nineteenth-century planners thought of as a respite from city congestion. The park was designed by America's foremost landscape architect, Frederick Law Olmstead, and his son, and it includes meandering walkways, little lakes, recreational fields for baseball and tennis, and small copses of trees and bushes.

There are now over 2,700 cherry trees, with the most luxuriant double-blossom variety clustered at the Belleville end of the park. The original trees were donated by Caroline Bamberger Fuld, back in 1923, but they have almost doubled in number since then. The

Japanese flowering cherry does not bear fruit and comes in several varieties, including the weeping cherry and the single and double blossom, all in white or pink. The trees are planted along the roadway, and people are allowed to park their cars by the road so they can get out and take pictures. The three-week season usually starts around the middle of April, depending on the weather, but of course the park is popular with locals all year round.

LOCATION: Rt. 280 to Newark; make a left on First St., a right on Park Ave., and then take the first right. **TELEPHONE:** 973-268-3500.

Colonial Park Gardens

There are several attractive gardens in this county park. The original rose garden, once part of the Mettler Estate, was developed and expanded by a horticulturist so that it now covers an acre. The Rudolf van der Goot Rose Garden displays over 285 species, with over 3,000 bushes that form a formal display garden to exhibit the A.A.R.S. Award Winning Roses each year. Included here are the original York and Lancaster roses, tea roses, floribunda, and more. They are all labeled to show type and date of introduction into the horticultural world. A flagstone walk makes for easy ambling.

Behind the rose garden is the Fragrance and Sensory Garden, which provides Braille plaques for the blind and a handrail for the handicapped. Set inside Colonial Park (one of those beautiful county parks that one comes upon so often in New Jersey) is also a 144-acre arboretum complete with meandering stream. Beyond that are tennis courts, paddleboats, and picnic tables for family get-togethers. A gazebo inside the 5-acre perennial garden is a popular picture-taking spot (formal pictures are by permit only).

Garden clubs, school classes, and other groups can arrange for guided tours for a fee. Otherwise the gardens are free. Major blooming at the rose garden occurs the first week of June and the first week of September.

HOURS: Daily for park. Call for rose garden hours. **LOCATION:** Franklin Twp. (Somerset County). Take Rt. 206 to Rt. 514 (Amwell Rd.) east, cross Millstone River to Mettlers Rd. **TELEPHONE:** 732-873-2459. **WEBSITE:** www.parks.co.somerset.nj.us.

Reeves-Reed Arboretum

A small estate is the setting for this arboretum, hidden by tall trees on one of Summit's stately old streets. You follow a winding path down to the parking lot, which has room for about fifty cars. The stone and shingle manor house on the rise above the lot is surrounded by trees, shrubs, and flowering plants. But the major part of the gardens is back behind the house. It is rather like visiting the house of a rich old aunt and being allowed to wander through the backyard by yourself. However, no picnicking, dog walking, or sledding is allowed.

You can follow the nature trails through marked oaks, maples, walnuts, and beeches. The open area of this hilly site is devoted to both flower and herb gardens. A deep depression (called a kettle hole in geological terms) is the setting for a spectacular flowering of daffodils in April, followed by summer field flowers. Azaleas, rhododendrons, a lily pond, and a small rose garden are also to be found along the walks of this 12.5-acre arboretum.

The main house offers a variety of classes and Sunday lectures. Among the brochures available there is a garden guide to help identify the species in the arboretum. Also on the premises are a greenhouse and a small gift shop.

> **HOURS:** Grounds, daily, dawn to dusk; office, Mon., Tue., Thu., Fri., 9–3. **ADMISSION:** Free. **LOCATION:** 165 Hobart Ave., Summit (Union County). Take Rt. 24 to Hobart Ave. exit. **TELEPHONE:** 908-273-8787. **WEBSITE:** www.reeves-reedarboretum.org.

James Rose Center

The James Rose Center for Landscape Architectural Research and Design is the former home and garden of James Rose, a founder of the modernist movement in landscape design. This site showcases Rose's ideas about interlocking indoor and outdoor spaces, combining architecture and art in a modernist residential setting. Rose designed everything here—the home, the furniture, sculpture, and garden. Three interconnected pavilions in an experimental landscape incorporate elements of Japanese design. Rose's goal was to create a radical approach to living on a small lot as an alternative to suburban tract housing. The site also shows photos of Rose's architecture and landscape designs at other locations. A self-guided brochure tour is available at the center. Some off-street and suburban street parking is available.

> **HOURS:** May–Oct., 10–4, 1st and 3rd Sat. of the month. Guided tours twice a day. **ADMISSION:** $$. **LOCATION:** 506 E. Ridgewood Ave., Ridgewood (Bergen County). Two miles west of Rt. 17. **TELEPHONE:** 201-446-6017. **WEBSITE:** www.jamesrosecenter.org.

The Camden Children's Garden

What's the latest thing in interactive education for moppets? Children's gardens. One of the most interesting is the Camden Children's

The Camden Children's Garden, with its many play elements, is a colorful addition to the aquarium and the waterfront. *(Photo by Barbara Hudgins)*

Garden, which spruces up the facade of the New Jersey State Aquarium. Although a separate entity, it adds much-needed color to the Camden waterfront. You can visit it alone or buy a combination ticket for the aquarium.

The Children's Garden is a pleasant spot for both kids and adults. There are lots of colorful play areas in this 4-acre attraction, many of which aren't just about flowers or plants. The Dinosaur Garden, for instance, offers a prehistoric environment of rock walls, waterfalls, and huge trees—not to mention a 35-foot-long Apatosaurus, created from recycled automobile parts by sculptor Jim Gary. Hand-painted benches and a painted wooden violet add color to the nearby Violet Plaza, which also features an interactive water fountain. Kids can also learn and play in the Red Oak Treehouse and nearby underground maze (which is really above-ground and at eye level for children).

The Storybook Gardens have three little houses made of straw, wood, and brick in the 3 Little Pigs Garden as well as fanciful topiaries and a chair made out of yews where children can hide and play. A giant watering can fronts the Giant's Garden, which is filled with oversize plants and foliage, and a slide sends children down a rabbit hole into Alice in Wonderland's Garden. Besides the many interactive play areas, there is now a small carousel. The Railroad Garden (fanciful plants inside small boxcars) also offers a working miniature train ride.

Grownups can enjoy the statue of Walt Whitman that stands in front of the Butterfly Garden. It is a fitting nod to the poet who lived his last years in this once-bustling city. And the enclosed, heated butterfly house nearby allows you to experience the winged creatures all year-round.

The garden offers a tented picnic area for reserved groups and parties. Individuals can picnic on the benches in the small waterfront park just outside the site. A small gift shop specializes in garden-themed items. Although this is primarily an outdoor garden, it does operate all year-round and has plenty of nonfoliage elements that can be enjoyed.

HOURS: Daily, 9:30–5:30. Shorter hours mid-Sept. to mid-Apr. **ADMISSION:** Adults: $$. Discounts: Children. Combo with aquarium: $$$. **LOCATION:** 3 Riverside Dr., Camden, near the Tweeter Center. Parking garage across street. **TELEPHONE:** 856-365-8733. **WEBSITE:** www.camdenchildrensgarden.org.

Well-Sweep Herb Farm

A commercial herb-growing farm, Well-Sweep lies in a scenic rural setting about 6 miles southwest of Hackettstown. It covers 120 acres and has almost 2,000 plant varieties lining the brick walkways of its display and perennial gardens.

Visitors may stroll down the paths of the formal herb garden and browse through the extensive display gardens at any time, but special tours are reserved for groups.

Owner Cyrus Hyde gives special lecture tours to groups by appointment. These tours offer fascinating insights into the many uses of plants. Did you know horsetail grass can be used for fine sanding? Or that tansy, planted next to the door, will keep ants away? Want the recipe for rose geranium sugar? No wonder this tour is popular with garden clubs. Special events also include guest presentations, lectures, slide shows, and craft classes. Just make sure to reserve your place in advance.

Since the principal activity here is growing and selling herbs and flowering perennials, there's always a wide selection at reasonable prices. Also sold in the gift shop are pottery, books, and other garden-related items.

HOURS: Apr.–Dec., Mon.–Sat., 9–5; Jan.–Mar., call for hours. Closed holidays. **LOCATION:** 205 Mt. Bethel Rd., Port Murray (Warren County). Off Rt. 629. **TELEPHONE:** 908-852-5390. **WEBSITE:** www.wellsweep.com.

New Jersey Botanical Gardens

The flowering preserve at Skylands Manor in Ringwood State Park is one of New Jersey's most popular garden attractions. The 96-acre site was designated the official state garden in 1984, but it is still known familiarly as Skylands Gardens. Because the mansion's original owner was an avid horticulturist, you'll find a large variety of flowering trees and bushes as well as flowering plants here. Most photographed is the long allee of crab-apple trees that blossom in the spring. However, the estate also has lilacs, azaleas, geraniums, and peonies among its many varieties. The formal garden with its stone urns includes fall flowers and foliage.

Skylands, the forty-four-room Tudor-style mansion (q.v.), has limited visiting hours, but you may peruse the plantings that surround the house. From the back of the house you can see the classic terraces dotted with statues and greenery. There's quite a bit of walking to do if you want to see all the garden areas. Many of these are aligned to provide a vista; the reflecting pool especially is set up this way. A winter garden, an octagonal garden, a lily pond, formal terraces with stone balustrades, and scenic vistas make this a beautiful place year-round. Since there are only a few gardeners on hand, compared to eighty in the days of the millionaire owner, not all sections are kept up to par. However, the volunteer group, the Skylands Association, does yeoman work here.

The association holds garden tours on Sundays at 2 from May through October. They also offer garden tours for groups and hold a Holiday Open House at the mansion the first weekend in December. If you'd like some hands-on fun in the gardens, they offer Saturday morning volunteer garden work on various weekends in season. Manor tours are held the first Sunday afternoon of each month (except Jan. & Feb.) There are Friday evening concerts in summer on the grounds as well as other seasonal events throughout the year.

> **HOURS:** Daily, 8–8, for park and gardens. **ADMISSION:** Parking fee, $ in season; manor fee, $. **LOCATION:** Ringwood State Park (Passaic County). Rt. 511 to Sloatsburg Rd., then Morris Rd. **TELEPHONE:** Park, 973-962-7031; Association, 973-962-9534. **WEBSITE:** www.njbg.org.

Leonard J. Buck Garden

The former estate of a wealthy Far Hills mining engineer, this 33-acre garden features native and exotic plants displayed in a naturalistic setting of woodland, rock garden, pond, and streams. A host of interesting wetland plants, perennials, flowering trees, and shrubs can be enjoyed year-round. The large fern garden features non-flowering hardy ferns intermingled with unusual shade plants.

Plenty of walking here, since the terrain varies from a low-lying stream to steep hillsides, but you can pause at well-placed benches to enjoy the vista.

The rock gardens are at peak bloom in the spring, when thousands of tiny flowers peek out from designed rock formations. There are plenty of irises, azaleas, and rhododendrons and Japanese primroses in the spring, but you can find colorful autumn foliage, too. Unusual trees, a pleasant lake that is home to mallard ducks, and a small waterfall make for good picture taking. Pick up a garden map and bloom list (updated weekly) at the Visitor Center. There are many special programs and workshops at the main building, hosted by the Somerset County Park Commission, which administers the garden.

> **HOURS:** Mon.–Fri., 10–4; Sat., 10–5; Sun., 12–5. Closed weekends & major holidays, Dec.–Mar. **LOCATION:** 11 Layton Rd., Far Hills (Somerset County). Off Rt. 512 about a mile south of Rt. 202. **TELEPHONE:** 908-234-2677. **WEBSITE:** www.park.co.somerset.nj.us/buckgarden2.htm.

Other New Jersey Gardens

Presby Iris Gardens: From the last week in May to the second week in June, an outstanding display of irises can be found in this lovely suburban park in Upper Montclair. Hilly terrain and gracious homes are the setting for this local park where a Mr. Presby began his iris beds many years ago. Every color in the rainbow is reflected in irises. There are thousands of varieties of these bearded and straight-stalked flowers, planted in long linear beds that parallel the street. Peonies can be found at the adjoining headquarters. Free. **LOCATION:** Mountainside Park, 474 Upper Mountain Ave., Upper Montclair (Essex County). **TELEPHONE:** 973-783-5974.

Davis Johnson Park: This pleasant city park in the town of Tenafly covers 7 acres and features a rose garden, a sunken garden, and a small herb garden. Like many other local parks, it is a popular spot for photographers taking wedding pictures. **LOCATION:** 137 Engle St., Tenafly (Bergen County). **TELEPHONE:** 201-569-7275.

Deep Cut Gardens: Once the property of a mafioso chief in the 1930s, these well-kept gardens still have a slight Mediterranean flavor. The 1952 ranch-style house is now a Horticultural Center where you can find a good library and some plant specimens in the enclosed porch. There are 52 acres of gardens and greenhouses that are planned as a living catalog of cultivated and native plants. Two ponds (one sporting lily pads) are home to brightly colored Koi. An azalea and rhododendron walk is a springtime favorite, while the butterfly and hummingbird garden attracts visitors in summer. Greenhouses, shade gardens, cascading pools, and a long meadow make this a pleasant place to meander. Free. **LOCATION:** 352 Red Hill Rd., Middletown (Monmouth County), 1.5 miles north of Garden State Parkway, Exit 114. **TELEPHONE:** 732-671-6050. **WEBSITE:** www.mounmouthcounty-parksystem.com.

Sayen Gardens: Set in the heart of a charming town, this 28-acre park displays 2,000 azaleas and 1,500 rhododendrons among its many varieties. The gardens offer walking paths, benches, a scenic bridge over a lily pond, and a host of daffodils, tulips, and snowdrops in season. Three gazebos and a 1912 bungalow-style house are part of this personal garden now made public. A popular place both for weddings and wedding pictures. The Azalea Festival held here on Mother's Day attracts thousands. Free. **LOCATION:** 155 Hughes Dr., Hamilton Square (Mercer County). Rt. 33 to north on Old Trenton Rd. to Hughes Dr. **TELEPHONE:** 609-890-3543.

Cross Estate Gardens: Part of Morristown National Historic Park, the Cross Estate features a formal walled garden, vine-covered pergola, mountain laurel allee, shade gardens, and a native-plant area adjacent to the estate's mansion. There are also signs and a descriptive brochure covering examples of native trees important to the New Jersey Brigade, encamped here in 1780. **HOURS:** Daily, dawn to dusk. **LOCATION:** Jockey Hollow Rd., Bernardsville (Somerset County). **TELEPHONE:** 973-539-2016.

Rutgers Gardens: This 50-acre arboretum and display garden contains a wide variety of trees and flowers, including notable dogwood and holly collections as well as a rhododendron and azalea garden. These are not formal gardens, but are meant to display the variety of horticulture in the state. Among the displays is a water conservation terrace and a border of ornamental grasses. Across the street, there is a pavilion and patio where you can picnic, and beyond that are extensive virgin woods to explore. Open House days (spring, summer, and fall) feature lectures, plant sales, and garden tours. Free. **HOURS:** Daily, dawn to dusk. **LOCATION:** 112 Ryders Lane, New Brunswick (Middlesex County). Off Rt. 1. **TELEPHONE:** 732-932-8451. **WEBSITE:** http://aesop.rutgers.edu/~rugardens.

Frelinghuysen Arboretum: Tulips, azaleas, rhododendrons, a rose garden, and a wealth of flowering trees are part of the display at this 127-acre tract that was once the home of the Frelinghuysen family. Cherry trees, crab-apple and magnolia blossoms, along with a lilac garden and a dogwood copse bring color and contrast to the many evergreens in the collection. It serves as headquarters of the Morris County Park System, which uses the mansion for offices and library. Separate building for lectures, a nice lawn for concerts, and a gift shop specializing in garden items can all be found here. **HOURS:** Daily, 9 A.M.–dusk. **LOCATION:** 53 East Hanover Ave. (Rt. 511), Morristown (Morris County). **TELEPHONE:** 973-326-7600.

Willowwood/Bamboo Brook: The Willowwood Arboretum offers extensive walking paths and a conservatory. There are flowering gardens, wildflowers, a variety of trees, and long meadows on 130 acres of rolling farmland. Adjoins the Bamboo Brook Outdoor Education Center, which includes some formal gardens (originally created by a well-known landscape artist) and a white cedar allee. Walking trails and brook. **LOCATION:** Longview Rd., Chester Twp. (Morris County). **TELEPHONE:** 973-326-7600.

Cora Hartshorn Arboretum and Bird Sanctuary: This 16-acre refuge includes a small stone building used as a nature center. Once the estate of a millionaire's daughter, it is now a pleasant, hilly spot where you can walk on 3 miles of trails among the trees and listen to birdsongs. There are 150 species of wildflowers here as well as 45 tree species. It is known for its rhododendron dell and many rare ferns. Since there is no parking lot, you must park on the street. The nature center offers many programs. **HOURS:** Grounds open daily, dawn to dusk; stone house, Mon.–Fri., 9–4:30, Sat., 10–11:30; summer, Mon.–Fri., 9–12. **LOCATION:** 324 Forest Dr. South, Short Hills (Essex County). Rt. 24 to Hobart Ave., then to Forest Dr. **TELEPHONE:** 973-376-3587. **WEBSITE:** www.hartshornarboretum.com.

Sister Mary Grace Burns Arboretum: This former estate of railroad tycoon Jay Gould's son is now a college campus with four historic gardens—the Italian Garden, Sunken Garden, Formal Garden, and Japanese Garden. There is lots of statuary here as well as fountains, lagoons, and walkways plus a Japanese teahouse. **HOURS:** Daily, 8 A.M.–dusk. **LOCATION:** Georgian Court College, Lakewood (Ocean County). **TELEPHONE:** 732-364-2200, ext. 373. **WEBSITE:** www.georgian. edu/arboretum/index.html.

Van Vleck House and Gardens: These gardens feature rhododendrons, azaleas, and other woody plants, a wisteria-covered terrace balcony, and a small perennial and annual garden. The display greenhouse presents orchids and other tropical plants while a second greenhouse is used for various educational programs. The grounds also contain specimen trees and unusual hybrids, such as yellow rhododendrons. Donation. **HOURS:** Daily, 10–5, Apr. 15-Oct.

LOCATION: 21 Van Vleck St., Montclair (Essex County). Off N. Mountain Ave. three blocks north of Bloomfield Ave. and the Montclair Art Museum. **TELEPHONE:** 973-744-0837. **WEBSITE:** www.vanvleck.org.

NEARBY OUT-OF-STATE GARDENS
Brooklyn Botanic Gardens

New Jerseyans often combine a trip to these gardens with one to the Brooklyn Museum (which is right next door), since parking in the museum lot can serve for both places.

The Brooklyn Gardens are known for the cherry blossom walk—a wide swath of lawn with Japanese double blossoms, white and pink, that come out in mid-April. Another famous display is the Japanese Hill and Pond Garden, which was originally designed in 1914 and reconstructed in the 1990s. Here a vermilion Tori rises from the calm waters. The quiet meditation walks, the willow trees, and the stone turtles create a duplication of a Kyoto scene set down incongruously in the midst of urban high-rises.

The Brooklyn Gardens follow the natural cycles: daffodils in March, then the lilacs, then the cherry blossoms, then the wisteria and rhododendrons in May. The rose garden is spectacular but is only open certain months. The butterfly and hummingbird trail is a summer attraction. However, other features are available year-round: the formal prospect from Eastern Parkway, the rock garden and brooks, and of course the conservatories, which feature bonsai plants, cacti and tropical plants.

There are 50 acres to the gardens and lots of hills and dales. A terrace cafe offers sandwiches and drinks and the gift shop has a wide assortment of items. The requisite Discovery Garden for children is complete with a butterfly trail in season.

HOURS: Apr.–Sept., Tue.–Fri., 8–6; weekends and holidays, 10–6. Oct.–Mar., Tue.–Fri., 10–4:30; weekends and holidays, 10–4:30. **ADMISSION:** $. Discounts: Seniors, children. Under 16 free. **LOCATION:** Eastern Parkway and Washington Ave., Brooklyn, NY. **TELEPHONE:** 718-623-7200. **WEBSITE:** www.bbg.org.

New York Botanical Gardens

These 250 acres of grassland, trees, and formal gardens are the pride of the Bronx. Everything has been upgraded and prettified in recent years. The enclosed conservatories and an extensive new Children's Garden are popular draws here. A tram ride circles the park's interior—best take it early before the crowds come, but check your map first. The ride has four major stops, takes twenty minutes, and features live narration.

You can visit the ornate main building, a Beaux-Arts structure that is fronted by a landmark fountain statue. Inside are orchids, a herbarium, a library, and a gift shop. The beautiful rock garden with its pond, alpine meadow, and splashing waterfalls is another stop you should not miss. Of course, if you have kids with you, you'll want to stop at the garden created just for them. The children's garden features both outside topiaries, indoor interactive games, and all sorts of educational activities.

As for the Enid A. Haupt Conservatories, this 1903 "Glass Palace" with its Victorian-style rotunda and structural iron framework is most impressive. Inside, the tropical rain forests of the Americas (both North and South) are emphasized. Banana trees, native huts, and pineapple plants are in one section; the tall cacti of the Arizona and Mexican desert in another.

Outside the conservatory, there are nicely stylized perennial and herb gardens with brick walkways, shaded lattices, colorful flowers and plenty of benches. In June, the formal rose garden is lush with a variety of blooms. For lunch there is a pleasant cafeteria, or you can bring your own and eat at designated picnic spots. Tram rides, the conservatory, and children's garden are extra unless you buy a "Passport" ticket.

> **HOURS:** Tue.–Sun. & Mon. holidays, 10–6. **ADMISSION:** $. Discounts: Seniors, children. Wed. free. **LOCATION:** Bronx River Parkway and Fordham Rd. (Exit 7W). **TELEPHONE:** 718-817-8700. **WEBSITE:** www.nybg.org.

Wave Hill

A public garden located in the upper reaches of the Bronx in a quiet section called Riverdale, Wave Hill still gives the sense of a private estate filled with beauty and serenity. There are lovely vistas of the palisades and the Hudson from the many stone benches and Adirondack chairs on the "hill." Greenhouses are filled with tropical plants and desert cacti, and outdoor gardens are devoted to herbs and seasonal flowers. An aquatic garden, several pergolas, and many flowering trees dot the landscape.

Two houses stand on the estate. The one called Wave Hill was once rented to such notables as Mark Twain, Theodore Roosevelt, and Arturo Toscanini. The building currently houses a gift shop and a small lunchroom. French doors lead out to a stone terrace with yet another view. The Glynden Gallery features art shows and other events.

While Wave Hill was built by William Morris in 1840, it later became home to several millionaires. The gardens and conservatories, under constant restoration by horticulturists, allow the plebeian tourist a feel for the ambience of a private home landscaped for leisure and gracious living. Groups, families, mothers with children, and adult hikers all come to enjoy these pleasant grounds.

HOURS: Apr.–Oct., Tue.–Sun., 9:30–5:30. Rest of year, 9:30–4:30. **ADMISSION:** $. Discounts: Seniors, students. Under 6 free. Tue. & Sat. mornings free. **LOCATION:** 675 W. 252 St., Riverdale. Take George Washington Bridge to Henry Hudson Parkway to Exit 21. **TELEPHONE:** 718-549-3200. **WEBSITE:** www.wavehill.org.

Longwood Gardens

Without a doubt the most extensive formal gardens in the area (and considered among the best in the United States), this impressive display by the DuPont family offers an amazing variety. The gardens are open all year-round, and there is always something of interest whatever the weather. Over 1,000 acres are open to the public, including some beautifully laid out conservatories, so bring good walking shoes.

You enter through the main Visitor Center, which looks like a standard institutional building from the front but like an underground house from the back; it's cleverly concealed under a hillock of green. At the center you purchase your tickets and watch a four-minute film, which introduces you to the highlights of the gardens. There's a gift shop chock full of books and plants where you'll want to stop on your way out. But first, get a guide map at the information desk; you'll need it.

Here are some of the highlights. The conservatories are huge glass-enclosed rooms that surround a patio. Inside there are hanging basket mobiles sprouting flowers; stone herons in a pond surrounded by seasonal flowers; a ballroom featuring organ concerts; and the hot and humid Palm House with its banana and breadfruit trees. There is one room for insect-eating plants, another just for orchids. The main conservatory displays change four times a year. (The Christmas display alone attracts more than 100,000 people a year.) Nearby is an indoor Children's Garden replete with mazes, stepping stones, and hands-on activities for kids.

Outside, directly in front of the conservatories, is the main water fountain area. The fountain display, with its many spouting water jets, is framed by trimmed boxwood. Certain nights during the summer, colored lights and music from the carillon make a spectacular "Son et Lumiere." There are even fireworks added to the fountain displays on special Saturday nights—these must be reserved in advance. The carillon in its own little romantic nook with a cascading waterfall and a rock garden looks like something out of a nineteenth-century painting.

Further on are the Idea Garden, Heaths of Heather, the "Eye of God" (a low, circular water sculpture), topiary, and a rose garden. The right side of Longwood features a long walk bordered by seasonal flowers, and an open-air theater with display fountains. The Peirce-DuPont House is open to visitors for an extra fee. Beyond the restored house, there are wisteria and rose gardens, forest walks and meadows, a lake with gazebo and ducks, and, last of all, a complete Italian water garden in the manner of the Villa D'Este.

The Terrace Restaurant, located near the conservatories, offers both regular dining and cafeteria-style buffet. No smoking is allowed at the gardens, and no food can be brought in. However, there is a picnic area outside the parking lot.

HOURS: Apr.–Oct., daily, 9–6; Nov.–Mar., 10–5. Extended hours for special events. **ADMISSION:** $$$. Discounts: Seniors, children. Under 6 free. **LOCATION:** Rt. 1, Kennett Square, PA. **TELEPHONE:** 610-388-1000. **WEBSITE:** www.longwoodgardens.org.

Flea Markets and Outlets

The fields of New Jersey and Pennsylvania still host many open-air flea markets. *(Photo by Barbara Hudgins)*

OUTLETS

Flemington Outlets

Flemington is a pretty Victorian town in the middle of Hunterdon County, an area that still has a fair amount of farmland within its borders. Over the years Flemington has grown from a town that offered a few discount shops to a name that has become synonymous with outlet shopping.

If you're driving down Rt. 202 from the north, the first outlet you see is Dansk, which is on the Flemington Circle. This building includes Dansk modern design items, Samsonite, and other stores (plus the modern California Grill for eats). If you proceed onto Rt. 12 and then to Main Street you will find several shops including Mikasa (#95) and Flemington Glass (#156) and a number of nice lunchtime restaurants. Flemington Glass has sprouted annexes like crazy, so you can find not only glass there but also pewterware and dinnerware. The historic Main Street district also includes some nice Victorian Bed & Breakfasts and the the old County Courthouse if you want to combine some sightseeing with your shopping (see "Unique Towns" chapter).

Next stop is Liberty Village (follow signs—it has a huge parking lot behind the railroad tracks). Liberty Village started out in the 1970s as a restored colonial village, but converted into an outlet center not much later. The white clapboard buildings and brick walkways lend a pleasant air to the job of bargain hunting. Though the ambience is pleasant, the prices are higher these days, and the size of some of the sixty stores seems to have shrunk. At the Van Heusen outlet, for instance, men's jackets were once available at good discounts. Now, the jackets are gone and it's down to shirts and ties. Which is not to say you can't find bargains anymore—just that they won't be much different from department store sale prices. But Ann Klein, Hanes, Corning, Timberland, and many other outlet regulars are available here, and Ralph Lauren has a building all to himself. Somewhere along the way, pick up the shopping booklets that contain maps and discount coupons.

Next to Liberty Village is Turntable Junction, an old-fashioned green surrounded by specialty shops and a cozy English restaurant where you can stop for lunch or tea. And during the warmer months and at Christmas, the Black River and Western Railroad (an excursion train) runs along the tracks that separate the shops from the parking lot.

Over at Heritage Place (Rt. 31 and Church St.) you'll find another small complex of stores that includes Reebok, Rockport, Wamsutta, and a Levi's outlets. South of the Flemington Circle on Rt. 202/31 you pass yet another discount mall: this one called Circle Outlet Center, although it may be converted into a standard mall in the future.

As more and more outlet centers open, Flemington no longer has a monopoly on the franchise, but when it comes to pleasant surroundings and good, reasonably priced restaurants, this town certainly takes the prize. However, don't be surprised if particular stores have closed or moved elsewhere.

> **LOCATION:** Rt. 78 to Rt. 31 south, or Rt. 202. From Flemington Circle follow signs for "Business District." **TELEPHONE:** 908-788-5729; Liberty Village, 908-782-8550. **WEBSITE:** www.premiumoutlets.com.

Secaucus Outlets

Set in one of the busiest areas of New Jersey, just the other side of the Meadowlands Complex, the outlets here are dispersed over a huge area in between warehouses, office buildings, streets, and flat open spaces. You will definitely need a map. Fortunately, you can pick one up at the first outlet mall you hit (Outlets at the Cove), which is conveniently placed on Meadowlands Parkway. This small enclosed mall features air conditioning, clean restrooms, and a few designer outlets. At one of the stores here you can pick up a Secaucus booklet that includes a map and usually offers discount coupons as well.

As you drive farther to streets like Enterprise Avenue and Hartz Way, you will find several large outlet stores devoted to a single name. Mikasa China and Glassware and Liz Claiborne each have their own building, chock full of merchandise at a 20 to 30 percent discount. Of course, if you hit a sale you can realize even further savings, and many people put themselves on the mailing list to take advantage of these. You will also find a number of discount chains (such as Linens 'n Things) in the complex. The Syms clothing store takes up a full square block.

The Harmon Cove Outlet Center (20 Enterprise Ave.) is a large enclosed mall with a variety of shops of varying value. But it also contains a food court ringed by food counters where you can rest your feet and partake of pizza, chicken, ice cream, and other types of fast food. Further on, there's another small enclosed mall, called the Designer Outlet Gallery (55 Hartz Way), which includes designers like Anne Klein. If you check your map and drive around the maze of streets, you'll find that there are other little outlet enclaves within the general Secaucus territory. Even the MSNBC headquarters is located somewhere here.

Although the drive to Secaucus and the hunt for bargains can be exhausting, once you have found the store that fits your needs or carries the name brand you want, the trip will certainly seem worth it. And if you wait for the special warehouse sales (Mikasa has one, twice a year), you can stock up generously on all your gift needs.

HOURS: Daily. Individual stores vary. **LOCATION:** Secaucus. Take N.J. Turnpike, Exit 16W to Rt. 3 east to Meadowlands Parkway. **TELEPHONE:** 201-348-4780. **WEBSITE:** www.secaucusoutlets.com.

Jersey Gardens Mall

This is the ultimate Jersey experience—an indoor mall that is also an outlet mall. Since it's set in Elizabeth, right off Exit 13A of the Turnpike, it has the advantage of being in the special 3 percent tax zone (that's for nonclothing items). It also has bus service from NJ Transit, from Manhattan, and even from the Newark Liberty Airport. Since the mall is in close proximity to the huge Toys R Us outlet and the Ikea furniture store and also has a megaplex movie theater attached to one side and a Rex Plex sports entertainment center close to the other, you can assume that the parking lot here will always be full.

Inside the mall, there are plenty of tables at the food court, free strollers and wheelchairs to use, plus a huge play area for the kids and sporadic entertainment in the courtyard—so don't be surprised if people come here en famille. To shop? To camp out? Who knows?

The corners of the mall are anchored by mega-versions of discount chains such as Marshalls, Filene's Basement, Burlington Clothing Factory, and Cohoes. Between the anchors are outfits such as Off Saks 5th Avenue, Neiman Marcus Last Call, Daffy's, and Wilson's Leather Outlet besides the usual outlet lineup of Bass, Hanes, Dress Woman, and so forth. A few stores sport high-class names where you can buy a $250 Louis Ferragmo tie for $125. The mall also features a bar/restaurant, a concierge desk, and lots of special events.

HOURS: Open daily. Hours vary by season. **LOCATION:** 651 Kapkowski Rd., Elizabeth (Union County). Use N.J. Turnpike, Exit 13A. **TELEPHONE:** 1-877-SAY-VALU. **WEBSITE:** www.jerseygardens.com.

Other New Jersey Outlets

The Circle Factory Outlet Center: Located just off Route 35 in Manasquan at the Jersey shore, this center offers a smattering of outlets, including Corning Ware, Mikasa, and Geoffrey Beene. It's not in the most convenient place, right off a busy traffic circle. But it services shore tourists and locals alike. **TELEPHONE:** 732-223-2300.

Olde Lafayette Village: In the northern part of the state, where Rts. 15 and 94 meet just below the town of Lafayette in Sussex County, this "village" is half regular stores and half outlets. Colonial-style attached buildings feature bridal shops and fudge emporiums right next to such outlet regulars as Corning Ware, Cape Isle Knitters, and Van Heusen. TELEPHONE: 973-383-8323. Lafayette also has a nice antiques commune at the center of the town.

Princeton Forrestal Village: At the junction of Rt. 1 and College Rd. West is another addition to the outlet scene. This started out in the 1980s as a yuppie mall with all sorts of boutiques and gourmet shops. Now there are more than thirty-five outlets here, including many regulars plus Workbench Furniture, Lady Leslie, a tile shop, and some designer fashions. You'll find some nice eating places, too. TELEPHONE: 609-799-7400. WEBSITE: www.princetonoutlets.com.

Jackson Factory Outlets: A popular newcomer to the outlet scene is on Rt. 537 off Rt. 195 in Jackson (Ocean County), just a few miles west of Six Flags Great Adventure. It's not that big, but you can find Brooks Brothers, Big Dog Sportswear (they seem to be everywhere), and Samsonite, for example. Since this outlet was built from scratch, it has a convenient design. The connected buildings sport a late-Victorian beachhouse look and form a triangle around the parking lot, which makes a shorter walk for customers. The covered walkways are another plus. TELEPHONE: 732-833-0503. WEBSITE: www.jacksonoutletvillage.com.

Dutch Neck Village: This small country village of quaint specialty shops is built in colonial and country style on the grounds of the original Dutch Neck Landscaping nursery. Its brick paths and landscaped grounds include a display garden with 200 varieties of plants. Two small museums contain displays of old home furnishings memorabilia. Special sales and festivals occur throughout the year. HOURS: Mon.–Sat., 10–5; some shops open on Sun., 12–4. LOCATION: 97 Trench Rd., Bridgeton (Cumberland County). Rt. 49 to Fayette St.; go one mile south, then right on Trench Rd. TELEPHONE: 856-451-2188. WEBSITE: www.dutchneckvillage.com.

NEARBY OUT-OF-STATE OUTLETS
Woodbury Common

For people who live in the northeastern section of New Jersey, this is a popular shopping stop. It's in New York State, so you don't get the advantage of no sales tax on clothes that you do in New Jersey and Pennsylvania. What you do get is lots of stores—220 at the moment, and 25 of them are shoe stores! Scads of clothing stores and a little of everything else (Judith Leiber, Harry & David, Godiva). Also prominent are heavy names like Armani, Versace, and Prada, that undoubtedly attract people here.

The place is divided into color quadrants, with a Red Apple Court, a Green, a Blue, etc. But since this is an outdoor "common," you must walk from one store to the other in all sorts of weather. Directional maps are available. A trolley tram makes the rounds of the parking lot to take you to the different sections, because once you've managed to find a parking space there's no way you're going to give it up—not during the heavy pre-Christmas season, anyway! A fast food court in the Red section and a sit-down Applebee's are often crowded, but in warm weather there are many hot dog and ice cream vendors outdoors. Wear good walking shoes—there's lots of territory to cover here. Special events in summer.

LOCATION: Rt. 32, Central Valley, NY. Take Garden State Parkway to Rt. 87 (N.Y. Thruway) to Harriman, Exit 16. **TELEPHONE:** 914-928-4000. **WEBSITE:** www.premiumoutlets.com.

Reading

Reading is the grandaddy of outlet towns. It was here that someone decided to take old factory buildings and turn them into stores that would sell directly to the customer. For years people would drive from all over to get these manufacturer's goods at 50 percent off. Nowadays, with outlets everywhere, Reading has lost some of its draw. Still, the buses and cars come, and some real bargains can be found. Things have changed over the years. Outlets now take charge cards (they used to insist on cash or checks), and there are several decent eating places around. On the other hand, many of the shops are actually discount stores rather than true factory outlets.

The original Reading Outlet Center can now be found in a series of buildings, some of them of the old-factory, red-brick variety, where you have to walk upstairs. Others are new and low-slung. Building 1, the biggest, is on Windsor Street between N. 9th and Moss. Building 2 is across the street, while Building 3 is cater-cornered to 1. Others are on Douglass and Oley Streets. A variety of discount shops are stuffed into these buildings. In one or the other of them, you will find the Kleins (Calvin and Anne), the Jones New Yorks, Liz Claiborne, and many other "names."

A highly popular destination is the VF Outlet in the neighboring town of Wyomissing (801 Hill Ave.). This "village" includes three huge buildings and several smaller ones. The big Red and Blue Buildings offer racks and racks of Vanity Fair robes and nightgowns at half price, plus lots of other goods. The complex is surrounded by gates and parking lots (with preferred parking for tour buses). There's a food court in the basement of the Blue Building.

Companies owned by VF (Lee jeans, Jantzen sportswear, Health-Tex) sell their goods for 50 percent off. Other sections in the complex include American Tourister and Black and Decker, whose prices vary from 10 to 40 percent off. Across the street, the Designer Place sports a clean, well-lit interior. You'll find some high fashion names here, plus a cafe for noshes and a Godiva chocolate outlet.

The various buildings have colored flags, and their names are clearly marked. That's so you don't get lost in the shopping canyons forever and can find a landmark for your bus or car. On heavy shopping days at the VF Outlet, you may have to park blocks away and take a shuttle to the buildings.

HOURS: Most stores open Mon.–Sat., 9:30–5:30 or 9:30 and Sun. 12–5 (except Jan. and Feb.). **LOCATION:** Rt. 78 to U.S. 222 to Rt. 422 west to Reading, PA. VF Outlet is on Park and Hall Rds., Wyomissing. **TELEPHONE:** Reading, 610-373-549; VF, 800-772-8336. **WEBSITES:** Reading, www.outletsonline.com/roc; VF, www.vffo.com.

Franklin Mills Mall

While many outlet centers evolved from nearby factories or the conversion of unused buildings, Franklin Mills is a huge, superplanned, hi-tech mall designed as a magnet for shoppers from Philadelphia and New Jersey. It combines the convenience of an indoor mall with the bargain prices of discount stores and outlets.

Inside the 1.8 million square foot complex, you will find hundreds of stores, food courts (a square of tables ringed by numerous fast food eateries), plus entertainment and resting courts. Each corner of the huge complex is anchored by a large store, and each section of the mall is color coded and everything is on one level. The planners seem to have thought of everything, except (since undoubtedly they were men) enough ladies rooms!

You can also find a Levi Strauss outlet, plus chain discount shops like Linens 'n Things and Flemington Fashion among the many stores. There are arcades, movies, and other diversions for kids who are dragged along. Some courts have banks of TV screens.

HOURS: Mon.–Sat., 10–9:30; Sun., 11–6. **LOCATION:** Northeast Philadelphia, Rt. 95 to Woodhaven Rd. exit; turn right onto Franklin Mills Blvd. **TELEPHONE:** 215-632-1500; 800–336-MALL.

The Crossings

Another village created by Premium Outlets (which also did Liberty Village and Woodbury Common) and a popular favorite for those who live in northwest Jersey, the Crossings is right off Rt. 80, exit 299, as you drive west to Tannersville, PA. The left-hand turn into the complex is badly planned, but once inside, there are several streets of discount stores in this manufactured "town." People come here for Coach handbags or Stone Mountain bags, Petite Sophisticate, Carter's children's wear, and several women's plus-size places. Also, there's Timberland, Hanes, and many other outlet regulars. The place is growing, and parking can be a problem, so get there early. A few eating places like Au Bon Pain and a small food court may be joined by others as the place grows.

TELEPHONE: 570-629-4658. WEBSITE: www.thecrossings.com.

Rehoboth Outlets

If you live in or are visiting South Jersey, the trip across the bay on the Cape May–Lewes Ferry is an enjoyable outing in itself. But many people combine it with the determined business of shopping at outlet malls. If you go by car (taking either the ferry or the Delaware Memorial Bridge), you will be in a better position to take home the big-ticket items you might pick up. For Delaware is a state without any sales tax. Rehoboth is about 4 miles from Lewes, where the ferry lands, but in the summertime there are shuttle buses that meet each ferry and take passengers to the outlets. There are 140 stores altogether strung out along Route 1 in three different outlet centers (each resembling a long strip mall), about a mile from each other. Among the stores you will find are Royal Doulton, Britches Great Outdoors, VF Factory Outlet, Wicker Outlet, Big Dog, Black & Decker, and Harry & David. Rehoboth also has beaches that are popular in summer, but the outlets keep customers coming even in the fall and winter. Motels are close by in case you want to sleep over and shop some more.

TELEPHONE: 302-226-9223. WEBSITE: www.shoprehoboth.com.

See also Penns Purchase (under Lahaska in "Unique Towns" chapter).

FLEA MARKETS

Englishtown Auction Sales

This is one of the world's largest flea markets, a vast dusty field set on the edge of Monmouth County's farm country. What you find is something like 300 garage sales going on side by side with 700 New

York street hawkers, all of them set up on tables covering a huge field. Add to that several farm stands with bins of fresh corn, tomatoes, melons, apples, and pumpkins. Then add several buildings filled with discount clothing booths, kielbasa and knish stands, a great bagel place, hamburgers and oriental food, and a complete bar and grill. Then add a cast of thousands worthy of a Cecil B. DeMille movie, and you have some idea of the immensity of the place. In fact, Englishtown Auction Sales has everything but an auction, a term that refers to the old days when cows were sold here, too.

The flea market is open weekends only, and it opens early. What you will find is a mass of memorabilia, knickknacks, new shoes, and old tires and hubcaps—practically anything in the world can be discovered here. A new bell for your bicycle, a collection of porcelain doorknobs, and garage sale "junque" are all mixed in with bargain basement clothing and cosmetics.

Those who search for collectibles can certainly find something of interest. Depression glass, comic books, paperweights, and German World War I helmets and medals are some that can be found. More collectibles (along with food stands) are in the buildings called Red, Green, Blue, and Brown. Englishtown Auction Sales offers you a chance to buy that elusive whatnot you could never find anywhere else. But, of course, the mainstay is new merchandise sold at discount. Parking is free, with one close-by lot charging a couple of dollars.

HOURS: Sat., 7–5; Sun., 9–5. **LOCATION:** 90 Wilson Ave., Englishtown (Monmouth County). Garden State Parkway, Exit 123 to Rt. 9 south. Travel 7.5 mi., then turn right on Texas Rd. to Rt. 527. Turn left, then south 3 miles. **TELEPHONE:** 732-446-9644.

Dover Flea Market

A flea market that ran for many years in Chester, then relocated to Dover, has now transformed itself into its own unique style. While the usual venue for such endeavors in New Jersey is some dusty country field or the asphalt parking lot of a stadium, this flea market takes place on the sidewalks of a small urban town. Automobile traffic is roped off for several blocks where the vendors place their stands. One advantage is that you can take the train to Dover; the flea market is only a few blocks from the station (although trains run infrequently on Sunday). Another is that cafes and restaurants are open on the main street, so you can sit down and have a regular lunch if you like. Vendors sell a variety of new clothes, jewelry, unique items, crafts, collectibles, souvenir items, baseball cards, and such. And you can always find a hot dog or funnel cake stand.

Dover, by the way, has its own antique stores on W. Blackwell Street, including Berman's Auction Gallery and the Iron Carriage Antique Center, although they may not be open on Sundays.

HOURS: Sundays, May–Dec. **LOCATION:** Rt. 80 to Rt. 10 (Dover) exit (Morris County). **TELEPHONE:** 800-555-6263.

Columbus Flea Market

This started out as a farmer's market and just grew and grew. It has rows and rows of tables filled with pocketbooks, sweatshirts, sweaters, scarves, crazy items, knockoff perfumes, etc., as well as "garage sale" items. It's also a traditional farmer's market with fresh produce brought in from the neighboring countryside.

The indoor buildings include many permanent "niche" stores plus a number of eating spots (hamburgers, bagels, etc.). In one of the buildings you can also find several Pennsylvania Dutch delicatessen counters, where you can buy Amish-style cold cuts and breads and freshly grown produce. Don't be surprised to find furniture, window frames, and other large items in the indoor sections.

HOURS: Thu., Sat., Sun., dawn to 3 P.M. **LOCATION:** 2919 Rt. 206, just south of Columbus (Burlington County). **TELEPHONE:** 609-267-0400. **WEBSITE:** www.columbusfarmersmarket.com.

Meadowlands Flea Market

Even though the Garden State Race Track is out of business (along with the Garden State Flea Market that used to occupy its parking lot on weekends), don't think that asphalt vendors have disappeared from the Jersey scene. The parking lot behind the Giants Stadium had always been a venue for sporadic computer flea markets, along with a hundred other things. But for the past few years a regular flea market has been up and running on Thursdays and Saturdays. It's open year-round, with more vendors on hand on Saturdays. About 600 vendors at tables and trucks parked on the blacktop sell clothing such as sweaters, socks, and handbags, plus CDs, DVDs, and a large smattering of specialties such as antique telephones or African art. Of course, there are food stands, with twisted pretzels, kielbasa, Italian ices, handmade chocolates, and the Amish bakeries that always seem to pop up at flea markets. Many standard vendors come back year after year, so people can come back to their favorites. The small admission fee on Saturdays may be waived for seniors and bus groups. The flea market takes place even when some games are on (most Giants games are on Sundays) but closes on certain holiday Saturdays and for the Hambletonian race in August. If a new retail/entertainment complex rises in the Meadowlands, this market might be crowded out, but in the meantime, enjoy!

HOURS: Thu. & Sat., 9–5. **LOCATION:** Meadowlands Parking Lot 17, East Rutherford (Bergen County). Take New Jersey Turnpike, Exit 16W, then follow signs. **TELEPHONE:** 888-445-6543 or 201-935-5474. **WEBSITE:** www.meadowlandsfleamarket.com.

Other New Jersey Flea Markets

Neshanic Flea Market: This smallish (5-acre) homespun flea market is a favorite with many who come back year after year. Known for its garden equipment sales, it also has a number of household items. Various collectibles, but no food. **HOURS:** Sun., 7–2. **LOCATION:** 100 Elm St., Neshanic Station (Hunterdon County). **TELEPHONE:** 908-369-3660.

New Egypt Flea Market Village and Auction: A collection of eighty small shops and outside tables, with antiques, collectibles, crafts, clothing, tools, used books, furniture, and other used items. Individual shops in older buildings. Outdoor tables can have everything from foundry type to garage sale items. Hours are 7–2, Sun. & Wed. Auction Sun. at 1. New Egypt is 6 miles west of Six Flags in Ocean County (Rt. 537). **TELEPHONE:** 609-758-2082.

Berlin Farmer's Market and Shopping Center: A mix of traditional Jersey truck farm produce and flea market items. Indoor market houses more than eighty-five stores, while 300–400 vendors in outdoor spaces show new and used merchandise, including antiques, collectibles, crafts, and fresh produce. Outdoor flea market open Sat. & Sun., 8–4. Inside shopping center open Thu. & Fri., 11–9:30; Sat., 10–9:30; Sun., 10–6. **LOCATION:** 41 Clementon Rd., Berlin (Camden County). Just off Rts. 30, 73, and 42 between Atco and Voorhees. **TELEPHONE:** 856-767-1284. **WEBSITE:** www.berlinfarmersmarket.com.

Note: For information on the Golden Nugget and Lambertville Antiques Flea Market, see the Lambertville listing in the "Unique Towns" chapter.

NEARBY OUT-OF-STATE FLEA MARKETS

Rice's Flea Market

If it's Tuesday, it must be Rice's. That's the day this 30-acre flea market comes to life on a flat dirt field set on a back road near New Hope. They're open on Saturdays, too. Officially named Rice's Country Market and Auction, it has a reputation for quality. To the neophyte it doesn't look much different than any other flea market. In fact, many of the vendors who set up tables here can be found at other flea markets other days of the week.

The main virtue of Rice's seems to be its size. Although the dirt field where it is held is huge, getting past all the tables is not unmanageable. You can actually walk the whole market in a morning and get a chance to peruse all the bargains. Get there early, because by 1 P.M. most vendors are packing up. You can find specialty items here—one vendor sells only Guatamalan handmade goods; another specializes in ribbons and laces. There may be several booths of patterned sweaters. But the most common items tend to be college sweatshirts at reduced prices, tube socks, fancy scarves at ten or twelve dollars, and some brand-name toiletries.

Indoor stands sell coffee, bagels, doughnuts, and funnel cakes (giant intricately designed crullers with powdered sugar on top). There are also a few merchandise vendors inside the small buildings, but this is primarily an outdoor flea market. No real place for lunch, though there are some hot dog vendors and locals with fresh bread and fresh produce.

HOURS: Every Tue. & Sat. and some holidays. **LOCATION:** New Hope, PA. Rt. 202 to Aquetong, right on Green Hill Rd., then another right. **TELEPHONE:** 215-297-5993.

Pocono Bazaar Flea Market

One of the largest in the area, this flea market runs all year-round and has a smattering of everything. Since the place is one mile north of Marshall's Creek, lots of people stop by on their way to Pocono vacation spots. So when someone tells you she bought her bag at that "flea market—you know the one on 209," this is the place.There is a central indoor market with permanent booths and scores of outdoor tables. Collectibles such as porcelain dolls, old comic books, and Civil War mementos can be found at the permanent stands, while tables of white socks, T-shirts, sweaters, "designer" perfumes, and a hodge-podge of garage-sale items can be found outside.

HOURS: Sat., Sun., 9–5. **LOCATION:** Marshalls Creek, PA. Rt. 80, Exit 309, then Rt. 209 north for 5 miles. **TELEPHONE:** 570-223-8640. **WEBSITE:** www.poconobazaar.com.

Note: Flea market hours and offerings change constantly. Always telephone first.

Other Outings

The Sterling Hill Mining Museum includes many structures from the old working days plus a tour of an underground mine. *(Photo courtesy B. Kozykowski/Sterling Hill Mining Museum)*

POPULAR SITES

The State House

You don't have to be on a political mission to visit Trenton. The golden-domed State House is now open to the public after years of refurbishing, by guided tour only. One can see the architectural richness of this building, which predates the 1930s "institutional" style of many government structures. It is the second oldest state capitol that has been in continuous use.

Inside, the main hall is lit by Victorian-style chandeliers, once fueled by gas. There are arches of faux marble and pilasters of dark wood. One eye-catching piece in the center of the hall is a porcelain Boehm sculpture that features the state tree (the red oak), the state bird (the goldfinch), and even the state insect (the honeybee). The rotunda features paintings of the governors. If the legislature is not in session, you can visit the handsome Senate Chamber with its stained glass skylight or the General Assembly Room. Sometimes the Governor's Reception Room (which has even more portraits of governors) is open.

One also discovers some interesting Jersey facts on the tour. For instance—we don't have a lieutenant governor, and the legislature works only part time. Some past governors were George McClellan, the one-time Civil War general, and Woodrow Wilson, the only New Jersey governor to make it to the White House. Tours run hourly, and groups of more than ten should reserve in advance. There is a cafeteria on the third floor off the parking garage.

HOURS: Mon.–Fri., 10–3, Sat., 12–3. **ADMISSION:** Free.
LOCATION: 125 W. State St., Trenton (Rt. 29 to Calhoun St. exit).
TELEPHONE: 609-633-2709. **WEBSITE:** www.njleg.state.nj.us.

The Battleship *New Jersey*

The most decorated battleship in the United States was also one of the most fought-over in New Jersey as three different cities wanted the privilege of offering a berth to this refurbished ship. The Camden waterfront won out, and now the *New Jersey*, with its turret guns bristling, is docked close to the State Aquarium and across the river from Philadelphia (whose shipyards gave birth to it).

The *New Jersey* is one of the largest battleships ever built. Designed for a crew of 117 officers and 1,804 enlisted men in World War II, the ship had nineteen battle and campaign stars and served in World War II, Korea, Vietnam, and the Persian Gulf. Highlights of the two-hour guided tour include the ship's 16-inch gun turrets, Admiral Halsey's original cabin, the communications center, two mess areas, and crew quarters. You can watch a launch of a tomahawk missile and see how it's tracked in a virtual combat engagement room. There's also a multi-room museum where you can learn about duties on board. You also have the chance to crawl inside a gun turret, just as the crew did. The tour includes a lot of walking and climbing on ladders, both outdoors and inside. For those not up to ladder climbing, you can still walk on the main deck and enjoy a sitting room that features two 15-minute videos about the ship and about other parts of the tour. There is a snack bar onboard in the crew's mess, and there are two ship stores, one onboard and another on land.

HOURS: Apr.–Sept., Daily, 9–5; Oct.–Mar., daily, 9–3. **ADMISSION:** $$$. Discounts: Seniors, children, vets with ID. Active duty, free. **LOCATION:** Delaware River Waterfront, Camden (Camden County). **TELEPHONE:** 866-877-6262. **WEBSITE:** www.battleshipnj.org.

New Jersey Naval Museum

The New Jersey Naval Museum's USS *Ling* 297 submarine is only 312 feet long and 27 feet wide, and when you consider that eighty-one men and twenty-four torpedoes were aboard during its active career in 1945, you realize that this is no place for someone with claustrophobia. Nowadays, most of the torpedoes and many of the berths have been removed to allow tour groups to move about. Indeed, the inside seems surprisingly spacious. Tickets are bought at the museum building, which also houses a number of war pictures and paraphernalia, including the periscope prism from a Japanese sub.

Tours last about 45 minutes. You begin in the torpedo room, which still features two torpedoes. (No, they are not active.) These weapons were activated only after they left the tube; they also had to be aimed correctly, since a miss would give away the sub's position. Much of the time onboard the vessel was devoted to eating and cooking. When the *Ling* first left port, space was so dear that fresh fruit and vegetables had to be stacked in one of the showerheads. Tours include the Control Room, Maneuvering Room, Main Engine Room, sleeping quarters, and more; but the conning tower and its periscope are off-limits. You are allowed to handle certain equipment, including the wheels and gauges, and the guide sounds the diving signal, which may be memorable to some from a host of old war movies.

The Naval Museum complex also has a Vietnam-era patrol boat, a World War II Japanese Kaiten II suicide torpedo, and a German *Seehund* two-man coastal defense sub. An interesting place, both for older children and ex-servicemen. Birthday parties and scouting sleepovers are available.

HOURS: Thu.–Sun., 10–4; mid-Nov. to mid-Mar., weekends, 10–4. **ADMISSION:** $. Discounts: Children. **LOCATION:** 78 River Street, Hackensack (Bergen County). **TELEPHONE:** 201-342-3268. **WEBSITE:** www.njnm.com.

Sterling Hill Mine

The last operating zinc mine in New Jersey went out of business in 1986. You might wonder why anyone would want to keep and restore an old mine, but local people have put all their money and energy into it and for good reason. Besides the primary zinc deposits there are over 300 minerals in this area, half of which are found nowhere else. Dedicated townsfolk decided to keep the mine open for tours and use the buildings as a mining museum.

Tours of the mine are given at specific times (once a day during off-season, three times a day during summer). One thing you learn right away is to wear a jacket. It is 56 degrees all the time inside the mine, and it is often damp, too. Wear good, heavy shoes. Because the area of Ogdensburg and nearby Franklin has the world's largest deposits of fluorescent stones, an important stop on the tour is the "Rainbow Room." This is a wall that looks like ordinary rock when you first see it. The tour guide switches on an ultraviolet light and the red-fluorescent calcite and green-fluorescent willemite begin to glow in the half-dark. It looks like something from a science-fiction movie.

There is a lot of walking on this tour not only along the tracks of the mine itself, but in the other buildings as well. The museum— where the tour usually starts—includes one huge exhibit hall which was once used by the miners to change clothing. You can see the high metal baskets where they dumped their wet outer garments. Displays include dinosaur prints, rows of zinc products (including tires), and a whole range of mining paraphernalia. In the mine-office building you can buy hot dogs from the grill or peruse the gift shop, which offers plenty of mineral specimens. There is also an outdoor picnic area. An interesting tour, both for scout troops or for grown-ups, and it can easily be combined with a visit to the Franklin Mineral Museum, 3 miles away. You can also look for minerals yourself on the last Sunday of the month. The tour is not recommended for children under 6.

HOURS: Apr. 1–Nov. 30, daily, 10–5. **ADMISSION:** $$ **LOCATION:** 30 Plant St., Ogdensburg (Sussex County). Rt. 517 to Brooks Flat Rd. to Plant Rd. **TELEPHONE:** 973-209-7212. **WEBSITE:** www.sterlinghill.org.

Northlandz

"Northlandz" is a combination of the Great American Railway, doll museum, La Peep Dollhouse, art gallery, and a frontier-style music hall. All are housed in a Greek temple of a building that's a popular destination for grandparents, families, and railroad buffs.

The huge model railroad covers 52,000 square feet and uses enough wood to build forty-two houses and plenty of plaster to create small towns and great gorges. There are 115 trains and 8 miles of track that cut through looming mountains, deep quarries, and unique cityscapes. They go over bridges up to 40 feet long, above rivers, and past alpine scenes. Visitors walk about a mile as they travel on a ramp that rises 3½ stories to view the massive layout from different angles. You see Pennsylvania coal-mining towns, horses grazing on sloping hills, and marching bands. Some scenes are built with humor in mind. A hotel "with a view" perches precariously over a deep gorge. For drama there's a deep canyon with a complete mining town set beneath the looming railroad bridge. Some towns are peopled with miniature figures, while farms may have horses and cows set out to pasture.

The La Peep Dollhouse is not free standing but a series of ninety-four miniature rooms set into the wall, featuring home scenes including a library, indoor pool, and ballroom with doggie band. A doll museum of 150 large collectible dolls in fancy costume can be seen toward the end of the tour. The American Music Hall, in the style of a Western saloon, features a 2,000-pipe organ, which is played several times a day. Northlandz also includes a cafe and a gift shop filled with railroad memorabilia. Allow at least two hours. In good weather, there's also an outdoor three-quarter scale scenic railroad train you can ride for an extra fee.

HOURS: Weekdays, 10:30–4; weekends, 10:30–6. **ADMISSION:** Adults: $$$. Discounts: Seniors, children. Under 2 free. **LOCATION:** 495 Rt. 202 south, Flemington (Hunterdon County), 2 miles north of Flemington Circle. **TELEPHONE:** 908-782-4022. **WEBSITE:** www.northlandz.com.

New Jersey Renaissance Kingdom

This "faire" began in a large park in Somerset County, so the king and queen, knights and ladies still rule the Kingdom of Somerset, although this multiweekend Renaissance festival has moved to the South Mountain Reservation in Essex County. Follow a running storyline of love, knights, and knaves as costumed actors engage in swordplay and take various roles. A "living chess game" is part of the entertainment, as are storytelling and puppeteers for children. Grownups can join in a Maypole dance, run around the "forest," watch weddings, and so forth. A total of twenty different shows are put on each day. Food court and vendors are on hand. The Renaissance Kingdom runs on six weekends starting in mid-May. This group also hosts a Haunted Village at the Turtle Back Zoo in West Orange on weekends in October. Tour guides lead visitors through some scary places, filled with detailed scenery and special effects.

HOURS: Kingdom, late May–June, Sat.–Sun., 11–6; Haunted Village, Oct. weekends, 6:30–10 P.M. **ADMISSION:** Kingdom, $$$. Discounts: Seniors, children; Village, $$. Discounts: Children. **LOCATION:** South Mountain Reservation, South Orange (Essex County). **TELEPHONE:** 732-271-1119. **WEBSITE:** www.NJKingdom.com.

Medieval Times

Combine a horse show, a night club, a dinner theater, and a Renaissance festival, put it all in a circuslike arena inside a huge stucco castle, plunk it down near one of New Jersey's busiest intersections (right near the Meadowlands), and you have the northern version of Medieval Times. Here you get not one, but several jousts, a narrative of times gone by, and a chance to eat dinner without any utensils.

When you enter the cavernous castle to buy your tickets you are handed a paper hat with a special color. This color will determine which section you sit in, and which knight you root for. These colored hats are a great gimmick, for it is in cheering for a particular champion that the audience becomes part of the show. (The green knight is usually the villain.)

After a chance to look at medieval artifacts and inspect a torture dungeon (and buy such stuff as shields and banners at the gift shop), you are ushered into the arena where chairs are set against long banquet tables. These are set in tiers so that everybody in the huge oval arena can see the show.

And now, the menu. First, there is soup (served in a porringer), then chicken, potato, and barbecued ribs, plus dessert, coffee, or punch. Since you are supposed to eat this all with your fingers, the serving wench hands you a huge napkin that is best tucked into your collar in standard Henry VIII style.

As for the show—there is a story of sorts about a king who's come back from the war and orders a tournament. The show includes some fancy prancing by the horses and a display of skills by the knights. Then it's on to the jousts. The knights not only fight on horseback, but engage in swordplay after being unhorsed, and of course there are several good knights and one bad apple. After a few jousts and lots of clashing swords, the final victor is announced and the villain is sent to his doom. All this while the wenches are either serving supper or selling you pictures, banners, or wine.

After the show, some families stay around until their knight shows up to autograph the picture or shield their kids have bought. A popular spot for pre-teen parties and even dating couples, but skip the torture museum if you have young children along.

> **HOURS:** Wed., Thu., 7:30 P.M.; Fri., Sat., 8 P.M.; Sun., 4:30 P.M. **ADMISSION:** $$$$$. Discounts: Children. **LOCATION:** 149 Polito Ave., Lyndhurst (Bergen County). Rt. 3 to Rt. 17 south to Lyndhurst. **TELEPHONE:** 800-828-2945; 201-933-2220. **WEBSITE:** www.medievaltimes.com.

The Meadowlands

Interested in a behind-the-scenes look at the Meadowlands complex? Want to see how it feels to run out of the tunnel and onto the field at Giants Stadium, or view the field from the press box at Meadowlands Racetrack? It's part of the guided group tour of this complex, an insider's view that includes a visit to the locker room. Tours are by appointment and require a minimum of ten people, but they are free and last an hour and a half. **HOURS:** Mon.–Sat., 10 A.M. or 12:30 P.M. You must furnish your own transportation throughout the day, but this seems like a good one for youth activity groups. Call the NJSEA Office of Public Affairs at 201-460-4038. Most people, of course, head to the Meadowlands for the numerous sports and entertainment events held there throughout the year. These include the following.

Meadowlands Racetrack: Both harness and flat racing have their season at this major track, which is the home of the Hambletonian, harness racing's leading event. The facility offers a glassed-in, climate-controlled grandstand. There are restaurants for those who want to combine a night at the track with dining. The fancy one is Pegasus, on the top level, with a bird's-eye view of the race, buffet stations, and high prices. Or you can opt for the tiered restaurant, which gives a better view of the track but rather ordinary food. For those watching the race from the grandstand, a large 15 × 36 foot video matrix screen allows you to see the action on the far side of the track and also flashes results almost immediately.

Giants Stadium: The stadium is named for the NFL football team that makes its home there, but the Jets (so far) and college football teams also play on the same turf. The stadium has a seating capacity of 78,000 and has a video matrix scoreboard that delights the kids and skyboxes that delight corporations. The parking lot also hosts a flea market (q.v.) plus antique shows, petting zoos, and a three-week carnival in summer. Tailgating before football games is a tradition here. The stadium also hosts special headliner concerts and other events.

At press time the Continental Airlines Arena section of the Meadowlands was scheduled to be torn down and replaced by a retail/ entertainment complex. Check the Website for details.

PARKING: Fees vary. Come early, especially for football games. **LOCATION:** Off Rt. 3, East Rutherford (Bergen County). **DIRECTIONS:** From New Jersey Turnpike north, Exit 16W for direct access; from Turnpike south, take Exit 18W. **TELEPHONE:** 201-935-8500. **WEBSITE:** www.meadowlands.com.

Other Historic Outings

Doyle's Unami Farms: Learn the history of early settlers and Indians who once hunted these fields. Visits are tailored for each season. Take part in such activities as planting or harvesting crops, get hands-on demonstrations of farm machinery, and care for farm animals. Scenic hayrides and pony rides are offered. Indian field trips tailored for all age groups include a 30-minute presentation and a hayride to an Indian campsite to visit a fire pit discovered on the farm. Owner Richard Doyle is past president of the Archaeological Society of New Jersey and has collected thousands of Indian artifacts, some of which are included on the field trip. Open Apr.–Nov. Reservations required. **LOCATION:** 771 Mill Lane, Hillsborough (Somerset County), Rt. 206, west on Amwell Rd., right on E. Mountain Rd., then left on Mill Lane. **TELEPHONE:** 908-369-3187. **WEBSITE:** www.doyles-farm.com.

Eagle Rock 9/11 Memorial: A 160-foot-long granite wall with the names of the 9/11 victims inscribed on bronze plaques, plus several bronze monuments to the fallen at the World Trade Center, now stands at Eagle Rock Overlook. The park, which looks out on the Manhattan skyline, had become a spontaneous memorial after the tragedy, with flowers and flags placed on the stone wall. **LOCATION:** Eagle Rock Reservation, Eagle Rock Ave., West Orange (Essex County).

EXCURSION BOATS

The sight-seeing cruise has been with us for a long time; the fancier excursion cruise has become more popular within the last few years. Sightseeing usually involves some narration and access to hot dogs, soda, and beer. Excursion boats more often have cocktail bars, restaurant or buffet service, and music or entertainment. The entertainment may range from a single guitarist to a five-piece band. Here are some of the larger cruises that are currently afloat. The excursion-type vessel also caters to groups for birthdays, engagement parties, proms and business bashes.

Circle Line Tour: A standard sightseeing attraction for many years, the ferry leaves from Pier 83 at 42nd Street in New York City and travels around the island of Manhattan via the Hudson River, New York Harbor, East River, and Harlem River. There is the standard three-hour or a half-circle two-hour tour. (A one-hour tour departs from South Street Seaport for a ride around the harbor.) An announcer (or canned tape) points out the Statue of Liberty and all the monuments, skyscrapers, bridges, and churches, with appropriate anecdotes and facts. Too bad most of the tourists onboard don't understand English (although translation tapes may be available). Still, the big thrill is to wave at all the other excursion boats out there, and of course you do get to see New Jersey as well as New York when you're on the Hudson. Coffee and hot dogs available. Sailings vary by season and prices vary with the length of the tour. At one time the Circle Line picked up passengers on the New Jersey side in Jersey City. Who knows if they'll try it again someday. TELEPHONE: 212-563-3200. WEBSITE: www.circleline.com.

NY Waterways: It began as a commuter ferry between Weehawken and New York City. It filled a real need, leading to further service from Hoboken and Jersey City. A bus meets the ferry on the New York side and takes passengers to destinations within a confined loop. Now this popular line has expanded into limited cruises. You can take the boat from Weehawken to Kykuit, Sunnyside, and other Tarrytown destinations on weekends during warm weather— although you have to take a connecting ferry in New York City for these destinations. A popular ferry goes directly to Yankee Stadium and the Mets' Shea Stadium from Weehawken. There are also special outings on July 4, New Year's Eve, and for popular Broadway shows. TELEPHONE: 800-533-3779. WEBSITE: www.nywaterways.com.

The *Spirits*: The *Spirit of New Jersey* departs from Port Imperial in Weehawken (for a few years it was berthed at Liberty State Park) for a foray along the Hudson River. This popular cruise caters to individuals as well as diverse groups, including engagement parties, junior proms, and senior citizen groups. The two-hour lunch cruise includes a buffet, a narration of top tourist spots on both sides of the river (you can see both skylines at once), some cabaret-style entertainment, and a DJ for dancing. The dinner cruise is more party oriented, lasts three hours, and skips the narration but has more elaborate dance sessions. **TELEPHONE:** 866-211-3805. **WEBSITE:** www.spiritofnj.com.

The *Spirit of Philadelphia* departs from the pier at Penn's Landing (right across from the state aquarium) to cruise down the Delaware River and then circle back. The lunch cruise provides some historical narration for both sides of the river, and you pass the battleship *New Jersey* on one side and the historic ships on the Penn's Landing side. Cabaret entertainment, DJ, and dancing for lunch as with the *New Jersey;* evening parties available, too. **TELEPHONE:** 866-211-3808. **WEBSITE:** www.spiritofphiladelphia.com.

The *Cornucopia Princess* and *Destiny*: These are 130-foot dinner cruise ships that leave from the foot of Smith Street in Perth Amboy for champagne brunch and dinner cruises. Both the three-deck *Princess* and the two-deck *Destiny* feature "elegant" dining. Dinner and Saturday luncheon cruises go to Manhattan, while a shorter Sunday brunch cruise explores Raritan Bay. Live band for dancing on every cruise. Advance reservations required. Call for boarding times. **TELEPHONE:** 732-697-9500. **WEBSITE:** www.cornucopiacruise.com.

A. J. *Meerwald*: This is New Jersey's first and only tall ship! Actually, it's a 115-foot oyster schooner that has been restored and is berthed in Bivalve, not far from the project's small museum. Luckily, the schooner also visits other ports (such as Highlands, Philadelphia, and Cape May) during warm weather. From spring through fall, it takes on paying passengers, who can help hoist the rigging and trim the sails. Typical trips last 2½ hours. There are also sunset sails. In spring and fall, it's booked for school groups. Morning, afternoon, or evening sails: $$$$. Advance reservations recommended. Discounts: Children. **LOCATION:** 2800 High St., Bivalve (Cumberland County). **TELEPHONE:** 800-485-3072. **WEBSITE:** www.ajmeerwald.org.

EXCURSION RAILROADS

Black River & Western Railroad: New Jersey's best known excursion trains (both steam engine and diesel) operate from Stangl Road in Flemington, next to the outlet shops of Liberty Village, and travel to Ringoes and back three to four times a day. You can also board in Ringoes, get off in Flemington, and return on a later train. The trip meanders through the woods and farms of scenic Hunterdon County. **HOURS:** Thu.–Sun., July and Aug.; weekends, Mar.–June and

Sept.–Dec. 15. The Jack Frost Special operates Saturday afternoons, Jan.–Mar., between Ringoes and Three Bridges, with Flemington as the intermediate stop. Fare: $$. Discounts: Children. Under 3 free. Call 908-782-9600 for boarding times. **WEBSITE:** www.brwrr.com.

Pine Creek Railroad: This popular attraction at Allaire State Park (q.v.) takes riders on a ten-minute trip. This authentic narrow-gauge steam train ride is one of several park attractions. The train operates mostly during the summer season and is located on the left-hand side of the parking lot. **TELEPHONE:** 732-938-5524.

See also New Hope and Ivyland (in the "Unique Towns" chapter under New Hope).

WINERY TOURS

Let's face it, a winery tour is just about the most popular kind of industrial tour there is. The art of wine making is so ancient, and the slightly fermented air in the cellars so heady, that there is often a party air about these outings. And since wine tasting is involved, everyone seems to have a good time. But although most of the wineries have tastings, not all of them offer tours.

A fast-growing segment of New Jersey's agricultural scene, wineries seem to be popping up all over. New ones have sprung up in Warren, Hunterdon, and Somerset Counties. While many do not have traditional tours, all welcome visitors on weekends for tastings. And there are many festivals on tap. Even without a festival, tracking down wineries on fall weekends is a popular activity for many people. And tracking it is, because some of these places are pretty far out in the country where street signs don't exist. Luckily the New Jersey Wine Council puts out a map, complete with directions. Call 609-292-8853 for this or go to www.newjerseywines.com for a list and an online map of the "wine-tasting" trail.

As for tours, try the following.

The Renault Winery

This winery near Atlantic City used to call itself the best little tourhouse in New Jersey. It certainly is the oldest winery in New Jersey (and even the whole country, according to their brochure). It is situated way out in the Pine Barrens about 16 miles northwest of Atlantic City, where the sandy soil lends itself well to grape production. The entrance and brick patio give it a classic Mediterranean look. Now that the management books weddings and other catered affairs, the tours do not seem as imporant to them. However, they still run tours for groups, and if you show up during open hours you can latch on to one if it is just starting out.

The tour includes a sip of wine and some history of Renault. The original family brought the grapes over from Europe in the 1860s, but the winery is no longer owned by the Renault clan. Of the several rooms you visit, one is full of antique wine-making equipment, another is devoted to a collection of prized Venetian glassware. Then it's into the cellars, where giant vats store the wine. These oak and redwood vats are fifty and sixty years old and would have to be replaced today by stainless steel, as the old cooper's craft is lost.

The guide explains how the wine is poured off, and you see early wine presses and dosage machines. One salient fact they tell here is never to buy cooking wine. It seems that food companies buy the wineries' rejects, then add salt (that's a law), bottle it, and sell it. Of course, the tour winds up at the gift shop where there are many accesory items for sale as well as the wine itself.

Renault Winery also serves lunches at a charming bistro outside the main building called the Wine Garden. A gourmet restaurant, set in an old cask room, is open by reservation for dinner and brunch. For the casual tourist, there are still some down-home attractions like a grape-stomping festival in the fall and, of course, the tours.

HOURS: Open daily; tours Mon.–Sat., 10–4. **ADMISSION:** $. Under 18 free. **LOCATION:** 72 North Bremen Ave., Egg Harbor City (Atlantic County). Garden State Parkway, Exit 44 from north, right on Moss Mill Rd., then 6 miles to Bremen Ave. From Atlantic City, take Rt. 30 to Bremen Ave. **TELEPHONE:** 609-965-2111. **WEBSITE:** www.renaultwinery.com.

Other New Jersey Wineries

The newer wineries (which often look like suburban ranch houses) are run scientifically and feature fiberglass and steel equipment, so there isn't much to see on a tour and the information tends to be technical. The big thing is the wine tasting. At a long bar, an attendant will pour wine into little cups and explain its type and texture. Often he or she will start with light, dry wines and proceed to woody and fruit-flavored ones. Naturally, you are expected to buy a few bottles after all this work.

However, most wineries will go out of the way for a group and treat you to a full dissertation and perhaps a tour of the actual vineyards. One of these is the **Alba Winery** (908-995-7800), which we visited with a group. In this case, the winemaster addressed the group and explained the difference between brix and brie (pronounced the same way) and told us all about reading labels and sniffing corks. Of course, the group got a series of small cups of wine—fruit-flavored ones are big in this part of the state. The tastings take place in a special room set up with cafe tables and chairs. The winery is also a venue for parties, jazz festivals, corporate shindigs, and open-house events. **LOCATION:** 269 Rt. 627, Finesville. **TELEPHONE:** 908-995-7800. **WEBSITE:** www.albavineyards.com.

When it comes to special events, no one seems to have as many as the **Four Sisters Winery** in Warren County. They host a strawberry festival, an Indian pow-wow, hayrides in the fall, chocolate specials on Valentines Day and of course the ever popular grape-stomping parties. Spring, summer, and fall, something always seems to be going on here, right next to the Matarosso Vegetable Market (the same family operates both). As for the barefoot grape-stomping parties—these include food, wine, and the right to enter an open barrel and squish grapes through your toes. (Great anger therapy.) The Four Sisters also has regular visiting hours. **LOCATION:** 10 Doe Hollow Road (Rt. 519), Belvidere. **TELEPHONE:** 908-475-3671. **WEBSITE:** www.foursisterswinery.com.

Most of the eighteen or so New Jersey wineries combine forces for a large spring or fall wine-tasting festival, where food, entertainment, and wine are served in an open field. Most recently this event has taken place at Waterloo Village (q.v.), but sometimes a winery will host it.

Right across the river, in Pennsylvania, the **Sand Castle Winery** offers popular tours. This attractive building isn't quite a castle, but the view of the grape vines running in straight rows down the hill and the Delaware River beyond is quite reminiscent of Europe. In fact, the vineyard was developed by brothers from Czechoslovakia in the early 1990s and offers European-style wines. They haved a variety of tours: drop-ins can take the 20-minute quickie, while those who reserve tours can choose from a 45-minute barrel tour to longer versions that include cheese, crackers, or even lunch. Price varies with length of tour. **HOURS:** Open daily, except for winter months. **LOCATION:** 755 River Road, Erwinna, PA. **TELEPHONE:** 800-722-9463. **WEBSITE:** www.sandcastlewinery.com.

PICK-YOUR-OWN ORCHARDS

Who would have guessed that stooping over in the hot sun and picking strawberries, blueberries, etc. would become a "bonding" experience for young families? It's also attractive to people who want to save a little money and people who want to be sure their fruits and vegetables are fresh.

Usually you buy an empty basket and then fill it up, but arrangements vary. Also, weather conditions can throw off standard picking times. Most orchards are open from June until Halloween, when hayrides and contests often accompany the picking of pumpkins from the fields. Places that specialize in one fruit (such as blueberries) are open only during that season.

The best source for a list of picking farms is the Rutgers Cooperative Extension, which puts out a leaflet listing them by county and giving their farm specialties. In Burlington County, seven farms specialize in blueberries in Pemberton alone. The extension suggests calling first to see what is pickable at the moment, getting directions (most farms are out-a-ways), and learning prices. Most farms also have already-picked fruits and veggies for those who get tired or don't want to pick.

Some better-known farms include **Terhune's** (330 Cold Soil Road, Princeton, 609-924-2310), which also offers farm animals for petting and a busy cider mill. **Matarazzo Farms** (Rt. 519, Belvidere) runs a strawberry festival and a winery next door besides selling its own vegetables. You'll find Jersey peaches and sour cherries at **Battleview Orchards** at 91 Wemrock Road, Freehold, right next door to the Monmouth Battleground State Park (732-462-0756). The **Berry Farm** (732-294-0707), which specializes in raspberries, is in Colts Neck on Route 34, very close to **Delicious Orchards,** a gorgeous indoors market with fruits, vegetables, baked goods, and candies—definitely made for the gourmet who doesn't want the thrill of picking or making his own. Even in crowded Bergen County, you can find the **Demarest Farm** at 244 Werimus Road, Hillsdale (201-666-0472), for a little touch of country. And Mullica Hill in southern Jersey, known for its antique shops, also has several pick-your-own places.

You can get a county-by-county list from Rutgers Publication Distribution Service, Cook College, Rutgers University, Dudley Rd., P.O. Box 231, New Brunswick, NJ 08903-0231, or try their WEBSITE: www.ifplantscouldtalk.rutgers.edu. Also, your local county extension agent, and local newspapers and magazines, all carry listings of farms during the picking season.

THE HORSEY SET

Monmouth Park: Oceanport, Monmouth County (use Garden State Parkway, Exit 105). The oldest and to many, the most attractive of Jersey's racetracks, is close to the seashore. There are plenty of picnic tables along the outside track, so families often come and enjoy a day's outing. Indoor and outdoor seating at grandstand. Cafeteria, food stands, plus a restaurant in the clubhouse. Thoroughbred racing from late May through September. **TELEPHONE:** 732-222-5100. **WEBSITE:** www.monmouthpark.com.

Freehold Raceway: A beautiful track right in the heart of horse-breeding country. Standard-bred harness racing for trotters and pacers runs mid-Aug.–Feb., Tue.–Sat., and Mar.–May, Wed.–Sat. All post times 12:30 P.M. Also open days and evening year-round for simulcasting, so you can watch horse racing at other tracks around the country on TV monitors and place your bets on-site. **LOCATION:** 130 Park Avenue, Freehold (Monmouth County), junction of Rts. 9 and 33. **TELEPHONE:** 732-462-3800. **WEBSITE:** www.freeholdraceway. com.

Atlantic City Race Course: Very limited amount of thoroughbred racing. Call for schedule. Simulcasting daily. **LOCATION:** 4501 Black Horse Pike, Mays Landing (Atlantic County), junction of Rts. 40 and 322. Atlantic City Expressway, Exit 12. **TELEPHONE:** 609-641-2190.

Cowtown Rodeo: This is a real rodeo on the Professional Rodeo Cowboys Association circuit. It features bareback riding, calf roping, saddle bronc riding, steer wrestling, brahma bull riding, team roping, and girls' barrel racing. It's held every Saturday night from the last weekend of May to the last weekend of September at 7:30 P.M., rain or shine. The arena holds 4,000 on outdoor bleacher seats. There's also a farmer's market on Saturdays and Tuesdays that features more than 500 merchants. **ADMISSION:** Adults, $$. Discounts: Children 12 and under. **LOCATION:** 780 Rt. 40, Woodstown/Pilesgrove (Salem County). Eight miles east of Delaware Memorial Bridge, off exit 1 of the New Jersey Turnpike, or exit 4 off Rt. 295. **TELEPHONE:** 856-769-3200. **WEBSITE:** www.cowtownrodeo.com.

U.S. Equestrian Team Headquarters: Home of the USET Olympic training center and headquarters. Visitors can tour the 1916 stable, one of the largest and most lavish in the United States. The trophy room displays awards won by America's leading equestrians along with a pictorial timeline on the team's development. Guided tours by appointment. Several events are also open to the public. One, the Festival of Champions, includes show jumping, dressage, and things like four-in-hand competitions (for teams of horses). There is a charge for special events. **LOCATION:** Pottersville Rd., Gladstone (Somerset County). Just west of Rt. 206. **TELEPHONE:** 908-234-1251. **WEBSITE:** www.uset.org.

Horse Park of New Jersey: From March through November, equine events are held at this 147-acre park on most weekends and on many weekdays, including frequent multiday events. Events are frequently centered around horse shows, often on specific breeds like quarter-horses, Morgans, palominos, and Arabians. There are driving events, dressage, and even Olympic selection trials. The park has an indoor arena and five outdoor show rings. Food vendors are on site during show days. Most events are free and are usually held in daylight hours. LOCATION: Rt. 524, Stone Tavern (Monmouth County). Take Rt. 195, exit 11, then east on Rt. 524. TELEPHONE: 609-259-0170. WEBSITE: www.horseparkofnewjersey.com.

ARENAS AND THEATERS

PNC Bank Arts Center: Formerly known as the Garden State Arts Center, this beautiful white concrete amphitheater designed by Edward Durell Stone is the setting for nightly concerts and loads of special events throughout the summer. The "shell" is covered and offers seating for 7,000 while 10,500 more can be accommodated on the lawn. Lawn customers, however, can no longer bring their own chairs and must rent them from concessionaires. There are also strict rules about bringing in outside food and drink, although tailgating does take place in the parking lot. Shows range from pop and rock to jazz and country—everyone from the Beach Boys to operatic divas have appeared here. The season runs late May through September with ethnic festivals in June. LOCATION: Holmdel (Monmouth County). Take Exit 116 off the Garden State Parkway. TELEPHONE: 732-335-0400. Event and ticket hotline: 732-335-8698. WEBSITE: www.artscenter.com.

Ocean Grove Auditorium: A cavernous 7,000-seat auditorium built in the late Victorian age is one of the attractions of this quiet camp-meeting town just south of Asbury Park. The Great Auditorium, with its majestic organ, has been refurbished and restored. It is now home to many types of family-style entertainment plus a lecture series. Typical attractions are singers (including pop singers), choral groups, and festivals. Open for the summer. LOCATION: 21 Pilgrim Pathway, Ocean Grove (Monmouth County). TELEPHONE: 732-775-0035. WEBSITE: www.oceangrove.org.

Tweeter Center: On the Camden waterfront near the aquarium, this state-of-the-art facility presents premier artists and events year-round. It has a seating capacity of over 25,000 for rock groups and other entertainers. After the spring/summer outdoor season is over, the facility is enclosed for concerts, family entertainment, theatrical and cultural presentations, and special events. Flexible seating configurations range from 1,600 to 7,000. Secured parking is nearby. One Harbor Blvd., Camden (Camden County). **TELEPHONE:** 856-365-1300. **WEBSITE:** http://tweetercenter.com/philadelphia.

NJPAC: Opened in October 1997 and central to Newark's renaissance, the New Jersey Performing Arts Center is a beautiful building with a 2,750-seat auditorium worthy of the great opera houses and a small five-hundred-seat intimate theater, plus an indoor restaurant. Plenty of secured parking surrounds the center. This is a leading venue in the state for orchestras, ballet, jazz, tap, and traveling musicals. **HOURS:** One-hour guided walking tours for a small fee available by appointment Mon., Wed., and alternate Sun. **LOCATION:** One Center St., Newark (Essex County). Take Rt. 280 to Rt. 21 (McCarter Highway), follow signs. **TELEPHONE:** 888-GO-NJPAC. **WEBSITE:** www.njpac.org.

Albert Music Hall: Operated by the Pinelands Cultural Society to preserve the music of South Jersey's pines, the hall presents live shows every Sat. at 7:30 P.M., with occasional Sunday afternoon performances. This is the home of country music in New Jersey, with lots of bluegrass, country, and pinelands tunes. The hall, built in 1997, hosts local groups with names like Cedar Crick, Piney Hollow Drifters, and the Jersey Devil & the Sugar Sand Ramblers. There's even a Pine Barrens Festival and a Legend of the Jersey Devil Show. A snack bar and gifts are available in the hall. There's also a separate Pickin' Shed, where local musicians get together to swap songs. **ADMISSION:** $. Discounts: Children. **LOCATION:** 125 Wells Mills Rd. (Rt. 532), Waretown (Ocean County), one-quarter mile west of Rt. 9. **TELEPHONE:** 609-971-1593. **WEBSITE:** www.alberthall.org.

Other Arts Centers

State Theatre: Located in a cultural area next to the George Street Playhouse, this large, converted movie palace offers big-name musicals, operas, classical music, dance, divas, and occasional comedians, usually for one-night performances. **LOCATION:** 15 Livingston Ave., New Brunswick (Middlesex County). **TELEPHONE:** 877-STATE-11. **WEBSITE:** www.statetheatrenj.org.

Stockton Performing Arts Center: This professional theater on the Richard Stockton College campus includes the Performing Arts Center and the Experimental Theatre. Among the offerings are classic plays, from the Greeks to Shakespeare to contemporary works. Broadway classics as well as jazz, symphony, and dance troupes, and children's theater. **LOCATION:** Richard Stockton College, Pomona (Atlantic County). 609-652-9000. **WEBSITE:** www.intraweb.stockton. edu/pac/index.asp.

Patriots Theater: Owned by the state of New Jersey, this refurbished classical venue is the place for classical, folk, and rock concerts as well as plays and operas. The building is set in a large park near the Trenton waterfront. **LOCATION:** The War Memorial, Memorial Dr., Trenton (Mercer County). Information: 609-984-8400. Tickets: 800-955-5566. **WEBSITE:** www.thewarmemorial.com.

Community Theater: Housed in a former movie theater not far from the Morristown Green, this theater has undergone a major renovation, including a glass and limestone third floor, and has become one of the area's leading venues for both comedy acts and classical performances. Afternoon shows for kids. **LOCATION:** 100 South St., Morristown (Morris County). **TELEPHONE:** 973-539-8008. **WEBSITE:** www.communitytheaternj.com.

Count Basie Theatre: Features a wide range of shows, from musical revues and pop and rock stars to symphony, theater, and, of course, jazz and blues. There are also family-oriented matinee shows. All in a former 1926 movie theater and vaudeville house named for the legendary jazzman, who was born in Red Bank. **LOCATION:** 99 Monmouth St., Red Bank (Monmouth County). Garden State Parkway to Rt. 520 east, then left on Broad St. Follow to Monmouth St. and turn left. **TELEPHONE:** 732-842-9000. **WEBSITE:** www.countbasietheatre.org.

Theaters with Regular Seasons

McCarter Theatre: A leading regional theater, more than twenty new plays and adaptations have premiered at McCarter in the past decade. The theater season is complemented by music, dance, and special events. McCarter is the home of the Opera Festival of New Jersey and the American Repertory Ballet. **LOCATION:** 91 University Pl., Princeton (Mercer County). **TELEPHONE:** 609-258-2787. **WEBSITE:** www.mccarter.org.

Paper Mill Playhouse: New Jersey's leading venue for Broadway-style musicals and revivals, this 1,200-seat Equity theater produces notable works year-round, often with Broadway stars. Designated as the state theater of New Jersey. Art gallery upstairs and Carriage House restaurant next door. **LOCATION:** Brookside Dr., Millburn (Essex County). Take Millburn Ave. to Main St., then go right under railroad bridge to Brookside. **TELEPHONE:** 973-376-2181. **WEBSITE:** www. papermill.org.

George Street Playhouse: An intimate theater space with viewing good from all angles. The focus here is on new works for the American theater and revivals of Broadway dramas. Light refreshments in a cabaret/gallery area. Special after-show chats with performers on select Sunday performances. **LOCATION:** 9 Livingston Ave., New Brunswick (Middlesex County). **TELEPHONE:** 732-246-7717. **WEBSITE:** www.georgestplayhouse.org.

Shakespeare Theatre of New Jersey: Seasonal presentations from June to December by a repertory company that often includes Broadway names. Six plays per season with at least three by Shakespeare. Some touring done during the year. **LOCATION:** F. M. Kirby Shakespeare Theatre, Drew University, 36 Madison Ave., Madison (Morris County). **TELEPHONE:** 973-408-5600. **WEBSITE:** www.shakespearenj.org.

MINOR LEAGUE BASEBALL

Everyone knows the Yankees and Mets in New York and the Phillies in Philadelphia. But remember the old-fashioned park where you and the kids ate hot dogs and cheered the locals on? That seemed to be the stuff of movies rather than real life for many years. After decades of decline, however, there's been a resurgence of minor league baseball all over the country. Especially in New Jersey, stadiums have risen in the past few years from south to north. Some teams are affiliated with major league teams, at the A or AA level. Most are in independent leagues, including four that form the south division of the Atlantic League. Forget the old wooden bleachers; these are small versions of major league stadiums, with box and reserved seating, and some also offering glassed-in luxury suites. Many also offer lower-priced general admission tickets so you can sit on the grass beyond the outfield or picnic down the lines beyond the stands. Seating capacity generally runs around 6,000. Here are the minor league teams that play in the state.

Atlantic City Surf. Atlantic League (Indep.). The Sandcastle, Rt. 40 East, Atlantic City (Atlantic County). **TELEPHONE:** 609-344-7873. **WEBSITE:** www.acsurf.com.

Newark Bears. Atlantic League (Indep.). Bears & Eagles Riverfront Stadium, Bridge St., Newark (Essex County). **TELEPHONE:** 973-483-6900. **WEBSITE:** www.newarkbears.com.

New Jersey Cardinals. New York-Penn League (A). A St. Louis Cardinals affiliate. Skylands Park, Rt. 565, Augusta (Sussex County). **TELEPHONE:** 973-579-7500. **WEBSITE:** www.njcards.com.

New Jersey Jackals. Northern League (Indep.). Yogi Berra Stadium, One Hall Drive, Little Falls (Passaic County). On Montclair State University campus. **TELEPHONE:** 973-746-7434. **WEBSITE:** www.jackals.com.

Somerset Patriots. Atlantic League (Indep.). Commerce Bank Ballpark, East Main St., Bridgewater (Somerset County). **TELEPHONE:** 908-252-0700. **WEBSITE:** www.somersetpatriots.com

Trenton Thunder. Eastern League (AA). A Yankees affiliate. Waterfront Park, Trenton (Mercer County). **TELEPHONE:** 609-394-8326. **WEBSITE:** www.trentonthunder.com.

Lakewood Blue Claws. Southern Atlantic League (A). A Phillies affiliate. First Energy Park, Lakewood (Ocean County). Take Rt. 70 west, go right on Rt. 623. **TELEPHONE:** 732-901-7000. **WEBSITE:** www.lakewoodblueclaws.com.

Camden Riversharks. Atlantic League (Indep.). Campbell's Field, on the waterfront, Camden (Camden County). **TELEPHONE:** 866-742-7579. **WEBSITE:** www.riversharks.com.

NEARBY OUT-OF-STATE PLACES

New York Renaissance Faire

This festival, right over the New Jersey border, has been running for many years now and has become quite popular. For ten weekends from early August to mid-September, the greenery at Sterling Forest in New York is taken over by knights in shining armor, ladies, peddlers dressed in motley, jugglers, and mimes. A joust on horseback is the big attraction here (usually one at 2 P.M., the other at 6). Otherwise, a series of "shows" depicting outlaws, queens, and jesters are part of the festival—Robin Hood, for example, had a long run. However, the mud wrestling, juggling, belly dancing, and other attractions are operated by freelancers who expect the customers to come up with some coin of the realm, so bring extra money along. Rides (some simple ones) and games are extra, too. The main attractions, such as the living Chess Game, and the joust, take place at particular locations at specific times, so you must buy a program to enjoy everything. Vendors in tents offer such unusual items as brass rubbings and flower circlets for milady's hair. You can buy such victuals as steak-on-a-stick, turkey legs, lemonade, and beer, but no outside food or drink is allowed (strictness of enforcement varies).

HOURS: Aug. to mid-Sept., weekends, 10:30–7. **ADMISSION:** $$$$. Under 5 free. **LOCATION:** Sterling Forest, Tuxedo, NY. Rt. 17A west; look for signs. **TELEPHONE:** 845-351-5171. **WEBSITE:** www.renfair.com.

Crayola Factory

A popular outing for school groups, the Crayola Factory is also a place where parents can take their children for a few hours of entertainment and enlightenment. It's a combination of factory tour and children's interactive museum. The "Factory" takes up the second floor of a building called Two Rivers Landing, which also includes a Canal Museum on the upper floors. When you pay the admission price you are handed some Crayola "coins." Upon entering the factory floor you first see a docent who explains the crayon-making process and offers a little history. The hot wax mixture is poured into premade molds and allowed to cool. Then the paper wrapper is applied. Afterwards, you use your "coins" to buy a small four-crayon box. This is all for demonstration—the actual Crayola factory is 13 miles away.

As for history, Binney & Smith (the Crayola makers) started out as a paint company selling its distinctive red paint to Pennsylvania farmers for their barns. In 1903 they added paraffin to the color, creating their first crayons. They now sell Magic Markers and Silly Putty as well as all sizes and colors of crayons.

After the demonstrations, it's on to the interactive sections. These include arts and crafts plus interesting diversions. Really young kids will enjoy the Color Garden, where giant plastic vegetables can be planted, watered, gathered, and put into bins. One toddler picked up every onion, carrot, and apple in sight and piled them into her wheelbarrow. Other kids took produce out of bins and sold them at the sales register. Other sites include a small theater where you can put on a puppet show, a "shadow play" area, and several computers featuring arty concepts. There are also huge rooms where kids sit down and work with paper or clay to create anything they want. Traveling exhibits may vary the line-up, but there's always plenty of hands-on acitivities.

A visit to the Canal Museum upstairs is of interest if your children are not too young. The canals of the early nineteenth century were the main means of transportation in America and you can see a mock-up of a typical flatboat and plenty of interactive maps. The first floor of the building features local history and a small gift shop. The big gift shop, "The Crayola Store," is around the corner. The Factory can get crowded during the summer, so get there early, since it's first come, first served. Children under 16 must be accompanied by an adult.

HOURS: Summer, Mon.–Sat., 9–6; Sun., 11–6. Rest of year, Tue.–Sat., 9:30–5:30; Sun., 12–5. **ADMISSION:** \$\$. Under 2 free. **LOCATION:** 30

Centre Square, Easton, PA. **TELEPHONE:** 610-515-8000.
WEBSITE: www.crayola.com.

Culinary Institute of America

Want to run a day trip and fill up the bus? Try the Culinary Institute of America and seats will fill up fast. Groups often wait months for reservations. If you go on your own, you may find it easier to reserve a table at this school where budding chefs cook, clean, and serve in the restaurants on the first floor.

What makes CIA so popular? Since many of the graduates go on to found chic, ultra-expensive restaurants, there is the feeling of getting in on the ground floor of a good thing. But if the cooking is done by seniors, the waiters must be freshmen, because the service can vary from efficient to inept. The food, however, is always good, if not necessarily in the sublime category.

Set high on a hill overlooking the Hudson Valley, the red brick institute includes classrooms, student dorms, several restaurants, and a well-stocked bookstore. The Escoffier Room, which specializes in the formal, multicourse European meal, includes a large window that allows patrons to watch the chefs at meal preparation. A typical formal meal might include a light hors d'oeuvre, a soup, a main course followed by salad, and then a handsome dessert. The American Bounty Room offers faster service and includes such staples as roast beef and American pies.

Other eating areas (not always at the same level) include the St. Andrews Cafe and the Italian Caterina de Medici. A tour of the CIA is available if you can collect a group. You pass all the classrooms where students may be beheading fish or pushing pastry through a tube, and you will get the lowdown on how the institute works. If you are combining a trip to CIA with a visit to the neighboring historic houses at Hyde Park, be sure you allow plenty of time, since lunch can be a leisurely affair here. However, the Apple Pie cafe offers coffee, pastries, and sandwiches for a quick bite. Restaurants are closed when the school is not in session.

HOURS: Call first. **LOCATION:** Hyde Park, NY, 3 miles north of Poughkeepsie. **TELEPHONE:** 845-451-1588.

Fairs and Festivals

Here is a sampling of the most popular fairs, festivals, and parades in the Garden State.

FEBRUARY

1. New Jersey Flower and Patio Show. Indoor landscapes, flowers. Various venues. 800-332-3976.

MARCH

1. Atlantique City. Huge antiques fair inside Atlantic City's convention center. 800-526-2724.
2. St. Patrick's Day Parade, Belmar. 732-280-2648. (Others in Kearny, Newark, Morristown, Seaside Heights, etc.) On and around March 17.

APRIL

1. Branch Brook Cherry Blossom Festival, Branch Brook Park, Newark. Foot races, other events, usually mid-month. 973-643-1611.
2. Shad Festival, Lambertville. Food, crafts, sidewalk events, grilled shad. End of month. Telephone: 609-397-0055.

MAY

1. American Indian Arts Festival, on Indian Reservation, Westampton, South Jersey. Telephone: 609-261-4747.
2. N.J. Offshore Powerboat Races, in front of Point Pleasant Beach. Telephone: 732-583-8502.
3. Hoboken Arts and Music Festival. 201-420-2207.
4. Warren County Heritage Festival, Oxford. Nineteenth-century reenactments, fireworks. Third weekend. 908-453-4381.
5. Wildwood Kite Flying Contest, Wildwood. 609-523-0100.
6. Tour of Somerville, downtown Somerville. Memorial Day weekend bicycle race. Oldest bicycle race in USA. 908-725-0461.

JUNE

1. Appel Farms Arts and Music Festival, Elmer. All-day Saturday event. Heavy emphasis on folk music and classics. 800-394-1211. www.appelfarms.org.
2. N.J. Fresh Seafood Festival. Gardners Basin, Atlantic City. First weekend.
3. Red Bank Riverfest. Three-day jazz, food, events at Marine Park by the Navesink River. 732-741-0055.
4. Battle of Monmouth re-enactment. On battlefield grounds, Manalapan (Monmouth County). Weekend encampment. Costumed soldiers, overnight tenting. Third or fourth weekend. 732-462-9616.
5. U.S. Equestrian Team Festival of Champions. Dressage, horse-show events. Gladstone (Somerset County). 908-234-1251.

JULY

1. July 3 & 4. Atlantic City Fireworks. Philadelphia fireworks can be seen from Camden waterfront.
2. Night in Venice, Ocean City. Decorated boats parade on inland waterway. 609-525-9300.
4. St. Ann's Italian Street Festival, Hoboken. Food, vendors, entertainment. 201-659-1116.
3. QuickChek N.J. Festival of Ballooning, Solberg Airport, Readington (Somerset County). Three-day festival with balloon ascensions at dusk and dawn, plus bands, clowns, vendors; on an open field, usually fourth weekend of month. 800-468-2479.

AUGUST

1. Hambletonian. Meadowlands Race Track. Highest purse in trotter racing. Family events beforehand. East Rutherford (Bergen County). First Saturday. 201-935-8500.
2. Atlantic City Ocean Marathon Festival. Gardner's Basin. 609-343-3794.
3. NJ State Fair and Sussex County Farm & Horse Show. Combination old fashioned country fair and midway amusements. Augusta. 973-948-5500. www.newjerseystatefair.org.

SEPTEMBER

1. Garden State Wine Growers' Festival, Waterloo Village, Stanhope. First or second weekend. Food, wine, at restored village. 609-890-8188.
2. Miss America Pageant, Atlantic City. 609-345-7571.
3. Ocean County Decoy and Gunning Show, Tuckerton. Decoy carving, duck calling, vendors. 609-971-3085.

4. Wings 'n Water Festival. Wetlands Institute, Stone Harbor (Cape May County). Seafood, exhibits, decoys. 609-368-1211.

OCTOBER

1. Eighteenth-Century Field Day, Fort Mercer, Red Bank Battlefield, National Park (Gloucester County). 856-853-5120.
2. Cranberry Festival, Chatsworth (Burlington County). 609-726-9237.
3. Chowderfest Weekend. Beach Haven, Long Beach Island. Everybody samples soup. 609-494-7211.
4. Victorian Week, Cape May. House tours, costumes. 609-884-5404.
5. Far Hills Race Meeting, Moorland Farms, Far Hills (Somerset County). Steeplechase race on open field. Tailgate spectators. Bring your own food. Third Saturday. www.farhillsrace.org.

NOVEMBER

1. Annual Fall Antique Show, Allaire Village, Allaire State Park. 732-919-3500.
2. Cape May Jazz Festival, Cape May. 609-884-7277.

DECEMBER

1. Holly Walk, Morristown. Six historical houses with Christmas décor. First weekend. 973-631-5151.
2. Reenactment of Washington crossing the Delaware. Christmas Day. Titusville (Mercer County). 609-737-0623.
3. Reenactment of Battle of Trenton. Weekend after Christmas. 609-777-1770.

Index